D0919970

A History of the
Cuban Revolution

Viewpoints/Puntos de Vista
Themes and Interpretations in Latin American History

Series Editor: Jürgen Buchenau

The books in this series will introduce students to the most significant themes and topics in Latin American history. They represent a novel approach to designing supplementary texts for this growing market. Intended as supplementary textbooks, the books will also discuss the ways in which historians have interpreted these themes and topics, thus demonstrating to students that our understanding of our past is constantly changing, through the emergence of new sources, methodologies, and historical theories. Unlike monographs, the books in this series will be broad in scope and written in a style accessible to undergraduates.

Published

A History of the Cuban Revolution
Aviva Chomsky

Bartolomé de las Casas and the Conquest of the Americas
Lawrence A. Clayton

Mexican Immigration to the United States
Timothy J. Henderson

In preparation

The Last Caudillo: Alvaro Obregón and the Mexican Revolution
Jürgen Buchenau

Creoles vs. Peninsulars in Colonial Spanish America
Mark Burkholder

Dictatorship in South America
Jerry Davila

Mexico Since 1940: The Unscripted Revolution
Stephen E. Lewis

The Haitian Revolution, 1791–1804
Jeremy Popkin

A History of the Cuban Revolution

Aviva Chomsky

WILEY-BLACKWELL

A John Wiley & Sons, Ltd., Publication

This edition first published 2011
© 2011 Aviva Chomsky

Blackwell Publishing was acquired by John Wiley & Sons in February 2007. Blackwell's publishing program has been merged with Wiley's global Scientific, Technical, and Medical business to form Wiley-Blackwell.

Registered Office
John Wiley & Sons Ltd, The Atrium, Southern Gate, Chichester, West Sussex, PO19 8SQ, United Kingdom

Editorial Offices
350 Main Street, Malden, MA 02148-5020, USA

9600 Garsington Road, Oxford, OX4 2DQ, UK

The Atrium, Southern Gate, Chichester, West Sussex, PO19 8SQ, UK

For details of our global editorial offices, for customer services, and for information about how to apply for permission to reuse the copyright material in this book please see our website at www.wiley.com/wiley-blackwell.

The right of Aviva Chomsky to be identified as the author of this work has been asserted in accordance with the UK Copyright, Designs and Patents Act 1988.

Wiley also publishes its books in a variety of electronic formats. Some content that appears in print may not be available in electronic books.

Designations used by companies to distinguish their products are often claimed as trademarks. All brand names and product names used in this book are trade names, service marks, trademarks or registered trademarks of their respective owners. The publisher is not associated with any product or vendor mentioned in this book. This publication is designed to provide accurate and authoritative information in regard to the subject matter covered. It is sold on the understanding that the publisher is not engaged in rendering professional services. If professional advice or other expert assistance is required, the services of a competent professional should be sought.

Library of Congress Cataloging-in-Publication Data

Chomsky, Aviva, 1957–
    A history of the Cuban Revolution / Aviva Chomsky.
        p. cm. – (Viewpoints/puntos de vista : themes and interpretations in Latin American history)
    Includes bibliographical references and index.
    ISBN 978-1-4051-8774-9 (hardcover : alk. paper) – ISBN 978-1-4051-8773-2 (pbk. : alk. paper)   1. Cuba–History–Revolution, 1959.   2. Cuba–History–Revolution, 1959–Influence.   I. Title.
    F1788.C465 2011
    972.9106'4–dc22

                                                                2010019088

ISBN 9781405187732

A catalogue record for this book is available from the British Library.

Set in 10.5/13 pt Minion by Toppan Best-set Premedia Limited
Printed and bound in Malaysia by Vivar Printing Sdn Bhd

02   2012

Contents

Illustrations

Maps

Figures

Series Editor's Preface

Each book in the "Viewpoints/Puntos de Vista" series introduces students to a significant theme or topic in Latin American history. In an age in which student and faculty interest in the Global South increasingly challenges the old focus on the history of Europe and North America, Latin American history has assumed an increasingly prominent position in undergraduate curricula.

Some of these books discuss the ways in which historians have interpreted these themes and topics, thus demonstrating that our understanding of our past is constantly changing, through the emergence of new sources, methodologies, and historical theories. Others offer an introduction to a particular theme by means of a case study or biography in a manner easily understood by the contemporary, non-specialist reader. Yet others give an overview of a major theme that might serve as the foundation of an upper-level course.

What is common to all of these books is their goal of historical synthesis. They draw on the insights of generations of scholarship on the most enduring and fascinating issues in Latin American history, while also making use of primary sources as appropriate. Each book is written by a specialist in Latin American history who is concerned with undergraduate teaching, yet who has also made his or her mark as a first-rate scholar.

The books in this series can be used in a variety of ways, recognizing the differences in teaching conditions at small liberal arts colleges, large public universities, and research-oriented institutions with doctoral programs. Faculty have particular needs depending on whether they teach large lectures with discussion sections, small lecture or discussion-oriented classes, or large lectures with no discussion sections, and whether they teach on a semester or trimester system. The format adopted for this series fits all of these different parameters.

This volume is one of the two inaugural books in the "Viewpoints/ Puntos de Vista series. In *A History of the Cuban Revolution*, Avi Chomsky provides a compelling and fascinating synthesis of the Cuban Revolution – the first socialist revolution in the Americas, and significant in world history for its role in the Cold War. Drawing on historical literature and primary sources from both Cuba and the United States, the author takes the reader on a historical tour, from the beginning of the Revolution in the Sierra Maestra mountains up to the present day. Along the way she includes not only the preeminent actors in the drama – Fulgencio Batista, Che Guevara, Fidel Castro, Dwight Eisenhower, J.F.K., Robert Kennedy, and many others – but she also covers the Bay of Pigs invasion, the Cuban Missile Crisis, issues of immigration and emigration, political culture, and the social and cultural legacies of the Revolution in race, gender, and sexuality as well as in literature, film, music, dance, religion, sport, and food.

Jürgen Buchenau
University of North Carolina, Charlotte

Acknowledgments

Many thanks to Peter Coveney and Jürgen Buchenau, who proposed this project to me and who have helped it along at every juncture. Several anonymous readers provided welcome suggestions for both the proposal and the manuscript. Thanks also to copyeditor Tessa Hanford, and to my sister-in-law Amy Apel for indexing the book. Above all, I must thank Alfredo Prieto and his family. Alfredo has been my guide to Cuba and *socio* in Cuba-related intellectual and political endeavors over the past decade. Hundreds of hours of conversations in Havana, Maine, Massachusetts, and even Miami, have helped me better understand the complexities of Cuba's past and present. Alfredo also served as editor extraordinaire for this manuscript, catching errors, reminding me of what I'd missed, and pushing me towards new discoveries. ¡Muchísimas gracias!

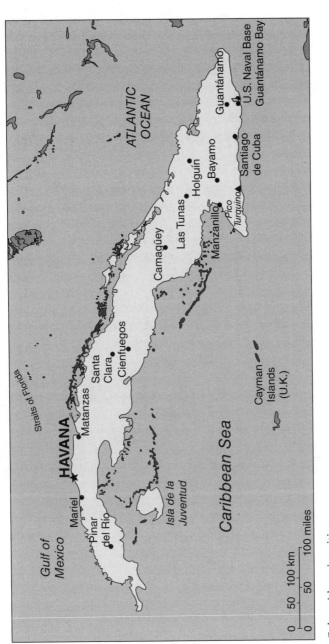

Cuba with major cities

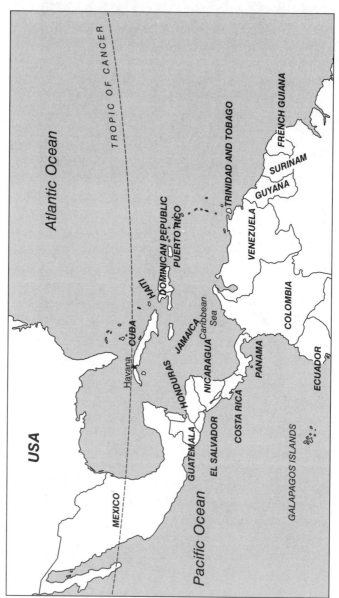

Cuba with respect to the Caribbean and the Americas

Introduction

Rarely does popular opinion in the United States diverge so strikingly from scholarly analysis as in the case of the Cuban Revolution.

It's one of the few events in Latin American history that U.S. students have heard of. When I ask my students to come up with names of important figures in Latin American history, the only one that reliably emerges is that of Fidel Castro. And students are fairly unanimous in their opinions of Castro: "Dangerous," "evil," "bad," and "dictator" are the words they most commonly come up with to describe him. Survey results show that my students' positions are widely shared among the U.S. population: 98 percent of those surveyed in the United States had heard of Fidel Castro, and 82 percent had a negative opinion of him.[1]

Fidel Castro has certainly inspired his share of scholarly attention, including numerous biographies. Some are by historians. Some are by journalists. One is by a doctor. There is even a graphic novel recounting Fidel's life. In a "spoken autobiography" the Cuban revolutionary recounted his own story of his life.[2]

Most serious studies of the Cuban Revolution, though, focus less on the figure of Fidel Castro and more on the process, the politics, and the people of the Cuban Revolution. Here we find a giant gap between what scholars, including historians, have to say, and what U.S. political leaders and the general public seem to believe. Most

A History of the Cuban Revolution. Aviva Chomsky
© 2011 Aviva Chomsky

historians frame the story of the Cuban Revolution with the long history of U.S. involvement in the island and in the rest of the Caribbean. But politicians and the general public have tended to see the USSR, rather than the United States, as the main factor explaining the nature of the Cuban Revolution. In this respect, U.S. scholars today have more in common with their Cuban counterparts than they do with the U.S. public.

Talking about Freedom

Both in Cuba and in the United States, the word "freedom" comes up frequently in describing Cuba's history and current realities. It's a word that incorporates many different meanings. U.S. policymakers tend to use it to refer to freedom for private enterprise, while for Cuban policymakers it generally means freedom from U.S. interference. This dichotomy is nothing new. "The Cuban people want to be free as much from the foreigners who abuse the flag as from the citizens who violate it and will end up burying it," wrote a Cuban nationalist organization in the 1920s, referring to the U.S. political and economic domination of the island, and to the Cubans who collaborated with the foreigners.[3] Around the same time, Cuban Communist Party founder Julio Antonio Mella published his pamphlet entitled *Cuba, A Nation That Has Never Been Free*.

And today, a billboard in Santa Clara proclaims "O libres para siempre o batallando siempre para ser libres," over a painting of two giant hands, one black and one white, breaking free of a shackle (Figure I.1). "Either free forever, or forever fighting to be free." The contemporary use of the image, and the quote by Cuban independence leader José Martí, clearly draws a parallel between Cuba's struggle for independence from Spain, its struggle for the abolition of slavery and for racial equality, and its struggle for national independence in the current era in the face of U.S. threats. "Freedom," a Cuban high school student at the "Martyrs of Kent" high school told U.S. educator Jonathan Kozol in 1976, "means when you are free of *international capitalistic exploitation!*"[4]

Figure I.1   Billboard quoting José Martí: "Either Free Forever, or Forever Fighting to be Free"
Source: Photo by Jackie McCabe

"Castro has taken no interest in international situation or in threat of international Communism," the U.S. Ambassador complained shortly after the Revolution. "I tried to explain significance of support of all peoples of free world in great struggle between freedom and slavery but do not believe he was particularly impressed."[5] The "freedom" that U.S. policymakers worried about incessantly in the first months of the Revolution was what the new revolutionary regime would mean for private enterprise. "'Real U.S. goals in Cuba', Assistant Secretary of State Roy Rubottom reiterated, included 'receptivity to U.S. and free world capital and increasing trade' and 'access by the United States to essential Cuban resources'."[6]

In late 2007, President Bush echoed the importance of private enterprise, the association of what he called "economic freedom" with political freedoms – and Cuba's failures on both counts. "One of the great success stories of the past century is the advance of economic and political freedom across Latin America," Bush explained in a major policy speech. "In this room are officials representing nations that are embracing the blessings of democratic government and free enterprise." However, "one country in our region still isolates its people from the hope that freedom brings, and traps them in a system that has failed them."[7] The one country, obviously, was Cuba.

In Barack Obama's first major speech on Cuba, before an audience of Cuban Americans in Miami in May 2008, he used the words "free" or "freedom" 33 times. "Never in my lifetime," he announced, "have the people of Cuba known freedom … My policy toward Cuba will be guided by one word: Libertad." He even quoted José Martí, saying "every moment is critical in the defense of freedom." While explicitly distancing himself from Republican policies, Obama nevertheless vowed to maintain the U.S. embargo against Cuba.[8]

Scholars Weigh In

Scholars of Latin America are less likely to share the U.S. administrations' infatuation with free markets. While economists are still divided on the issue, with the Chicago School holding fast to its free market principles, historians tend to be a bit more leery of automatically equating free markets with political freedom. Economic liberalism, they remind us, was implemented in much of Latin America in the late nineteenth century through "liberal dictatorships" like that of Porfirio Díaz in Mexico, who maintained repressive, undemocratic governments while warmly welcoming U.S. investors. Since World War II, dictatorships in the Southern Cone and authoritarian democracies like Mexico have followed neo-liberal economic advisers from the United States. And free market "economic miracles" in Latin America have often had disastrous effects on the poor.[9]

Latin Americanists have frequently found themselves at odds with U.S. policymakers towards the region. The interdisciplinary field of Latin American Studies came about in part as a result of the Cuban Revolution, as the State Department sought to create cadres of experts who could guide and implement U.S. policy by funding new Latin

American Studies programs at major U.S. universities. Historian Thomas Skidmore, in what Rolena Adorno called a "memorable and oft-repeated announcement," suggested in 1961 that "we are all sons and daughters of Fidel."[10] That is, the Cuban Revolution gave rise to an upsurge of government interest in Latin America, and funding for Latin American Studies programs in major U.S. universities. (Jan Knippers Black later revised this to suggest that U.S. Latin Americanists are Fidel Castro's "illegitimate offspring."[11]) In 1995 Stanford political scientist Richard Fagen echoed Skidmore's sentiment when, upon receiving the Latin American Studies Association's top scholarship award, he suggested "with my tongue only half-way into my cheek" that the Cuban revolutionary leader would be the most appropriate recipient because "at least in the United States, no one did more than Fidel Castro to stimulate the study of Latin America in the 60s and 70s."[12] "Many members of my generation," political scientist and former Latin American Studies Association (LASA) President Peter Smith reiterated in 2006, "went through graduate school with thanks to Fidel Castro."[13]

"U.S. officials," Smith continued, "expected the academic community to promote U.S. policy goals. The National Defense Education Act (note that name!) offered generous scholarships for the study of Latin America – on the mistaken assumption, of course, that newly trained area experts would figure out ways to prevent or defeat revolutionary movements."[14]

As Smith and the others have suggested, the attempt largely backfired. Instead, LASA took a strong stand early on: "Scholarship must never become a clandestine arm of U.S. policy."[15] New scholars trained in Latin American Studies who spent time working in Latin America as often as not turned into opponents of U.S. policy towards the region. LASA has been particularly critical of U.S. policy towards Cuba, passing resolution after resolution condemning the trade and travel embargo and calling for free academic exchange with the island. LASA has been especially rankled that the State Department has refused to issue visas for Cuban scholars to participate in its Congresses, and in 2007 the organization moved its meeting from Boston to Montreal so that Cuban scholars could attend unimpeded, vowing to boycott the United States until the organization received a guarantee that its Cuban members would be allowed to participate.

Nevertheless, the study of Cuba in the United States has frequently been criticized for its ideological divides. Several essays in the *Latin American Research Review* – the journal of the Latin American Studies Association – have noted the weight of politics in Cuban studies. Marifeli Pérez-Stable argued in 1991 that the Cold War construct of the "Cubanologist," modeled on monikers assigned to those who studied the Soviet bloc, should be replaced by "Cubanist," taking Cuban studies out of the Cold War paradigm and returning it to Latin America and following the pattern of "Latin Americanist" or "Mexicanist." Damián Fernández reiterated this stance a few years later, as did John Kirk and Peter McKenna in 1999.[16]

In addition to the ideological bent that it brought to the field, another drawback of the "Cubanology" approach has been an overemphasis on politics in studies of the Cuban Revolution. Historian Louis A. Pérez complained in 1992 that historians have woefully neglected the history of the post-revolutionary period. "After 1961, historians yield to political scientists, sociologists, economists, and anthropologists – to Cubanologists. The resulting anomaly is striking: for Cubanologists, there is no history before 1959; for historians, there is no history after 1959."[17] Clearly, the Revolution was a political event. But it was also social, cultural, economic, artistic, and many other things. Every revolution seeks to bring about change, and the Cuban Revolution is no exception. In some ways, people's everyday lives were fundamentally changed by the Revolution. In other ways, the Revolution grew out of, and drew on, longstanding aspects of Cuban history and culture. A social history of the Revolution grows from the intersection of structures, policies, and the actions of ordinary people.

Why Revolution?

If historians' main objective is to understand change over time, we tend to be especially attracted to the study of revolutions because, by definition, they offer concrete examples of a lot of change occurring in a rather limited time period. We want to know when and why revolutions occur, why they take the forms they do, and what their results are. Social historians in particular want to know how and why ordinary people mobilize for revolution, to what extent they are actors and participants in revolutionary change, and how revolutions affect their lives. Both the Cuban revolutionaries themselves, and the historians who have studied the Cuban Revolution, have utilized historical understandings of what they know about other revolutions.

Uprisings by oppressed people – like slave and peasant rebellions – have existed as long as civilization has existed. But revolutions are more than just uprisings – they are concerted attempts to reorganize society.

Historians often categorize revolutions into political versus social revolutions. The former focus on changing the structures of governance and the access of the population to political institutions; while the latter emphasize creating a new social and economic order.

Cuba's revolution in 1959 drew on a long revolutionary tradition, both in Cuba and globally, at the same time that it responded to the immediate realities of Cuba in the 1950s. The revolutionary traditions included European political and social revolutions of the nineteenth and early twentieth centuries, American anti-colonial revolutions, and Cubans' own attempts from the mid-nineteenth century on to achieve national independence and social change.

The global "Age of Revolution" marked by the American and French Revolutions at the end of the eighteenth century was accompanied by revolutions in thought and political philosophy known as the Enlightenment, when (primarily) European intellectuals began to argue that the social order is man-made, rather than God-given, and thus subject to human agency. Enlightenment thought invited people to question existing political and social systems and try to imagine better ones.

Out of this philosophical or intellectual movement grew a wide variety of political philosophies, and political and social movements to try to put the ideas into practice. The "Glorious Revolution" in England in 1688 established a constitutional monarchy with a bill of rights, while the American Revolution beginning in 1775 established national independence and did away with monarchy altogether. While these two were primarily political revolutions, the French Revolution in 1789 went further in challenging the social order as well as the political system. The Haitian Revolution may have begun as a political movement, but it quickly became a profound social revolution and war of national liberation in 1791, as slaves rose up and dismantled the slave plantation system and declared independence from France.

None of the Latin American wars of independence that followed the Haitian Revolution were quite as revolutionary. But it's also notable that in the colonies most heavily reliant on slavery – Cuba and the other islands of the Caribbean, as well as Brazil – there were no wars for independence in the early nineteenth century. Instead, the elites closed ranks with the colonial powers. The example of Haiti soured them not only on social revolution, but on any challenge to the political or social order. It took another 75 years – and the abolition of the slave trade and a global repudiation of the slave system – before national liberation and republicanism found any allies among the upper echelons of the slave colonies. Men like Washington and Jefferson fought for national liberation in Britain's northern colonies when they believed it could come about without threatening their social position, which rested on the slave system. Their counterparts in Brazil and the Caribbean, chastened by the Haitian example, decided that colonial status, and monarchy, were not so bad after all. Cuba would remain a Spanish colony until 1898, and even during and after its wars of independence, the threat of becoming "another Haiti" was raised repeatedly.

Many of the social revolutions of the twentieth century drew on the ideas of the German philosopher Karl Marx. The Communist Manifesto, which he authored in 1848 with Friedrich Engels, argued that the constitutional and representative political systems that were replacing Europe's monarchies were not universal ideals, but rather the manifestation of bourgeois rule. Feudalism and monarchy represented the rule of the landed elites, who were being overthrown by a new urban, industrial class that sought political power in order to enforce its new economic order, industrial capitalism. But, they argued, "all history is the history of class struggle." Capitalism was based on the exploitation of the working class. These working masses were politically and socially excluded, and would be the next class to rise up and overthrow the system that oppressed them, creating a new socialist state that would represent their interests rather than the interests of their bosses. Instead of protecting the private property amassed by the industrial elites, the state would use the wealth created by industrialization – and by the labor of the working classes – for the benefit of all.

The Cuban Revolution, then, was made by people who believed they could change their society and their world. By overthrowing the old, unjust social order, and challenging the legacies of colonial rule, they could make history, rather than being passive victims of their history. National independence and social justice were two fundamental goals, and they were understood as two sides of the same coin: it was colonial and neo-colonial rule that had created the poverty and inequality of the present. And just as poverty and inequality were the product of human actions, so they could be transformed by human actions.

Comparing Capitalism and Socialism

Capitalism and socialism are often assumed to be two opposing economic systems. In some ways, this is accurate. The two systems operate according to very different economic rationales. But in other ways, when we try to define the two as polar opposites we lose sight of how real economies work. In fact, almost every economic system incorporates aspects of both logics, and it might make sense to imagine the two as ideal types at different ends of a spectrum, rather than as exclusive and contained systems.

Capitalist logic is based on private ownership of the means of production – that is, the tools, the factories, the farms – everything that is used to produce goods. Capitalists invest money in the means of production, and employ labor to carry out the work. Workers get paid a wage, and the items they produce belong to the capitalist, who sells them in a market governed by supply and demand. The owner of the goods sets the price, calculating between the benefits of a high price – which means higher profit on each item sold – and a low price, which means that more items will be sold. It's generally in the capitalist's interest to lower the costs of production as much as possible, often by investing in improved technology that can cut the cost of labor.

It's also in the capitalist's interest to sell as much as possible. Increased sales mean greater profits. Because it's in the interest of the businesses to produce and sell as much as possible, they go beyond producing what people actually need. It's to their benefit to produce things that may be useless and even things that are harmful, as long as they can find a way to sell them.

Capitalist systems are best at increasing production and variety of goods. They are less successful at distributing the goods to those who may need them most. In pretty much every capitalist society, even the wealthiest, there are people who are hungry. Not because there isn't enough food, but because the people who are hungry don't have the money to buy it. They may want and need food, but in capitalist logic, they don't represent a "demand" for food because "demand" isn't created by human need, it's created by the economic means to buy something. A penniless person may *want* a gallon of milk as much or more than a rich person, but under capitalism, only the person with money to buy the milk represents a "demand" for the product.

Every capitalist society recognizes this contradiction in the meaning of "demand," which is why every capitalist society incorporates other, non-capitalist means of distributing what it produces. For example, within every capitalist society there are some people who do not work and earn a wage: children, the elderly, those who are unemployed for other reasons. But the system is organized to provide for the needs of these people, even if they can't purchase what they need on the open, "free" market. In the United States, society collectively – through national and local governments – provides education to all children, outside of the capitalist supply-and-demand system. Some needs, society implicitly or explicitly decides, are so important to the well-being of all that they should not be left to the imperfect capitalist system of distribution – the state must step in and ensure a fair distribution that meets human needs, rather than just the ability of people to pay. Every capitalist society has some sort of public sector that is organized with human priorities, rather than profit, as its governing logic.

Socialist logic is based on the idea that human needs, rather than profit, should govern what and how much is produced. In a democratic system, the decision-making process is in the hands of the population, through various forms of democratic mechanisms like the election of representatives, or town meetings. In an autocratic system, governing elites may make the decisions about production. Either way, though, the decisions are based not on how much potential profit can be made by producing something, but rather on what needs it fills. This is why socialist governments make economic plans and production goals.

Of course governments – especially non-democratic governments – can be arbitrary and unrealistic in setting production priorities. Like Stalin in the USSR or Mao in China, they can prioritize a long-term goal of industrialization above the short-term need for the population to feed itself, leading to social and economic catastrophe. But capitalism is no guarantee against famine and economic disaster either. In twentieth-century Africa, most famines have been caused by capitalism rather than by socialism. A system of supply and demand leads countries to export food to wealthy consumers in the First World while their impoverished citizens starve.

But if the strength of the socialist logic is in distribution, its weakness is in production. Specifically, if everybody's needs are guaranteed, what's the incentive to work, and to push oneself to increase production? Socialist systems have come up with two answers to this. One is to mix in an element of capitalist logic. Many socialist systems guarantee certain basic needs, but leave other aspects of consumption to the free market. The other is Che Guevara's idea of moral incentives. According to Che, humans have been shaped by capitalism to value greed and consumption. But we are also capable of being motivated by unselfish goals – by the desire to contribute to and participate in one's society.

Most people in both capitalist and socialist societies can recognize both elements in themselves. Most of us seek both material comforts and possessions *and* some kind of more meaningful fulfillment in our lives. Che's argument is that while capitalism fosters materialism, socialism should instead foster unselfish, participatory values.

Neither capitalism nor socialism exists in the world as a pure replica of a theory. Rather, every modern society incorporates capitalist and socialist elements, just as every individual is capable of both selfish materialism and of caring about the needs of others.

Likewise, it makes little sense to ask whether capitalism or socialism "works" better. In the United States capitalism seems to work remarkably well: our standard of living is higher than anywhere else in the world. But other countries, just as capitalist as our own, are not faring so well. If we use Haiti or Rwanda as our measuring stick, capitalism seems to be quite a failure as an economic system. Conversely, a heavy dose of socialism has not doomed Sweden or Norway to economic collapse, nor to authoritarian excesses.

In a world historical view, what "works" best seems to be having been a colonial power, while what "works" worst is having been colonized. The former colonial powers, with ample resources, seem to be able to make a variety of economic and political models work successfully. The former colonies, with a history of foreign ownership and the export of primary goods, social and racial inequality, and authoritarian politics, have struggled mightily to achieve a better standard of living, a measure of social equality, and some kind of participatory political system. Despite experimentation with a large variety of economic and political forms, and numerous so-called economic miracles, no formula has yet been found that could reliably and effectively overcome this colonial legacy. The Argentinean sociologist Carlos M. Vilas wrote in 1990 that "although socialism is facing profound crisis, capitalism – whether flowering or in crisis – has been unable to handle the economic, social, and cultural problems of impoverishment, oppression, and marginalization of the rapidly-growing populations of what were once called developing societies."[18]

Despite his critique of capitalism's ability to function in the Third World, Vilas also takes a critical stance towards the manner in which socialism has developed there. Marx, he reminds us, imagined socialism – i.e., a state-controlled economy – as a stage that highly industrialized countries would pass through on the way to communism – when the state would "wither away" and the means of production (i.e., industry and land) would be collectively owned and managed by their own workers. A state-controlled economy would come about, he argued, in highly industrialized societies in which most people worked in industry, and industry could produce more than enough of what people needed.

While Marx predicted that these socialist revolutions would come about in the most advanced industrialized countries, this is not exactly what happened. Instead, the "bourgeois" governments in the industrialized countries (primarily in the United States and Europe) began to gradually extend political and social rights to the dispossessed working classes. By the beginning of the twentieth century, the revolutionary option had faded into marginal status in Western Europe and the United States. In Europe, communist and socialist parties remained politically active, but they ceased to be revolutionary, choosing instead to compete in the electoral arena.

Instead, Marxist ideas came to shape movements for national liberation over the course of the twentieth century. The Chinese Revolution fused Marxism with anti-imperialism, challenging both Japanese and Western control in China. Like in Russia, the Chinese also tried to use Marxist ideas to push forward an industrial revolution. Throughout Asia, Africa, and Latin America, national independence movements used Marxist ideas to challenge colonial masters and the ways that European imperialism had distorted, exploited, and depleted their resources. Especially in the middle of the twentieth century, as the Great Depression made capitalism seem ever less viable and the Soviet Union achieved great international legitimacy as the main challenge to Nazism, Soviet communism seemed to offer an alternative for hope in the world's colonies.

Besides, it was the Western European countries, and the United States, that were the colonial oppressors in Africa, Latin America, and much of Asia. For all that they may have admired the standard of living in the United States and Europe, many people in these colonies found it hard to take very seriously Western claims to be promoting democracy, freedom, and human rights. For them, capitalism meant conquest, repression and exploitation, not freedom. Increasingly over the course of the twentieth century, revolutionary movements in these colonies linked national independence to some form of socialism. Cuba's was one of them.

Socialist revolutions, then, occurred in societies with very little industry: Russia, China, Cuba, and other Third World countries in Africa, Asia, and Latin America. "As a consequence of the economic realities of Third World societies, developing the productive forces has become the central goal of transition to socialism," Vilas wrote. Socialism became no more than "a species of left-wing developmentalism, a method for accelerating modernization."

In addition, the economic backwardness of Third World revolutionary countries forced them to seek economic support from outside. This "outside" became, inevitably, given the geo-political realities of the twentieth century, the USSR. Reliance on the USSR and the Council for Mutual Economic Assistance (COMECON) became "the central element in the conceptualization of these regimes as 'socialist,' in an epoch in which the USSR was waging an aggressive political competition with U.S. expansion in the Third World. From this point onward, the socialist-oriented, or at least non-capitalist, road that these countries were walking was more a function of the friends they could gather abroad than of the policies they were pushing at home. Or to put it a different way, the political classification of Third World regimes become more an issue of international politics than of political economy. Not infrequently, such 'socialist-oriented' regimes were highly authoritarian, and their only connection to socialism was their orientation toward the foreign policies of the Soviet Union."[19]

Latin American Attitudes

"Fidel Castro is a symbol," one of my Cuban colleagues tried to explain in a talk at a college in Maine a few years ago. For many in

Latin America and elsewhere, he is a symbol of speaking truth to power. When he stood up at the Group of 77 "South Summit" in 2000 and attacked neoliberal economic policies and corporate globalization – what he called "the neoliberal race to catastrophe" – for the poverty and suffering that they have created in the Third World, he was cheered for precisely those words.

> In over 100 countries the per capita income is lower than 15 years ago. At the moment, 1.6 billion people are faring worse than at the beginning of the 1980s.
>
> Over 820 million people are undernourished and 790 million of them live in the Third World. It is estimated that 507 million people living in the South today will not live to see their fortieth birthday.
>
> In the Third World countries represented here, two out of every five children suffer from growth retardation and one out of every three is underweight; 30,000 who could be saved are dying every day; 2 million girls are forced into prostitution; 130 million children do not have access to elementary education and 250 million minors under 15 are bound to work for a living.
>
> The world economic order works for 20 percent of the population but it leaves out, demeans and degrades the remaining 80 percent. We cannot simply accept to enter the next century as the backward, poor and exploited rearguard.[20]

To many in Latin America, these words ring patently true, and eloquently express their outrage at an unjust global order.

Although public opinion polls have their limitations – especially in Latin America, where they are often conducted by telephone in countries where most of the poor do not have telephones – their results often look surprising to those who have lived and been educated in the United States. In Cuba, for example, 47 percent approved of their government in a 2006 survey (based on face-to-face interviews in Cuba's two major cities), while 40 percent disapproved. Ninety-six percent of those surveyed believed that health care was accessible to all Cubans (as opposed to only 42 percent in other Latin American urban areas, when asked the question about their own countries), and 75 percent expressed confidence in their country's health care system (as opposed to 57 percent elsewhere in Latin America). Ninety-eight percent believed that education was available to all (as opposed to 52 percent in other Latin American cities), and 78 percent were satisfied with the educational system (as opposed to 59 percent in other Latin American cities).[21] When asked to identify the biggest problem in Cuba, 42.5 percent chose "low salaries, high cost of living," while only 18.2 percent chose "lack of freedoms, political system." The largest proportion (42 percent) gave no answer to the question of what kind of government would best solve their country's problems. Only 32.1 percent believed that a democratic form of government would be the best solution.[22]

People in Latin America tend to be more ambivalent about democracy than those in the United States. In almost every country, significant majorities view the role of the United States in the world as "mainly negative." Overall, the majority approves of democracy, but these are often slim majorities: in Mexico 54 percent believed that democracy was the best form of government; in Colombia, 53 percent; and in Brazil, only 46 percent.[23] By large majorities, Latin Americans preferred socialism to capitalism in a 2008 Gallup poll. Only in two countries, Mexico and Panama, did slightly more people prefer capitalism. "Any U.S. policy toward Latin America," Gallup concluded, "needs to recognize that 'socialism' is not a dirty word in the region."[24]

Clearly, a huge gap in knowledge, beliefs, and attitudes exists between the United States and Latin America. One of the keys to understanding why is the Cuban Revolution.

This book engages with multiple perspectives in writing a history of the Cuban Revolution. It looks at the positions of policymakers and the media in the United States and Cuba, as well as at popular opinion and popular movements in Cuba and beyond. It brings in the views of a variety of historians and other scholars who have approached the Cuban Revolution with a variety of assumptions and a variety of questions. Most of all, it tries to illuminate the experiences and actions of Cuban people from many different walks of life and what the Cuban Revolution meant for them.

It is also, inevitably, informed by my own perspective. As a scholar who has traveled numerous times to Cuba, including taking three groups of students there as part of a class I teach on the Cuban Revolution, I am a strong opponent of U.S.-imposed travel restrictions. As a Latin Americanist who has studied and witnessed the deleterious effects of U.S. policies and foreign investment in countries such as Nicaragua, Haiti, and Colombia, and especially on the poor in those countries, I cannot help but admire the audacity of a government, and a country, that has tried to invent a radically different path to economic development, and has openly challenged U.S. imperialism in the hemisphere.

1

Cuba through 1959

Did the Cuban Revolution begin on January 1st, 1959, when the dictator Fulgencio Batista fled the island, leaving a new revolutionary government to take power? Or did it begin on July 26th, 1953, when Fidel Castro's guerrilla force attacked the Moncada Barracks in its first dramatic action? Or in the various revolutionary uprisings in 1844, 1868, 1895, 1912, or 1933, unfinished or aborted revolutions that failed to achieve their goals, but contributed to the island's revolutionary identity?

Colonial History

Some Cuban accounts argue that the Cuban Revolution began in 1511 when the Taíno Indian Hatuey (who had fled to Cuba, pursued by the Spanish, from neighboring Hispaniola) took up arms against the Spanish colonizers. A statue of Hatuey in Baracoa, Cuba (Figure 1.1), proclaims him "the first rebel of America."[1] Clearly the Cuban revolutionaries, and Cuban historiography, emphasize a long tradition of anti-colonial struggle on the island leading up to 1959.

Estimates of Cuba's indigenous population prior to 1492 range from a low of 100,000 to a high of 500,000. Within a few genera-

A History of the Cuban Revolution. Aviva Chomsky
© 2011 Aviva Chomsky

Figure 1.1   Bust of Hatuey in the main plaza of Baracoa in eastern Cuba. "Hatuey: The First Rebel of America. Burned at the Stake in Yara, Baracoa." Oriente Workers Lodge
Source: Hinz, Felix: "Baracoa. 'Cortesillo' y la ciudad española más antigua en Cuba" (2008), www.motecuhzoma.de/Baracoa-es.htm

tions, a combination of military conquest, enslavement, and above all, diseases introduced by the Spanish, had virtually wiped out the natives as a distinct people. Nevertheless, both biologically and culturally, indigenous survivals shaped the society that emerged from the ruins. The Spanish adopted Taíno words for places, products, and phenomena that were new to them. (Some of these words, like *hurricane*, *barbecue*, and *canoe* also made their way into English.) By choice or by force, indigenous women intermarried and reproduced with Spanish men. Indigenous foods and customs shaped the Spanish-dominated culture that emerged on the island.[2]

During much of the colonial period, the Spanish focused their attention on their mainland empires based in Mexico and Peru. The Caribbean was important strategically and geopolitically, because Spanish fleets carrying gold and silver from the mines on the mainland had to pass through there, and French, Dutch, and British pirates sought their share of the booty. These latter countries also succeeded in establishing control of some of the smaller islands, although the Spanish managed to hold on to Cuba, Puerto Rico, and half of Hispaniola. (The French took the eastern half, calling it Saint Domingue, while the Spanish dubbed their half Santo Domingo.) Although Cuba was the largest island in the Caribbean, its population was small: in 1700, only 50,000 people lived there.[3]

The British, French, Dutch and Danish, lacking the source of riches the Spanish had found in the mainland, set about establishing sugar plantations on their islands. The Portuguese did the same in Brazil. Together they imported millions of slaves between the mid-1600s and the early 1800s. Brazil, St. Domingue, Jamaica and Barbados in particular became huge exporters of sugar. The Spanish islands, though, were imperial backwaters until the late 1700s, with smaller populations, and more diversified and subsistence production.

The big influx of African slaves in Cuba, and the sugar export economy, started towards the end of the 1700s, as the Spanish attempted to increase their empire's economic efficiency through a series of measures knows as the Bourbon Reforms. Meanwhile the American and French Revolutions, followed by the Haitian Revolution, dramatically altered the global economy. The world's largest sugar producer, St. Domingue (which restored its Taíno name, Haiti, after the slave rebellion that freed it from France) retreated entirely from global markets, and soon Spain's mainland colonies followed the United States and Haiti in fighting for and eventually achieving independence. In the nineteenth century Spain turned its full attention to its much-reduced Caribbean empire, with Cuba as its centerpiece.

Over a million slaves were brought to the island in less than a century. African slaves continued to pour into Cuba until 1866, and slavery itself was not abolished until 1886. Between 1790 and 1867,

780,000 arrived.⁴ A substantial proportion of today's population of Cuba is at least partly descended from these Africans: estimates range from 30 percent to 60 percent.

Others arrived in Cuba also. As British pressure to end the slave trade increased, Cuban planters turned to China, and in the middle of the nineteenth century some 100,000 Chinese were imported to work in conditions not far removed from slavery. Large numbers of Spaniards continued to arrive both before and after Cuba gained its independence in 1898. U.S. investors, including both individual planters and well-known companies like Hershey and the United Fruit Company, began to take over the production of sugar in the late nineteenth century. In the early years of the twentieth century, the United States orchestrated a large influx of migrant workers from U.S.-occupied Haiti to labor on the plantations. Sugar workers also migrated from Jamaica. Refugees came from Europe, including Jews fleeing the Nazis and Spanish Republicans fleeing the 1936–39 Civil War and subsequent Franco dictatorship.

In an influential body of work in the 1940s, Cuban anthropologist Fernando Ortiz argued that Cuba's population was characterized by the phenomenon of *transculturation*. Each successive group of migrants, he explains was "torn from his native moorings, faced with the problem of disadjustment and readjustment, of deculturation and acculturation." Cuba's history, "more than that of any other country of America, is an intense, complex, unbroken process of transculturation of human groups, all in a state of transition."⁵

The United States may seem to share Cuba's multiracial, transculturated character, and in many ways it does. There are, though, some major historical differences. Africans formed a far greater proportion of Cuba's population, and they continued to arrive in large numbers during most of the nineteenth century. This presence meant that African languages, religions, and cultures remained much more alive in twentieth-century Cuba than in the United States.

In the United States, the independence movement was carried out by whites – many of them slaveholders – and the nation established in 1776 committed itself to maintaining the slave system. Not until almost a hundred years later were blacks granted citizenship. Even then, the country's white leadership was committed to a policy of territorial expansion and racial exclusion.

In Cuba, colonial rule lasted over a century longer, and slavery was understood as a part of the colonial system, firmly rejected by many leaders of the independence movement. "To be Cuban comes before being white, before being black, before being mulatto," white independence leader José Martí announced in an oft-repeated phrase. Independence would create a country "with all, and for the good of all."[6]

The Cuban War of Independence began in 1868 when plantation owner Carlos Manuel de Céspedes issued the "Grito de Yara," freed his slaves, and called upon them to join him in fighting for Cuba's independence. He was soon joined by Antonio Maceo, the "Bronze Titan" – the mixed-race son of a Venezuelan farmer and a free Afro-Cuban woman, Mariana Grajales. Together with José Martí these three formed the pantheon of Cuban independence leaders, highlighting for future generations the diversity that the movement represented. The Mayor of Havana officially named Grajales as "the mother of Cuba" in 1957. Each of these heroes of independence today has a Cuban airport bearing his or her name: Cuba's main international airport in Havana is named after José Martí (as are its National Library and other important institutions), while the airports in Santiago, and Guantánamo and Bayamo are named, respectively, after Maceo, Grajales, and de Céspedes.

National independence, then, and national identity, were associated with ideas of racial equality and racial unity in Cuba in a way very different from in the United States. This does not mean, of course, that anti-black racism did not, and does not still, exist in Cuba. No society whose history is based on centuries of racially-based exploitation can free itself overnight from the structures and ideas built into this kind of system. Even within the independence movement some, like Céspedes, argued for a gradual abolition that would accommodate the interests of the sugar plantocracy. Still, the relationship of anti-black racism to nationalism, and the relationships of blacks to the independence movement and ideology, were very different in Cuba from in the United States. After 1902, nationalist ideas about the integral connection between foreign, colonial domination and racial inequality only strengthened.

The experience and meaning of independence in Cuba were also shaped by the role of the United States in the process. Cuba fought for and obtained independence in a continent that was increasingly dominated by its northern neighbor. Martí echoed the sentiment of Simón Bolívar, leader of the Latin American independence movements three-quarters of a century earlier, who famously stated that "The United States ... seem[s] destined by Providence to plague America with torments in the name of freedom."[7] In 1823 the Monroe Doctrine announced U.S. intentions to police the hemisphere (for its own good, of course). The United States extended its control westward, challenging newly independent Mexico and climaxing in a war that added over half of Mexico's territory to the United States in 1848. In 1891, Martí penned the similarly oft-quoted essay "Our America" in which he warned of the U.S. threat. He used the phrase "Our America" to refer to Latin America, which he contrasted to the other America – the United States.

"Our America is running another risk that does not come from itself but from the difference in origins, methods, and interest between the two halves of the continent ... The scorn of our formidable neighbor, who does not know us, is Our America's greatest danger ... Through ignorance it may even come to lay hands on us ..." To challenge the threat of U.S. domination, Martí argued, Latin America must embrace its non-European origins – the very origins that the United States rejected. Latin America must "make common cause with the oppressed, in order to secure a new system opposed to the ambitions and governing habits of the oppressors" and, in particular, reject the "wicked and unpolitical disdain for the aboriginal race" that characterized the United States, which "drowns its Indians in blood."[8]

Nevertheless, Cuban attitudes towards the United States were decidedly mixed. Significant numbers, especially of white Cubans, saw the United States as a beacon of freedom and progress, and believed that Cuba's best hope for the future lay in becoming a part of the nation to the north. While Cuba's historians have tended to downplay or demonize annexationists (just as U.S. historians have de-emphasized the many Americans who supported the British rather than the independence movement at the end of the eighteenth century), they constituted an important voice both before and after independence. Czech scholar Josef Opatrný argued that in the mid-nineteenth century, annexationist sentiment was in fact a first step towards a move for independence, as it sowed the seeds of imagining a Cuba separate from Spain.[9] Cuba's tri-color national flag was in fact designed in 1848 in the United States by the Venezuelan émigré Narciso López, who modeled it after the Texas Lone Star, and led several annexationist incursions into Cuba.[10] But the United States was also home to many Cuban émigrés, like Martí himself, who were some of the strongest fomenters of the idea of independence.[11]

The outcome of Cuba's wars of independence, on and off between 1868 and 1898, consolidated what President McKinley called "ties of singular intimacy" between Cuba and the United States.[12] Refusing to recognize Cuba's independence fighters as belligerents, the United States invaded the island in 1898, and established a four-year military occupation. When U.S. forces withdrew in 1902 they left in place the Platt Amendment, which turned the island into a virtual U.S. protectorate. The Amendment, written by the U.S. Secretary of War and included in Cuba's new constitution as a condition for U.S. withdrawal, gave the United States control over Cuba's foreign and economic policies, the right to intervene militarily to protect U.S. property in Cuba, and the right to develop coaling and naval stations on the island. Under the last provision, the United States established its base at Guantánamo Bay, which it retains to this day over Cuban protests.

U.S. political, military, and economic influence dominated the island over the period leading up to 1959 and oversaw the economic distortion, political corruption, and repression that characterized that 60-year period. Except for Puerto Rico, no other Latin American country enjoyed – or endured – such a lengthy and intense relationship with the United States. The relationship shaped Cuban culture, the Cuban economy, Cuban politics, and Cubans' sense of national identity. Cubans refer to the period after 1902 as the "neo-colonial" period, or the "pseudo-republic" to indicate the compromised nature of the country's independence.

The Colony in the Republic

"The colony lives on in the republic," José Martí had written in 1891. Cuba was then still a colony, but he was referring to the cultural and intellectual adherence in other countries of Latin America to European ideas, including ideas about European racial superiority. Martí, who was killed in 1895 shortly after returning to Cuba to fight in the island's war of independence, did not live to see the colony living on in the Cuban republic. But he surely would have agreed with some of the critiques and protests regarding the new social order that emerged there during the first decades of the twentieth century.

The abolition of slavery in 1886, Afro-Cuban participation in the independence movement and army, and the very experience of the wars opened some doors towards challenging racial inequality and white racism. Post-independence developments, though, did much to restore white supremacy. The occupying U.S. army wasted no time in demobilizing the notably multiracial independence army, and adding U.S.-style racism to the complex mix that already existed in Cuba. Plantation owners, both Cubans and from the United States, sought to re-establish control over their labor force in the aftermath of abolition and black mobilization.

Some blacks adopted the ideas of another important independence fighter, Juan Gualberto Gómez, who argued after independence that through education and self-improvement blacks could individually overcome racial inequality. Others believed that blacks had to organize for social change, and formed the Independent Party of Color (PIC) to promote black interests. The slaughter of some 3000 blacks in a wave of military and paramilitary violence, ostensibly aimed at the PIC, put an end to black political organizing for many years.[13]

Still, as Cuban American historian Alejandro de la Fuente has argued, despite deep racial prejudices and inequities imbedded in

Cuban society by slavery, the independence ideology emphasizing racial unity led, among other things, to the establishment of universal (male) suffrage after independence. Universal suffrage meant that white politicians had to take black voters and their interests into account, and that mainstream political parties were open to black candidates. An official commitment to Martí's anti-racist stance meant that certain forms of institutionalized racism could not be implemented in Cuba as they were in the United States. In some ways, the situation in pre-revolutionary Cuba resembled that in the United States today. Racial discrimination was outlawed and officially disavowed, including at the voting polls. Nevertheless, racial inequality was widespread, and racism continued to permeate attitudes and institutions.[14]

An influx of Haitian and Jamaican migrants to the U.S.-owned plantations in eastern Cuba added another ingredient to the complex national and racial landscape. Despite their ostensible commitment to anti-racism, some white Cuban intellectuals argued that the influx of blacks threatened Cuba's racial balance. They even tried to woo Afro-Cubans into a nationalist, anti-imperialist, anti-immigrant stance that was based on anti-black stereotypes and racism. They argued that Cuban blacks were *not really black* because of their Cuban nationality, but that an influx of foreign blacks would destroy Cuba's racial harmony. And they invoked the colony, recalling the old association of colonial status with slavery. Once again, white foreigners were bringing blacks into the country to work on their plantations. Racial ideas and realities in Cuba presented a complicated landscape, but one in which the colonial heritage seemed very alive.[15]

The colony also lived on in the export economy and the economic distortions it entailed. Foreign capital and foreign products poured into the country after independence, but they did not create a rising tide that lifted all boats. Instead, the sugar boom displaced small farmers and provided meager wages. Rural folk flocked to the cities in search of jobs and a better life, but urban infrastructure served the wealthy and the small middle classes, not the burgeoning slums. With little in the way of a manufacturing sector, informal employment was the only path open for many poor migrants. Independence from

Spain had not brought the economic independence or prosperity that many had hoped for. Historian Louis A. Pérez echoed Martí's prophesy in his own analysis of the results of independence. "Many contradictions of colonial society remained unresolved," he wrote in 1995. "The United States had ... rescued and revived the moribund colonial order ... In all its essential features and in its principal functions, the republic gave new political form to the socio-economic infrastructure of the old colony."[16]

Cuban politics remained hostage to the United States, while U.S. companies and investors took control of the major sectors of Cuba's economy. By 1905, 60 percent of Cuba's rural land was owned by U.S. citizens or companies. U.S. investors also controlled 90 percent of Cuba's tobacco trade, the country's iron, copper, and nickel mines, its railroads, and its electricity and telephone systems.[17] U.S. economic historian Leland Jenks analyzed U.S. economic control in Cuba in his provocatively titled book *Our Cuban Colony* in 1928. Scott Nearing and Joseph Freeman used Cuba as a key example in their *Dollar Diplomacy: A Study in American Imperialism.*[18]

In the United States, the critical approach offered by Jenks and Nearing and Freedman was superseded in the mid-century by a more triumphalist narrative that framed U.S. foreign policy as benevolent and disinterested. Samuel Flagg Bemis famously opined, in 1943, that while "the United States has been an imperialistic power since 1898," its "comparatively mild imperialism was tapered off after 1921 and is fully liquidated now ... United States imperialism ... was never deep-rooted in the character of the people, that it was essentially a protective imperialism ... against intervention by the imperialistic powers of the Old World. It was, if you will, an imperialism against imperialism. It did not last long and it was not really bad."[19]

William Appleman Williams's *The Tragedy of American Diplomacy* (1959) initiated what came to be known as the revisionist school of U.S. diplomatic history, which dismissed Bemis and others' idealized interpretation and once again argued that U.S. policies were guided by imperialist and economic motives. Historians like Philip Foner and Louis A. Pérez developed this perspective with respect to Cuba. With the U.S. intervention in 1898, Pérez argued, "a Cuban war of liberation was transformed into a U.S. war of conquest."[20] In numerous works focusing on the pre-1959 period, Pérez explored the impact of U.S. political and economic control in Cuba.

Cuban historians also developed a critique of U.S. colonialist policies in the 1920s. As David Healy points out, Cuban historiography followed a more consistent trajectory, building on those early works to develop an analysis of Cuban history as a prolonged struggle for independence, beginning in 1868 and continuing through 1959. The U.S. intervention in 1898 crushed the possibility of independence that Cubans had been fighting for since 1868, and U.S. economic control, and repeated military interventions, in the first half of the twentieth century, maintained Cuba's neocolonial status until the Revolution.[21]

Political and economic turmoil also characterized the first half of the twentieth century. When the price and demand for sugar were strong, the economy boomed. When prices and demand crashed, as in 1921, the results were devastating. The 1921 crash led to a bank collapse, and a preview of the Great Depression. Prices shot up while unemployment skyrocketed. The population responded with strikes, demonstrations, and protests.[22]

Even in boom times, the fruits of economic growth were not evenly divided. For many Cuban workers and peasants who had supported or fought for the cause of independence, Pérez explains, "the dream of *patria* turned quickly into a nightmare." "The Cuban proletariat discovered that, for them, the transition from colony to republic meant a descent into destitution."[23] The boom and bust was inherent in the economy's overdependence on one product.

Foreign domination and widespread poverty contributed to another essential characteristic of pre-revolutionary Cuba: corruption. With few economic alternatives, Cubans turned to an increasingly corrupt public sector for enrichment, or for survival. "By 1925 corruption was an integral part of republican Cuba's daily economic and political life," write Sergio Díaz-Briquets and Jorge Pérez-López. "Low-level officials, often appointed as political patronage, depended on petty corruption to supplement meager salaries or accumulate savings, given their lack of job security in a highly politicized civil service. And just as petty corruption was rampant, so was grand corruption. To survive and prosper, businesses had to 'take care' of public officials. The most ambitious and entrepreneurial, ironically, looked to political corruption."[24] In the 1920s, "the spectacle of republican politics was played before an incredulous national audience. There seemed to be no limit to political abuses, no end to revelations of spectacular graft and accounts of official corruption in all branches" of government.[25]

Resentment against the status quo, and especially Cuban subordination to the United States, coalesced in the 1920s in a number of artistic and intellectual movements that challenged both Eurocentrism and U.S. domination with a revitalized Cuban nationalism. Cuban intellectuals were finally following José Martí's advice, and concentrating not only on Martí himself, but on a spectrum of authors from "Our America," challenging the idea of U.S. and European superiority. They were also reading critical U.S. and European authors, ranging from Marx, Engels, Trotsky, and Stalin, to those in the United States like Scott Nearing, Joseph Freeman, and Leland H. Jenks, who denounced U.S. imperialism in Cuba.

The intellectual currents of the 1920s incorporated a new valorization of things African, including, especially, the African-influenced musical genre of *son*. "In the context of the barrage of North American merchandise, films, literature, sports events, and music that entered Cuba during these years, *son* represented an important symbol of national identity" notes ethnomusicologist Robin Moore.[26] In this respect, Cubans played a part in the worldwide phenomenon of *négritude*, in their own way. *Négritude* drew together blacks in the French-speaking world, from independent Haiti to the French colonies of the Caribbean and West Africa, asserting the value and promotion of black experiences and cultures.

Black Cuban intellectuals also looked to the Harlem Renaissance of the 1920s and the flourishing of black intellectual and cultural life that it encompassed. Afro-Cuban writers like poet Nicolás Guillén and newspaper columnist Gustavo Urrutia developed close ties with U.S. colleagues like poet Langston Hughes and Afro-Puerto Rican Arthur Schomburg, curator of his own African-themed collections at the New York Public Library. White Cuban intellectuals like Fernando Ortíz and Ramiro Guerra y Sánchez were deeply influenced by these currents in black thought as they struggled to analyze Cuba's colonial history and its ongoing economic and political dependence. Critiques of U.S. imperialism in Cuba, of white supremacy in the United States, and of Cuba's own history of racial inequality, were all intertwined.

Numerous organizations grew out of the ferment of the 1920s. University students founded the FEU, or Federación Estudiantil Universitaria, in 1923. Cuba's Communist Party had its roots in the Cuban labor movement of the 1920s. The country's growing labor organizations formed a national federation, the Confederación Nacional Obrera de Cuba (CNOC) in 1925, and some of its leaders founded the Partido Comunista de Cuba (PCC) later the same year. During its first decade the PCC followed the lead of the Comintern (which it had quickly affiliated with) in focusing its activities on developing political influence in the urban labor movement, in which it played a major role. Stalin had declared the Comintern's "Third Period" in 1928, instructing the world's Communist parties to create militant labor unions based on the philosophy of class struggle. In the early 1930s, the Party expanded its reach into the rural areas, organizing agricultural workers and peasants, becoming one of the largest and strongest Communist parties in Latin America.

The Depression hit Cuba's export-dependent economy brutally. Wages and employment contracted, and organized protest grew. The corrupt government of Gerardo Machado, who had stretched his term in office first by pressing Congress to extend it, and then by running unopposed for a second term, increasingly resorted to violent repression of peaceful protests. By the early 1930s, Cubans ranging from sugar workers to urban workers to students and intellectuals were moving to direct action and armed rebellion.

The PCC and the labor movement affiliated with it played a major role in a series of political upheavals in 1933. While the Communists concentrated on labor organization and protest, other groups like the ABC Revolutionary Society and the Directorio Estudiantil Universitario took up arms against Machado. The government responded with growing repression, including outlawing both the

PCC and the CNOC as well as other political and social organizations. Even the United States came to see Machado as a liability, and began to work behind the scenes to orchestrate his removal.

Intense backroom maneuvering between the U.S. Ambassador, Sumner Welles, and the Cuban military, resulted in Machado's resignation and his replacement by Carlos Manuel de Céspedes, a little-known outsider, in 1933. The new government lasted less than a month before it was overturned by another military revolt, quickly joined by students and others. This time a group of radical reformers took the helm, with former university professor Ramón Grau San Martín as President and revolutionary anti-imperialist Antonio Guiteras as Minister of the Interior.

The new government called itself revolutionary, and proceeded to implement a series of social, political and labor reforms, including unilaterally abrogating the Platt Amendment. U.S. Ambassador Sumner Welles deemed it "frankly communistic."[27] "For one hundred days," historian Louis Pérez writes, "the provisional government devoted itself to the task of transforming Cuba with exalted purposefulness … This was the first government of the republic formed without the sanction and support of the United States. Under the injunction of 'Cuba for Cubans,' the new government proceeded to enact reform laws at a dizzying pace."[28] The new government implemented pro-labor policies that echoed – and in some cases prefigured – those of the New Deal in the United States, including creating a Ministry of Labor, raising wages, legislating the eight-hour day, and creating a system of Workers Compensation. These changes challenged U.S. political control, as well as the interests of U.S. investors on the island. But the new government went still further to challenge foreign economic control, with measures that cut the rates charged by (U.S.-owned) utility companies, and an agrarian reform. "The defense of Cuban interests," Pérez states bluntly, "jeopardized U.S. interests."[29] Meanwhile the labor uprising had taken on a life of its own. Sugar workers – many of them affiliated with the PCC – seized the plantations they worked on and established self-governing soviets. The United States quickly concluded that the new government was far too radical for its purposes. Increasingly alarmed, Welles turned to the Cuban army.

The 1933 revolt against Céspedes had been set off by a group of low-level officers led by Sergeant Fulgencio Batista. Grau San Martín quickly promoted Batista to Colonel and turned the command of the army over to him. But Welles too had his eye on Batista as a potential, more controllable, replacement for Grau. While refusing to recognize the new government, Welles privately cultivated Batista, suggesting to him that "the very great majority of the commercial and financial interests in Cuba who are looking for protection ... could only find such protection in himself" and that the United States would look approvingly on an overthrow of the revolutionary government.[30] Batista did just that in January of 1934, and this time, it lasted. The United States helped by immediately offering recognition to the new Batista regime. Directly, or behind the scenes, Batista would remain a power-maker until 1959. From 1934–44 and 1952–59 he ruled directly.

While Batista succeeded in crushing the armed opposition to his takeover, he eventually made peace with Cuba's Communist Party. In a 1935 about-face, the Comintern abandoned the Third Period for the idea of the Popular Front, in which the parties were urged to participate in elections and ally with what they termed bourgeois political parties and organizations to form a Popular Front against the threat of fascism. The Cuban Communist Party interpreted this dictum as a mandate to work with the Batista government. In return, Batista enacted some of the labor reforms that the CNOC had been demanding and even invited two Communist leaders, Juan Marinello and Carlos Rafael Rodríguez, to serve in his Cabinet.[31]

Reformism remained in the air, but the gap between reformist goals and ideologies, and political and economic realities, only grew. For example, a wide spectrum of Cuba's political groups participated in the writing of a new Constitution in 1940. The Constitution enshrined many of the reformist goals of 1933, including political and economic freedoms and guarantees. With no enforcement mechanisms, however, it remained a document representing dreams rather than realities.

In 1944 Batista stepped down when the opposition Auténtico Party won the elections. But reformist hopes gave way to an if anything more corrupt and unequal reality. "Embezzlement, graft, corruption, and malfeasance of public office permeated every branch of national, provincial, and municipal government. The public trust was transformed into a private till," Pérez concludes.[32] When Batista led a second coup in 1952, there was little organized opposition.

The new military government also had little to offer in the way of solution to Cuba's deep structural problems: overdependence on a single crop (sugar), political and economic subordination to the United States, and grinding poverty and inequality. What it did provide was repression. Opposition was banned. The Communist Party, with which Batista had previously collaborated, was declared illegal in 1953, partly to adhere to U.S. Cold War policy. The Cuban labor movement was taken over by pro-government leaders. Other organizations, like Afro-Cuban clubs and societies, followed suit as collaboration became necessary for survival.

While all agree that Cubans of African descent were dispropor-tionately represented among the country's poor, scholars have also disagreed about the relationship of the Batista government with Cuba's black population. Black social organizations in the 1950s – like most formal organizations in Cuba – had been purged, coopted, and were essentially controlled by the Batista government. Thus it is not surprising that they expressed support for Batista. Batista himself was of mixed race, and some of his conservative opponents attacked him on the basis of his race, using epithets like "el mulato malo" and the "black beast" to refer to him.[33]

One could say that there were at least two Cubas in the 1950s. One was the 1.5 million who were jobless or who belonged to the rural poor, including landless workers and *campesinos* with small plots. These impoverished Cubans survived mostly on rice, a few beans, and sugar-water, creating the "naked children, their swollen stom-achs testifying to an unbalanced diet and infection from parasitic worms" that sociologist Lowry Nelson found everywhere in rural Cuba in 1950. At the other end of the spectrum, the 900,000 or so wealthiest Cubans controlled 43 percent of the country's income. These were the people who had money to spend on frequent shop-ping jaunts to Miami, luxurious, air conditioned homes, and even mausoleums complete with "elevators, air conditioners, and tele-phones" to make sure they continued to enjoy a high level of comfort in the afterlife. In between, another 3.5 million struggled to make ends meet. Cuba's close integration with the U.S. economy meant that almost everything Cubans bought was imported from the United States, and the cost of living was as high or higher than in the United States. But Cuban wages were much lower, and Cubans had none of the social services and guarantees that U.S. citizens enjoyed.[34] In many ways, the country was ripe for revolution.

Revolution: A War, or a Process?

A song by Carlos Puebla, a troubadour who chronicled the events of the early revolutionary years, captures some of the heady optimism of the revolutionary victory and its rejection of the past:

> They thought they could go on forever here, earning their 100% profits
> With their apartment houses, and leaving the people to suffer.
> And go on cruelly conspiring against the people
> To continue exploiting them... And then Fidel arrived!
> The party was over:
> The Comandante arrived and order it to stop!

Many of the actors and events in Cuba's revolutionary history have been elevated to mythical status, not only in Cuba, but around the world. In 2000, *Time Magazine* named Che Guevara as one of the 100 most important figures of the previous century. "His figure stares out at us from coffee mugs and posters, jingles at the end of key rings and jewelry, pops up in rock songs and operas and art shows," *Time* notes.[35] In Cuba, it is impossible to pass a day without confronting Che's image. Schoolchildren chant "¡Seremos como el Che!"– we will be like Che – to launch the school day (Figure 1.2).[36] The United States has its American Revolution, Declaration of Independence, George Washington, Abraham Lincoln, and Statue of Liberty as symbols of what many believe to be the essence of the country and

Figure 1.2   Print by Cuban artist Sandra Ramos, "Seremos Como El Che"
(We will be like Che)
Source: Sandra Ramos, 1993, "Seremos Como El Che". Etching/aquatint
40 × 50 cm. © Sandra Ramos

its national identity. Cuba elevates figures from its nineteenth-century
revolutionary war against Spain to heroic status, and it does the same
with many of the people and events central to the 1959 Revolution.
None quite reaches the iconic status of José Martí, whose bust is
ubiquitous in public places and whose name graces Havana's international airport and the country's national library. But the leaders of
the 1959 Revolution have also achieved outsized status in Cuba.

   Che Guevara became the most mythologized leader for several
reasons. Unlike the other revolutionary leaders, he was not Cuban.
Rather, he was a Marxist physician from Argentina, who left his
country to devote his life to the revolutionary cause. He was also

something of a revolutionary philosopher, leaving his mark on Marxist thought with his ideas about guerrilla warfare and, even more, about the goals and nature of socialism. He was the architect of some of the most radical and utopian economic reforms implemented in Cuba in the early 1960s, when it seemed to many that virtually anything was possible. He also came to symbolize the Revolution's commitment to internationalism, to solidarity with revolutionary movements from Africa to Latin America. Finally, he died, a martyr, trying to bring his revolutionary theories to the mountains of Bolivia, in 1967. Thus his image has forever remained associated with the sense of infinite possibility of the early days of the Revolution, rather than with the compromises made through the decades of revolutionary power.

Behind the various heroes are the organizations and movements they participated in or led, and the many others whose work, and names, did not make it into the history books. The July 26th Movement that initiated a revolutionary war against the Batista government in 1953, a year after the coup, and led the final victory march into Havana on New Year's Eve, 1958, brought together a diverse and complex set of leaders and organizations.

The group took its name from its first action: the July 26th, 1953 attack on the Moncada Barracks in eastern Cuba that initiated the uprising against Batista. Fidel Castro, who led the attack, like most of the other predominantly young men who joined him, was involved with the student movement and the Ortodoxo Party, founded in 1947 by former student leader Eduardo Chibás to resurrect the ideals of the 1933 reform movements. "The Moncada showed us the road to follow," Carlos Puebla sang, "And since that great example, for us it is always the 26th."[37]

The plan was to take the barracks, and call upon the population to rise up in rebellion. It was a miserable failure in military terms. The attack was repelled, and 61 out of the 160 or so attackers were killed. Many of the others were captured on the spot or, like Fidel, shortly after escaping the scene. Cuba's Communist Party condemned the attack as "adventurism guided by bourgeois misconceptions" and for suffering "lack of theoretical cohesion and ideology."[38]

But as Puebla's lyrics suggest, Moncada came to occupy an exalted spot in revolutionary historiography, as symbolizing the beginning of a complete break with Cuba's past. For its audacity, its youthfulness, and its sheer drama, as well as for launching Fidel Castro's long career as a revolutionary, the meaning of Moncada has expanded over the years. Even the bullet-holes in the building have been recreated and maintained as a tourist attraction. In a further symbolic gesture, the barracks were converted, after the revolutionary victory, into an educational complex.

From prison, Fidel penned his own defense. He freely admitted his participation in the attack, but turned the speech into a wide-ranging denunciation of the Batista regime and defense of the right to resist illegitimate authority, citing everything from Cuba's 1940 Constitution to Montesquieu to St. Thomas Aquinas and Martin Luther. The U.S. Declaration of Independence, he reminded the court, declared that a government's authority rested on the consent of the governed. "Condemn me – it does not matter!" he concluded stirringly. "History will absolve me."[39]

The document also outlined a revolutionary project. Castro appealed to Cubans who were unemployed, to the *campesinos* and farm laborers, and to the urban professionals for whom political corruption closed all opportunity. He laid out the five "revolutionary laws" that the Moncada attackers intended to implement: restoration and implementation of the 1940 Constitution, an agrarian reform putting land in the hands of those who tilled it, obligation of employers to share profits with workers, guaranteed markets for small sugar farmers, and confiscation of all enterprises obtained through fraud and corruption. All of these revolutionary laws, he emphasized, were based on the Constitution itself, which restricted large landholdings and provided labor rights.

It was a program that could unify Cuba's fragmented opposition – but during most of the 1950s, various organizations and ideologies competed for the population's support in bringing about political change. Some advocated armed uprising, while others, like the now-banned Communist Party, believed that the organized labor movement must be the chief protagonist. It was not until 1958 that the

July 26th Movement emerged as the conclusive leader of the struggle. "To reach January 1st, 1959," Julia Sweig suggests, "the 26th of July not only had to mount a two-year military campaign [two years, because it began in 1956 when Castro returned from exile] but also a political campaign against many of the forces that were also seeking an end to the Batista regime."[40] In a way, it's a backwards-looking history that now proclaims the Moncada attack as the first shot of the Revolution. At the time, it appeared to be one more crazy, failed scheme.

If the Moncada attack came to symbolize the opening of the Cuban Revolution, Fidel Castro's return to the island after being released from prison and sent into exile in Mexico, with some 80 other revolutionaries on the yacht *Granma* in 1956, constitutes the second act. The *Granma* today rests proudly in Havana's Museo de la Revolución, and Cuba's main daily newspaper, the official organ of the Communist Party's Central Committee, takes its name from the boat.[41]

As a military expedition, however, the *Granma* landing was not much more successful than the Moncada attack. An uprising planned in the city of Santiago to coincide with the boat's arrival was quickly crushed, and government forces greeted the *Granma* as it landed and succeeded in killing most of the 82 would-be rebels. Fidel and his brother Raúl Castro, along with Che Guevara, escaped into the Sierra Maestra mountains of eastern Cuba. "They thought they could go on, swallowing up more and more land," sang Carlos Puebla, "Without even knowing that there in the Sierra, the future was dawning."[42]

The mountains of eastern Cuba proved fertile ground for rebellion. Since colonial times they had harbored their share of outlaws, squatters, and rebels.[43] The expansion of the U.S.-dominated sugar plantation economy into eastern Cuba during the early twentieth century only increased the ranks of the dispossessed and the discontented.

The rural rebellion has held the place of pride in Cuban historiography. Che Guevara's *Guerrilla Warfare* promoted and popularized the idea of the *foco* – the theory that a small group of dedicated guerrilla fighters could set off a mass uprising through spectacular acts, and that peasant uprising was the key to revolution in Latin America. The sierra strategy was to defeat Batista's army in the countryside.

One reason that the sierra became so important in Cuban historiography of the Revolution is because of how it shaped revolutionary ideology and programs. Leaders like Fidel Castro and Che Guevara were fighting for radical change before they spent time in the sierra. But it was during those sierra years that the goals of the July 26th Movement developed and crystallized. "Among the factors influencing the development of the postrevolutionary health ideology, the single most important was the guerrillas' confrontation with the abject poverty and enormous health problems of the rural population," Julie Feinsilver argues.[44] Rural poverty had to do with lack of money, but it also had to do with lack of jobs, lack of social services, and lack of education. From an urban, middle class vantage point, it was not so easy to see the deeply imbedded, structural nature of rural poverty. Living with the rural poor was a consciousness-raising experience. Two key aspects of the later revolutionary program grew from the sierra: one, the need for a fundamental redistribution of resources that focused on the countryside; and two, the need for nation-building and consciousness-raising, by bringing urban Cubans face to face with the realities of rural poverty.

The sierra was also important to the revolutionary ideology that linked the 1950s uprising directly to the failed struggles for national independence and social justice of the past. Eastern Cuba was where the Wars of Independence had begun, where it had radicalized, and where the Cuban cause found its "first and most ardent supporters."[45] The July 26th Movement aimed to fulfill the project that José Martí and so many others had died for. In 1898, U.S. occupation forces prevented the Cuban rebel army from entering the eastern capital of Santiago. "What happened in 1895 will not happen again," Fidel proclaimed on the verge of entering Santiago on December 31, 1958. "This time the *mambises* will advance on Santiago de Cuba!"[46]

Still, the sierra may have been less key to the Revolution in military terms than the historiography has suggested. Recently historians have turned to the urban organizations and emphasized their important role in the July 26th Movement. The *llano* (plains, in contrast to the sierra or mountains) strategy aimed to force Batista's resignation through urban insurrection. Julia Sweig argues that from 1957–58 the urban underground wing of the Movement, led by middle class youth and focusing on acts of sabotage leading up to a general strike, held center stage in Cuba's revolutionary war. It was only after the general strike planned for April, 1958 failed that Fidel and Che's sierra movement emerged preeminent in the revolutionary coalition.[47]

Curiously, a U.S. journalist, writing for the *New York Times*, gave Fidel Castro's sierra guerrillas' revolt an unexpected boost and contributed to the sierra's mythmaking qualities. *Times* reporter Herbert L. Matthews travelled into the sierra to interview Fidel in February, 1957, just months after the failed *Granma* expedition. His explosive report appeared on the front page of the *Times* and brought Castro into U.S. living rooms. "He has strong ideas of liberty, democracy, social justice, the need to restore the Constitution, to hold elections," Matthews reported. Another *Times* reporter would later dub Matthews "the man who invented Fidel."[48]

Until March of 1958, the United States stood behind its ally Batista, supplying his government with arms and ammunition. Just as the rebels were unifying and gaining strength, the government lost its most important pillar of support when the United States cut off military aid. What Batista hoped would be a final offensive against the rebels in the summer of 1958 failed, and the rebel counteroffensive that begin in August proved inexorable. Batista's army, though large and well equipped, was poorly trained and poorly motivated. As 1958 drew to a close, the rebel armies took city after city and moved in on the capital, as the United States scrambled ineffectually to derail a July 26 victory or to impose an alternative that they believed would be more amenable to U.S. control.[49]

Much ink has been spent in the United States trying to pinpoint when, exactly, the Cuban Revolution became a socialist revolution, or when Fidel Castro became a Communist. It's important to remember that Communist and other Marxist political parties and organizations have been active in Latin America throughout the century. The Communist parties are generally those that historically have been allied with the Comintern, while other independent Marxist parties and organizations have followed different leaders, methods, and goals. Despite U.S. preoccupation with Communism, the Soviet Union and the Comintern have not supported the idea of armed revolution in Latin America, and they did not support the revolution in Cuba in the 1950s. Soviet-aligned parties like the Cuban PSP have been involved in labor organizing, and often in electoral politics, but generally not in armed resistance. The PSP was a late and reluctant participant in the July 26th Coalition that led Cuba's armed revolution, joining it only in the summer of 1958, when the fall of the Batista regime was virtually assured.

Much more important to Latin America's revolutionary movements has been the ideology and legacy of Che Guevara. Mexican commentator Jorge Castañeda, author of a popular study of the Latin American Left as well as a biography of Che Guevara, argues that Che's legacy for Latin America lies primarily in his commitment to revolutionary violence and guerrilla warfare, and in the obstacles that his larger-than-life romanticism places in the way of more "modern" leftist alternatives.[50] In this perspective, Che and his Marxist thought have only served to lead many Latin Americans – both would-be revolutionaries, and even more so, those unwillingly caught up in their struggles – to their deaths.

But Che's legacy, and his place in the Cuban and the global popular imagination, go beyond his military feats and his theorizing about guerrilla warfare. Just as important was his reformulation of socialist ideas. In his many and well-translated writings, Che argued that Communism could not be reduced to a mere reformation of the economy. Rather, "Communism is a phenomenon of consciousness" – a means of overcoming alienation, of creating a "new man." "I am not interested in dry economic socialism," Che wrote. "We are fighting against misery, but we are also fighting against alienation ... Marx was preoccupied both with economic factors and with their repercussions on the human spirit. If communism isn't interested in this too, it may be a method of distributing goods, but it will never be a revolutionary way of life."[51]

Cuban historian and philosopher Juan Antonio Blanco echoed this strain in Che's thought in an interview in 1993: "Che's criticism of the Soviet Union and the socialist camp was that they were obsessed with the economic construction of socialism and that they were disregarding the moral and spiritual factors of socialist societies. Che once said in an interview that he was not interested in economic socialism. If you disregard the spiritual factors and only attempt to deal with economic factors, you are not going to get rid of alienation. For both Che and Fidel, socialism was not simply a matter of developing a new way of distribution. It was a question of freeing people from alienation at the same time."[52]

The idea of the *hombre nuevo* or New Man found strong echoes in alternative and revolutionary movements around the world, even after the idea of guerrilla warfare had faded. Historian Van Gosse has argued that the New Left in the United States took more than a little inspiration from Cuba's attempt to create a new, humane form of socialism.[53] From the Counterculture of the 1960s to the New Age movements of the 1990s, critiques of the spiritual and human poverty of capitalism and materialism referred to Che's positions. Most recently, President Hugo Chávez in Venezuela announced the country's commitment to creating the *hombre nuevo* there: "The old values of individualism, capitalism and egoism must be demolished," he declared.[54]

Although public U.S. pronouncements on the Cuban Revolution emphasized the issue of "Communism," a close look at internal U.S. government correspondence at the time shows a somewhat different concern. In the early years of the Revolution the issues of Soviet influence, human rights, or military threat to the United States rarely surface in U.S. diplomatic correspondence. Instead, what the State Department and the diplomats on the ground worried about was what kind of economic model Cuba was going to pursue, and in particular, how U.S. businesses in Cuba would be affected. Further, they were quite concerned about how the Cuban example might inspire other Latin American countries to attempt similar economic transformations to the detriment of U.S. investors. As J. C. Hill of the Bureau of Inter-American Affairs at the State Department put it in September, 1959, "There are indications that if the Cuban Revolution is successful other countries in Latin America and perhaps elsewhere will use it as a model and we should decide whether or not we wish to have the Cuban Revolution succeed."[55]

When Fidel Castro's troops made their triumphant entrance into Havana on New Year's Day, 1959, the war was over, but the revolution was just about to begin. In Cuba, "the Revolution" refers to a 50-year process of consciously creating a new society with many different phases, twists and turns.

2

Experiments with Socialism

This chapter begins with the economy, and looks at how Cuba has experimented with bold economic change, beginning with agrarian reform and leading to virtually complete nationalization of the economy. It highlights everyday issues of production and consumption in areas like food, housing, education, and health care, in the context of domestic and global politics. It focuses on social and ideological, as well as economic, aspects of Cuba's version of socialism. Voluntarism, massive incorporation of women into the workforce, socialization of child rearing, and rationing all characterized Cuba's "socialism with pachanga."[1]

The July 26th Movement began its experiment at governance on January 1st, 1959, with an enormous popular support and legitimacy. Its diverse supporters, though, had very different ideas about what kind of new system should replace the old. Some wanted merely an end to Batista's corrupt rule and a restoration of constitutional order, with little fundamental social change. Others saw a more revolutionary opportunity in the collapse of the old order and the overwhelming popular mandate behind the new government. Could a revolution overcome dependency, poverty, and underdevelopment? Could it create a new society, and a new man?

Certainly, dependence on the USSR came to characterize socialist Cuba. But the Revolution encompassed many other political, social,

A History of the Cuban Revolution. Aviva Chomsky
© 2011 Aviva Chomsky

cultural, and economic changes as well. Most historians periodize the Cuban Revolution by its economic phases, shifts, and landmarks. Such a periodization would characterize the 1960s as the decade of experimentation, starting by trying to shift the economy away from sugar, but returning to it later in the decade. The radically experimental phase ended with the failed attempt to achieve a record 10 million ton harvest in 1970. The years 1970–86 saw increasing political and economic dependence on the USSR, institutionalization and bureaucratization, and, starting in 1980, market openings. The 1986 Rectification Campaign has been much debated by those who have analyzed it, but all agree that it halted the experimentation with markets.

The fall of the Soviet bloc drastically undercut Cuba's economic model, and the Special Period in Time of Peace declared in 1991 began a series of major economic reforms. Once again, it's difficult to capture the trend since 1991 in a single generalization. Sociologist Susan Eckstein usefully characterized the post-1990 reforms as falling into three categories: socialist, capitalist, and pre-capitalist.

Chapters 7 and 8 will examine the post-1990 period. The rest of this chapter will trace Cuba's domestic political–economic development during the first 30 years of the Revolution. It will pay special attention to identifying where radical changes have taken place over the course of the Revolution, and what ideas and policies can be said to characterize the Revolution as a whole.

Analyzing the Situation: Economic Backwardness

The idea that the Revolution must bring about political independence and social justice was deeply rooted in Cuba's own revolutionary history. As the new leaders analyzed their country's situation and began to develop and implement policies, they drew on a wide range of revolutionary and reformist ideologies to develop their programs. In addition to those described in the Introduction, Cuban revolutionary leaders looked to, and contributed to, contemporary debates about the meaning and nature of economic development.

After World War II social scientists developed several kinds of critiques of the state of the world, and different ideas for how to improve living standards in its poorer areas. *Modernization* theorists explained the higher standard of living in what came to be called the First World – Europe, the United States, Canada, Australia – as the result of its economic development. They saw development as a linear process, and argued that the "backward" or "underdeveloped" countries needed to move forward along the same path to industrialization in order to catch up with the "developed" world.[2]

Dependency theorists, primarily coming from Latin America and influenced by Marxism, challenged this linear view. They argued that the industrialized countries had benefited from their colonial relations with Latin America and Africa, and that they had developed in tandem – but different – ways. The colonies had undergone *dependent development* based on foreign domination of their economies and the production of primary goods for export to the industrializing colonial powers. Dependent development was skewed in a number of ways. Landed elites maintained a near-feudal control in the countryside, profiting from the labor of a large and extremely poor peasantry. Modern urban areas served the needs of a small elite linked to foreign capital. Income was squandered on luxury consumption by this elite, rather than invested in production. Foreign capital controlled key sectors of the economy. Democratic institutions were weak or nonexistent. This meant that foreign capital reigned supreme, and major decisions about the use of the country's resources were made by outsiders, for the benefit of outsiders.[3]

Cuba's economy exhibited many of the characteristics associated with economic dependency. Three-quarters of the country's arable land was used to produce sugar, which accounted for 80 percent of its exports. Forty percent of the farms and 55 percent of the mills were in the hands of U.S. companies. U.S. investors also controlled 90 percent of Cuba's telecommunications and electrical services and half of the country's railroads, as well as significant portions of the banking, cattle, mining, petroleum, and tourist industries.[4] Almost a quarter of those with jobs worked in the sugar industry, and most of these only seasonally. Technical development helped planters reduce

the time of the harvest from 10 months at the beginning of the twentieth century to only three months by the 1950s, meaning that sea-
sonal unemployment skyrocketed.[5]

While Cuba's small middle and upper classes, who resided primarily in Havana, enjoyed reasonably high levels of access to education,
health care, and urban amenities, the majority of the population was
rural and poor – what Cubans called *guajiros*. Swedish economist
Claes Brunendius described a typical *guajiro's* life this way: "He
lived in a *bohío*, a small house with an earthen floor and a roof made
of palm thatch. For 90 percent of the *guajiros*, a kerosene lamp
was the only form of lighting, and 44 percent of them had never
attended school. Only 11 percent drank milk, only 4 percent ate meat,
and only 2 percent ate eggs. The daily diet, which had a deficiency
of 1,000 calories, was the main reason for a constant increase in the
number of cases of tuberculosis, anemia, parasitic diseases, and other
illnesses."[6]

Dependency also affected the relatively privileged urban sectors,
though. "The modern Cuban eats hot dogs, hamburgers, hot cakes,
waffles, fried chicken and ice cream," commented an American journalist in 1957. "It has become almost impossible in Havana today to
find native foods such as *malanga, yuca, picadillo* or *ajiaco*."[7] Though
something of an exaggeration – in fact small food stands continued
to offer traditional Cuban foods throughout the city – the observa-
tion reflected an overall reality that many Cubans saw as a decidedly
mixed blessing. "The Cuban is unfortunately fading into the distant
past," wrote one commentator in the 1920s. "Soon ... there will be
nothing remaining except a stylized caricature of the *yanki* ... where
chewing gum and tortoiseshell eye glasses will complete our conver-
sion into puppets 'Made in the U.S.'"[8] It was the same problem José
Martí had critiqued in the 1870s: "Our youth go out into the world
wearing Yankee- or French-colored glasses and aspire to rule by
guesswork a country they do not know." And his solution: "Statesmen
who arise from the nation must replace statesmen who are alien to
it ... Make wine from plantains, it may be sour, but it is our wine!"[9]

Breaking the economic and psychological dependency on the
United States was clearly to be an overriding goal of the Revolution.

But Cuban planners were also keen to avoid some of the darker side of industrialization in backward countries. In both the socialist bloc and in capitalist Latin America, the push to industrialize had been funded by a super-exploitation of the peasant class. In the USSR and China, peasants starved in famines. In Latin America, there was no widespread famine, but peasants still starved – slowly. In the twentieth century they also fled the countryside, in desperate hope of improving their livelihoods in the cities. They flooded into sprawling urban slums and shantytowns.

Many of the leaders of Cuba's guerrilla war came from middle class, urban, educated backgrounds. Castro himself was the son of a sugar planter, educated at Catholic boarding schools and with a law degree from the University of Havana. Their experience fighting in the mountains of eastern Cuba was key to their political formation. In the sierra they were confronted with realities of the agro-export economy, with rural poverty, and with the desperate needs in the countryside.

So another pillar of the Cuban development model was to reduce inequalities between city and countryside by privileging rural development. Schools, universities, health clinics, theaters, electricity, running water – all of these so-called urban amenities would come to the countryside. Yet another aspect of the rural orientation was the idea that urban Cubans must have their consciousness raised by directly experiencing the rural realities. Until the 1990s, this position remained a constant, despite the many twists and turns in the economy.

The 1960s: Experimentation and the Great Debate

The first weeks and months after January 1st, 1959, were characterized by a series of radical reforms that drastically redistributed Cuba's wealth and income. "Expectations ran high, were met, and then raised higher again," writes historian Louis Pérez. "Labor received wage increases, the unemployed received jobs. The urban proletariat received rent and utility rate reductions. Peasants received land and credit ... The effects were visible. A significant redistribution of income had taken place. Real wages increased approximately 15 percent through a corresponding decline in the income of landlords and entrepreneurs. In the short space of six months, hundreds of thousands of Cubans developed an immediate and lasting stake in the success of the Revolution."[10] Social services were vastly expanded, and made available free of charge or at very low cost. "Basic social services" that were cost-free included "schooling, medical care, medicines, and social security, but also water, burial services, sports facilities, even public phones." Rates for utilities and public transportation were slashed.[11]

Restructuring production into a viable, egalitarian economy, however, was a lot harder than the initial redistribution of existing resources. The problems were exacerbated by two factors that all such experiments have faced: capital flight, and social capital flight. In a capitalist economy, investment comes from private individuals or institutions (like banks) that invest their money based on where they believe a profit can be made. If a revolutionary government starts to limit the ability to make a profit – by raising wages or placing legal restrictions on businesses – capitalists will start to look elsewhere. They may place their money in foreign banks, or invest in enterprises overseas. In other words, capital flight.

Second, the formerly privileged classes, who generally have high levels of education, skills, business contacts, and other forms of what social scientists call *social capital* often decide to flee the country themselves when they see their privileges evaporating. The institutions (like private schools, maids, and fancy restaurants) and the luxury items that their status depends on are no longer available. Their comfortable lifestyles are threatened or undermined. They may have relatives or friends abroad, they may even have attended private school or college in the United States. They have the resources to leave – and many of them do. Half of Cuba's 6,000 doctors, for example, emigrated in the years immediately following the Revolution.[12] The country loses their *social capital* – the very skills, education, and contacts that it most needs to restructure its economy.

Cuba's new leaders vowed to break the island's historic dependence on sugar exports. Sugar, Cuban anthropologist Fernando Ortiz had argued in 1940, meant foreign, colonial domination; it meant slavery and dispossessed workers; it meant dependence, backwardness, and underdevelopment. Many economists and other social scientists in the 1960s agreed. Cuban leaders vowed to modernize the economy and overcome the island's historic dependence by diversifying agriculture and by promoting industrialization. It was not an unprecedented goal – but Cuba intended to do it simultaneously with a Revolution that was redistributing the country's wealth and resources.

The Revolution would accomplish this by relying on two techniques: government distribution systems, ranging from land reform to rationing, which guaranteed that the poor got an equal share of whatever resources there were; and popular mobilization, which increased the availability of certain kinds of services even when resources were lacking. Education and health care were two areas in which human resources could, to a certain extent, make up for the lack of material resources.

The first years of the Revolution were characterized by an ethos of voluntarism and redistribution mobilized in the service of national redemption. While some Cubans objected, and left the country, many more were inspired by the opportunity to remake their society. The literacy campaign, the formation of mass organizations, and the reform of the health system marked this initial period of intense mobilization.

"The attack on illiteracy," Richard Fagen explains, was "not simply a technological or pedagogical problem. It was seen as a profoundly political effort, one tied intimately to the revolutionary transformation of society and the economy."[13] Illiteracy and lack of education meant silence, marginalization, and oppression. Mass education was a key means of overturning centuries of inequality and empowering the poor. The mobilization of some 250,000 urban Cubans, including 100,000 students, was also a part of the project of political education, or *concientización*, for the urban, educated sectors of the population who had lived in relative material comfort under the old order. The campaign "vividly demonstrated a fundamental and repeatedly stated value of Cuban society – namely, that revolution *equals* education."

Figure 2.1   Literacy Museum in Ciudad Libertad outside of Havana, 2000
Source: Photo by Aviva Chomsky

Banners throughout the country exhorted "The path up from underdevelopment is education," and "The school plan is your responsibility."[14] The Museo Nacional de la Campaña de Alfabetización, housed in a former military complex in the outskirts of Havana, commemorates the achievements of the campaign (see Figure 2.1).

The literacy campaign, like the massive infusion of resources into education, especially for the rural poor, also invoked José Martí's "radical ideas for rural, vocational, lyrical, and adult education." Private schools were closed, and basic, vocational, and technical education was spread to every corner of the country.[15] Urban students were required to spend time working in the countryside. In the 1960s, this took the form of two-week mobilizations for agricultural labor; in the 1970s, urban high school students who wanted to follow the pre-university track were sent to rural boarding schools that combined classroom work with manual labor.

Economic and social marginalization meant that Cuba's poor had little access to health care before the Revolution. Like wealth and education, health care was concentrated in the urban areas. In January

1960 the new government created the Rural Health Service, establishing rural health facilities and requiring every medical school graduate to spend a year doing social service work in an underserved rural area. Dental service was added in 1961.[16] Like education, improving access to health care was not seen as a technical problem, but rather as a revolutionary transformation of society.

The overt hostility of Cuba's powerful neighbor, the United States, to the revolutionary process contributed to the sense that the Revolution had to continue with a state of mobilization and alert even after the military victory. In late 1960, in the context of ongoing attacks and sabotage – which Castro called "imperialist campaigns of aggression" – the Cuban leader called for the population to "set up a system of revolutionary collective vigilance." "When the masses are organized," he exhorted, "there isn't a single imperialist, or a lackey of the imperialists, or anybody who has sold out to the imperialists, who can operate."[17] The response was the creation of the CDRs or Committees for the Defense of the Revolution.

"The first committees began to form almost immediately following Castro's speech, despite the absence of official guidelines for the program," explains Richard Fagen. "Groups of enthusiastic citizens went ahead and organized their own committees without much attention to procedural niceties. Like so many other institutions of the early years of the Revolution, the first CDR displayed more energy than order, more enthusiasm than discipline."[18]

The Revolution called on everybody to participate in creating the new society. The CDRs carried out the country's first vaccination campaign, in 1962. They supported the implementation of the Literacy Campaign. When the U.S.-backed exile army invaded Cuba at the Bay of Pigs in April, 1961, the CDRs were ordered to round up counterrevolutionaries and their sympathizers. "While the Revolutionary Armed Forces and the Militia were engaging the exile troops ... the committees, in a frenzy of activity in the cities and towns, were reporting and rounding up persons suspected of counterrevolutionary sentiments and behavior."[19] Although tens of thousands were detained – often on flimsy evidence – most were released when the three-day invasion was decisively defeated. The events prefigured an aspect of Cuba's revolutionary mobilization that would be repeated over the decades: the greater the external threat to the government and the country, the greater was the pressure exerted on the population to close ranks, refrain from criticism, and conform and obey.

By 1963 the attempt to diversify the economy by abandoning sugar production had proved disastrous. Nevertheless, the revolutionary project of redistributing the country's resources, raising the standard of living of the poor, and popular mobilization to create a new, equal country, had succeeded in bringing about fundamental social changes. Despite what looked like a downturn or failure in macroeconomic terms, things got much better for the poor.

By the mid-1960s Cuban leaders, and their advisors, agreed that returning to sugar production in order to finance grander economic projects was an inevitable necessity. But they continued to debate the shape, and the pace, of the grander economic project. Soviet advisors, and members of the Cuban Communist Party who adhered to a Soviet model, argued for Soviet-style "market socialism": a combination of central planning and capitalist-style market incentives. Investment, and rewards in the form of wages and benefits, should reflect productive capacity. Eventually, increased production would benefit everyone.

But Che Guevara's alternative vision, which argued for abolishing the market altogether, won out initially. According to this idea, the socialist *hombre nuevo* would be motivated by moral incentives rather than material reward. Voluntarism was an important part of this model, based on the success of the literacy campaign. But revolutionary mobilization would be based on decisions made from above. With sufficient revolutionary zeal, the impossible could be achieved.

Part of the idea of abolishing material incentives and the market was that people shouldn't need money to get access to goods and services. The private economy was virtually abolished. The agrarian reforms of 1959 and 1963 abolished all private farms over five *caballerías* (67 hectares). With the Urban Reform Law in 1960, the state took over all rental housing and set rents at no more than 10 percent of a family's income. Between 1965 and 1967 private doctors, hospitals and clinics were brought into the new socialized medical system, so that all health care became public. And in 1968, the "revolutionary offensive" nationalized the remaining small private businesses. Pretty much everything people needed was now provided by the government, not the private sector. And much of what the government provided was provided free, or at heavily subsidized rates: health care, education, telephone service, public transportation, and day care, for example.

In return for having basic needs guaranteed, the population was expected to contribute and participate. The victory over Batista, and the early revolutionary campaigns, showed what a mobilized, committed popular effort could accomplish. Now, this kind of effort would be dedicated to building the economy. Fidel Castro summarized the need for sacrifice in a 1968 speech. "Investing in development necessarily implies not consuming everything we might consume," he explained. "A good example for us: Our foreign exchange. If we spend it all on consumer goods and nothing on a single machine, irrigation equipment, or machinery to build drainage systems or water conservation projects, the sure result is all too clear. We would eat today, but it is certain that we wouldn't be able to eat next year … In other words, with foreign credit we can buy bulldozers or powdered milk, one or the other."[20]

Another example was the attempt to reach a 10 million ton sugar harvest in 1970. The entire society was mobilized. Tens of thousands of volunteers left their jobs to cut cane. The legitimacy of the Revolution itself seemed invested in the goal.

The campaign was both a success and a failure. It was a success, in showing Cubans, and the world, people's capacity to work, and achieve collective goals, for rewards that went beyond individualism and material gain. But it was an economic failure, in more ways than one. The harvest failed to reach 10 million tons, although at 8.5 million tons it was the largest sugar harvest in Cuba's history. The larger failure, though, was what happened to the rest of the economy when everything was concentrated on sugar. With little investment and with labor diverted to sugar, other sectors collapsed.

The 1970s: Institutionalization and the Soviet Model

Susan Eckstein called this period the "retreat to socialism," which in some ways captures the shift. The radical, utopian goals of the 1960s were scaled down. Juan Antonio Blanco mourns the Sovietization that occurred during this period. Socialism was in some ways reduced, as Che had warned, to "a method of distributing goods," or, as Vilas suggested, "a form of left-wing developmentalism."

But the concept of Sovietization is only useful up to a point. Cuba is a Caribbean society, and even the driest bureaucrats could not erase the *pachanga* inherent in Cuban culture. Political and economic structures may have been based on a Soviet model, but society and culture were still decidedly Cuban.

Furthermore, the Soviet model became associated, since the 1930s, with famine, with a huge repressive apparatus, with gulags, terror and political prisoners. Cuba may have followed the Soviet model of centralized economic planning, but it did not create anything remotely akin to the human rights disasters that occurred in the USSR. In fact, while the "retreat to socialism" meant a return of markets and a retreat from the radical economic egalitarianism of the 1960s, it came with a growing democratization of the political sphere. Existing mass organizations took on new roles, and new institutions were created for participation.

Despite more than a decade of Sovietization, and five decades of economic blockade by the United States, the latter remained a much more decisive influence on Cuba than did the former. Cubans learned English, watched U.S. movies, and longed to visit relatives in Miami. In contrast, as one Cuban scholar described the popular response to the Soviets: "The Cubans kept their distance because of certain cultural practices, like the fact that the Russians did not use deodorant or, in the case of the women, shave their legs ... Moreover, they spoke a strange and distant language, indecipherable by most Cubans no matter how much they stretched their imaginations, and they dressed as if time had stopped at some point in the past between the Yalta

Conference and the end of World War II ... The technology they brought was efficient and sturdy, but also wasteful and unviable, heavy and ostentations; in other words, just too *Russian*."[21]

Institutionalization in the 1970s included the creation or strengthening of institutions for democratic participation, like labor unions and elected assemblies. The heady optimism and commitment that forged popular participation in the 1960s gave way to more everyday, systematic means of participation. The Cuban Revolution's vision of democracy was quite different from U.S.-style electoral democracy, but avenues for popular participation certainly existed in Cuba.

Democracy: U.S. and Cuban Style

"Before 1959 we had plenty of political parties, but no democracy," Cubans like to explain. For those raised in the United States, the type of democracy that has developed in this country sometimes seems to be the only, the inevitable, or the ideal form of democracy. But democracy has in fact taken many different forms over space and time. It's worth taking a moment to look a bit more deeply at what we mean by "democracy."

In essence, democracy has to do with systems or mechanisms for the people of a society to be involved in making decisions about how their society will function. Political scientists distinguish between *representative* and *direct* democracy. In a representative democracy, people participate in decision making by electing representatives to make the actual decisions; in a direct democracy, decisions are made by some sort of collective assembly in which all can participate. Most modern democracies also rely on some sort of constitution or founding document that sets the ground rules.

Democracy can be measured on several different axes. For example, who gets to participate? What kind of rights does the system guarantee? What kinds of decisions are subject to the democratic process?

Using the first axis as a measure, it is clear that U.S. democracy has become more democratic over time. In the early Republic, political rights were restricted to a small portion of the population; gradually, these restrictions have been eliminated. The Voting Rights Act of 1965, which eliminated literacy restrictions and poll taxes, was the last major reform to expand political participation in the United States by ending the disenfranchisement of African Americans in the South.

Most analysts agree that without some basic protections guaranteed to individuals and organizations, democracy has little meaning. Freedom of speech and organization, and freedom from arbitrary arrest, for example, are considered key democratic rights. When opposition figures are jailed or murdered, an election is not considered very democratic.

Still, most democratic countries place some kind of restrictions on these political freedoms. No government allows groups to try to overthrow it. In the United States, Alien and Sedition Acts of 1798, the Sedition Act of 1918, the Smith Act of 1940 and the PATRIOT Act of 2001 are examples of how the U.S. government has tried to strengthen its ability to prosecute actual or potential challenges to its authority or existence, especially when national security is threatened.

Finally, political systems can vary in terms of what spheres are subject to democratic controls. This is where capitalist and socialist systems can diverge significantly. Socialism argues that economic decisions should be made by the government; capitalism is based on the idea that economic decisions should be made by private individuals and institutions. In a democracy, socialism could be more democratic, because democratic institutions can make decisions about the economy. If a government is undemocratic, though, leaving the economy in private hands at least offers a potential counterweight to the government.

Cuba in the 1970s: How it Worked

Closer ties to the USSR, and a system of economic planning based on the Soviet model, characterized the 1970s. Cuba joined the COMECON in 1972, and implemented its first Five-Year Plan in 1975. Politically too, the Cuban government reorganized itself on the Soviet model. The Cuban Communist Party (*Partido Comunista de*

Cuba, or PCC) held its first Congress in 1975, and in 1976 Cuba's government approved a new, socialist Constitution. The Constitution established a system of *Poder Popular* or People's Power. Cubans voted for municipal assemblies with a significant degree of control over local affairs. Municipal delegates then elected delegates to the provincial and National Assemblies.

Closer ties with the socialist bloc were accompanied by closer ties to the capitalist world as well. Not the United States, which maintained its economic blockade of the island. But Cuba joined the International Sugar Organization and the Latin American and Caribbean Sugar Exporters' Association, and sold a good portion of its sugar to Western countries: 41 percent in 1974. Towards the end of the 1970s the government began to encourage foreign investment from the capitalist countries. As Eckstein explains, "sectors opened to foreign investors included tourism, light industry, medical equipment, medicine, construction, and agro-industry. Investors were promised tax-free use of land, tax exemptions on imported materials, and free repatriation of profits." In 1982 Cuba passed a foreign investment code to guarantee the rights of investors. Eckstein argued that the opening to the West was initially a more significant factor in the economic upturn of the 1970s than was Cuba's integration into the Soviet bloc. Falling sugar prices towards the end of the 1970s, though, made Cuba more dependent on its relationship with the Soviets.[22]

Sugar exports and Soviet credit – and petroleum imports – also helped to finance industrial growth. The sugar industry was increasingly mechanized. Cuba increased production of machinery as well as of consumer goods. Cuban factories produced farm machinery, fertilizers, and pesticides, as well as ships and processing facilities for the fishing industry, and machinery and infrastructure for nickel mining.

High sugar prices during the early 1970s contributed to the government's ability to carry out its social goals. Significant investments in health and education, in rural electrification, and in cultural institutions meant that the population in general had a high degree of access to both material and cultural goods. Cuba's nascent foreign aid programs, begun in the 1960s, also mushroomed in the 1970s, as the island sent large numbers of teachers, doctors, and construction workers abroad on aid missions, and lent military support to liberation movements in Angola and elsewhere in Africa.

The rationing system may have provided for the population's basic needs, but increasing production to satisfy consumer demand was a constant challenge. Outside of the state-controlled system, black and gray markets flourished. On the "gray" market, a non-smoker, for example, might exchange cigarettes received through the ration with a friend for some other items, with no harm done to anybody. On the black market, people sold imported or scarce goods at inflated prices.

Money made an official comeback in the 1970s, to address the problem of low production and insufficient goods. The government restored some material incentives. Wages and bonuses would be linked to worker productivity, and charges were implemented for services formerly provided free by the government.

By the mid-1970s some small-scale experiments with markets were reintroduced – what political scientist Jorge Domínguez called a "gradual desocialization of minor social services."[23] These experiments reached their height in 1980 with the creation of private markets in a much more important sector: food. Private farmers, cooperatives, and state farms were authorized to sell produce directly to the public, and set their own prices.

The idea was to add what Food First analysts Medea Benjamin and her co-authors called "a dash of capitalism" to stimulate production.[24] It worked – in that the markets thrived and offered a good quality and variety of produce. But if the experiment resolved some of the problems created by socialism – lack of incentives, and low productivity – it also brought some of capitalism's problems back. High prices meant that only some people could afford what the markets had to sell, and that sellers could make inordinate profits.

Capitalism also came into the country through an official opening to Cubans who had left for the United States. Towards the end of the 1970s the government stopped using the epithet *gusano* – worm – for those who had left. Émigrés were invited to visit Cuba, and allowed to shop in special dollar-only stores and bring gifts to their relatives on the island. The government even set up a system for bank transfers from abroad. All of these measures carried restrictions, though. In particular, Cubans were not allowed to have or use dollars. Gifts had to be in kind, and currency had to be deposited in the National Bank and exchanged for pesos.

Experiments with incentives that fostered inequality only went so far. The government's commitment to equality continued to reign in other sectors, particularly in the area of health. Institutionalization in health care meant the creation of regional structures following the Soviet model. But, unlike the Soviets, the Cubans continued to invest heavily in their health system, and to emphasize primary care and community health initiatives. Cuba's innovative and comprehensive system of polyclinics not only put accessible clinics everywhere in the country, it "projects the polyclinics services into the neighborhood. Not only do the physician–nurse teams attend patients in the polyclinic, but they also visit patients in their everyday environment: the home, school, day-care center, and workplace."[25] In 1984 the country implemented a new "family doctor" program – a drive to train thousands of primary care doctors and place a doctor in every neighborhood of the country. The idea was to integrate primary medical care into the community. The number of health care workers tripled between 1970 and 2005, while the number of doctors rose from "one doctor for every 1,393 people in 1970 to one doctor for every 159 people in 2005."[26]

Human capital was also maximized through voluntarism and the mass organizations. Workers were asked to volunteer for "microbrigades" to construct housing. CDRs and the FMC (Federación de Mujeres Cubanas, or Federation of Cuban Women) played a key role in the health system. "Together, they can reach into all neighborhoods of Cuba, since CDRs exist in every block and every little town," an education official explained to Jonathan Kozol in 1976. "If an elderly person, for example, is not seen out on the street for several days, it is the obligation of the CDR to go upstairs into that person's home and to find out if he or she is incapacitated somehow. The CDR and the FMC work in close cooperation with the Ministry of Health.

Proper prenatal care depends upon the use of polyclinics, but poly-clinics can be of no use to anyone if women do not recognize the need to keep appointments … If a woman fails to show up for appointments, someone from the CDR goes to her home and tries to find out what has prevented her from keeping the appointment."[27]

1986: Rectification

The Rectification campaign of 1986 seemed in some ways to hark back to the early days of the Revolution. In a series of speeches Fidel decried the inequalities and privileges that had emerged as a result of the market reforms, and the loss of revolutionary idealism. Che Guevara's ideas were resurrected. The farmers markets were closed, as were other small private businesses. Exile visits were curtailed.

Cuban sociologist Haroldo Dilla described the essence of the Rectification campaign as "characterized by a strong anti-market rhetoric, the recovery of national autonomy (in contraposition to both the United States and Soviet *perestroika*), and a strong reliance on ethical and nationalist arguments that had as their emblematic figures José Martí and Che Guevara."[28]

Rectification coincided with what seemed like an opposite trend in the Soviet Union: the era of *glasnost* and *perestroika*. Some analysts of the Cuban scene concluded that Cuba was reacting to the growing economic and political openness in the USSR by cracking down with a hard line.[29] Others saw the Rectification campaign in more positive terms, and argued that Cuba was returning to the indigenous roots of its Revolution, rather than obediently following the Soviets down a path towards growing inequality, poverty, and corruption. This was certainly how Cuba's leaders presented the situation to the public. Still others argued that Cuba's leaders were responding in the only way possible to a crisis caused by the falling price of sugar and increased foreign debt: they had to take steps to decrease domestic consumption and increase exports.[30]

The Rectification campaign did not have long to experiment, however. The collapse of the Soviet bloc in 1989 meant that the premise that had guided Cuba's economic path at least since the middle of the 1960s – that it could rely on Soviet aid and a guaranteed market at a "fair price" in the eastern bloc for its sugar – shattered.

How Democratic was Cuban Socialism?

Cuban officials argued that their political and economic system was extraordinarily democratic. Most Western governments believed just the opposite, claiming that Cuba suffered from an extreme lack of democracy. Scholars in both countries examined the system implemented in the 1960s and1970s and its evolution through the 1980s and 1990s.

To many Americans, the idea of socialism has become almost synonymous with political repression, restrictions on freedom of speech and other political freedoms, arbitrary rule, and human rights violations. Censorship, repressions, and gulags play a key role in how Americans view socialism.

If the July 26th Movement enjoyed almost unanimous support when it took over the country in January 1959, those unanimous supporters were far from unanimous about the direction they believed the Revolution should take. Antipathy to the old order did not necessarily mean agreement about the new. The Revolutionary Tribunals that condemned hundreds of former Batista police, army and security officers to death in the months following the Revolution received far greater condemnation abroad than in Cuba. But as the July 26th Movement consolidated its hold on power, liberals lost their initial enthusiasm for the revolutionary project. As the government expropriations of property expanded, property owners, and often their workers, were alienated. Voluntary labor, and support for the Revolution, became conditions for employment. Citizens were urged to join the Committees for the Defense of the Revolution, the Federation of Cuban Women, and the civilian militia. Those who doubted, hesitated, or chose not to participate found themselves increasingly marginalized.

It was not only liberals who became disenchanted, or whose ideas were squeezed to the margins of the revolutionary project. By the early 1960s the revolutionary leadership, pressed on one side by the increasing U.S. aggression, and on the other, by the need for capable and experienced cadres to develop and run its institutions, drew closer to the country's old Communist Party, the PSP. Paradoxically, the PSP was one of the most conservative forces in the revolutionary coalition. Historic Party members tended to hold a hard line and a narrow view of what revolution could mean and could encompass. They scorned intellectual and cultural experimentation.

The Revolution's policies towards intellectual freedom were summarized by Fidel Castro in 1961 in an oft-quoted speech entitled "Words to Intellectuals." "Within the Revolution, everything; against the Revolution, nothing," he said. That is, a distinction is made between intellectual work, from art to literature to academics, which *opposes* the Revolution, and work which does not oppose it – and work which opposes the Revolution is not permitted. (This is essentially the same distinction enshrined in the Cuban Constitution: "freedom of speech" may not be exercised against the Constitution, the laws of the country, or socialism.)

This position, however, leaves much room for interpretation, and in fact the boundaries of what is considered "within the Revolution" and what is "against the Revolution" have changed considerably over time. American journalist Lee Lockwood, who spent several months traveling on the island and studying the Revolution in 1965 and 1966, was impressed that "under the loosely administered patronage of the Revolution, the arts have flourished in Cuba and remained refreshingly free of the ideological influence and restraint common to other socialist cultures."[31] In the 1970s the limits shrank considerably, and many intellectuals and ideas that had up until then been encompassed "within the Revolution" suddenly became defined as "against the Revolution" as the government became more closely aligned with the Soviet Union. Cuban intellectuals now refer to the five-year period between 1971 and 1976 as the "gray five years" because of the intense Sovietization of cultural life. "Socialist realism" as imposed during that period, explained Cuban author Ambrosio Fornet later, required a "literature as pedagogy and hagiography, aimed at developing 'positive heroes' erasing any possible conflicts in the 'bosom of the working class'."[32] The bounds started to ease after 1976 with the appointment of Armando Hart as Minister of Culture, and what has generally been seen as a "new openness" through the 1980s.[33] Most intellectuals felt that the Fourth Party Congress in 1991 was an important positive step in further legitimizing debate and critical thought. Indeed, for Cuban intellectuals, the collapse of the Soviet bloc, while bringing a virtual economic collapse, also heralded an era of increased intellectual openness and debate. Chapter 5 will explore in more depth the issue of intellectual and artistic freedom under the Revolution, while Chapters 7 and 8 will examine all of these different aspects of the Special Period.

3

Relations with the United States

Cuba's Revolution, of course, did not happen in isolation. Both Cuba's historical development up to 1959 and the experiences and ideas of its revolutionary leaders were imbedded in a global context. The Revolution itself had major global impacts – some purposeful, and some unintended. Decisions and events in other parts of the world also had significant impacts on Cuba. The Cuban Revolution developed an active foreign policy that both responded to and affected global events.

Fernando Ortiz offered the term "transculturation" back in 1940 to analyze the diversity of Cuba's peoples and how they interacted and became Cuban. In contrast to the United States, where Anglo culture was dominant, in Cuba an entirely new, mixed culture had emerged. People from Africa, America, Europe, and Asia, "each of them torn from his native moorings, faced with the problem of disadjustment and readjustment, of deculturation and acculturation – in a word, of transculturation," he wrote in his epic *Cuban Counterpoint: Tobacco and Sugar.*

Most of the figures that have come to symbolize Cuba's national identity had strong ties to other places as well. Hatuey, the indigenous rebel who stood up to the Spaniards in the early 1500s, came from Hispaniola. Antonio Maceo's father was Venezuelan. Carlos Manuel

A History of the Cuban Revolution. Aviva Chomsky
© 2011 Aviva Chomsky

de Céspedes went to university and law school in Spain, while José Martí was the son of Spanish immigrants and spent much of his adult life working, writing, and organizing in the United States. Che Guevara hailed from Argentina, and Fidel Castro's father was an immigrant from Galicia, in northern Spain. The July 26th Movement was plotted in exile in Mexico. To be quintessentially Cuban, it seems, means to be a citizen of the world.

People from around the world went to Cuba after the Revolution – some to support the revolutionary process, and some to try to undermine or overthrow it. Cubans also went around the world – some to escape the Revolution, some to work against it, and some to act in solidarity with revolutionary movements elsewhere, especially in Africa and Latin America. Cuba after the Revolution achieved a high diplomatic profile as well, becoming a leader in the Non-Aligned Movement. And the foreign policies of other countries – in particular, the United States and the USSR – were influenced by, and in turn influenced, the Cuban Revolution.

This chapter and the next look at how Cuba's relations with the world shaped the Cuban Revolution, and how the Cuban Revolution shaped the country's relations with the world. We will also look at the global importance and impact of the Revolution. Because the relationship with the United States was so fundamental to the shape and direction of the Revolution, we'll begin there.

The United States and Cuba

Accounts of United States–Cuba relations since 1959 tend to fall into two categories. Some privilege the Cold War context, emphasizing the Communist nature of the Revolution, Cuba's ties with the USSR, and the Cold War ideologies that motivated U.S. policies during the second half of the twentieth century. Other, revisionist histories in the United States – as well as the majority of Cuban historians – consider the U.S. imperial stance towards the Caribbean and Latin America, which predated both the Cold War and the Revolution, as the most important context.

Cuban singer-songwriter Silvio Rodríguez exemplified the latter stance in a song about the 1979 Nicaraguan Revolution and the U.S. response. "Now the eagle is suffering from its greatest pain," he wrote. "It is hurt by Nicaragua because it is hurt by love. It is hurt by children being healthy and going to school, because it can't sharpen its spurs that way."[1] According to this perspective, the United States seeks economic gain from Latin America, and often opposes real democracy and economic development there because these would reduce the U.S. ability to exploit its neighbors.

In many ways, conflict between the United States and the Cuban Revolution was inevitable. In its emphasis on nationalism, and on redistributive social justice, the Revolution challenged half a century or more of U.S. domination of the island, and the economic and political model that it had imposed. Immediately after the Revolution, U.S. officials hoped and believed that they could manipulate and rein in the new Cuban government, in particular with regard to how it would treat U.S. investors. Over the course of 1959, policymakers grew increasingly discouraged about their ability to control the course of events. By the end of 1959, the U.S. government had moved to implacable hostility towards the Revolution and determination to overthrow it.

Between 1959 and the present, the United States has attempted a dizzying array of tactics and methods in its attempt to control, and then to undermine, overthrow, or destroy the Cuban revolutionary experiment. Many of them were covert. The Ministry of the Interior Museum in Havana offers a testament to the many attempts at sabotage and assassination carried out by U.S. agents. The U.S. public knew little about these until 1975 Senate Hearings where CIA and other officials testified to their involvement in assassination attempts against Fidel Castro. Despite the publicity at the time, this history remains relatively unknown in the United States, although it is common knowledge in Cuba.

What is best known to the U.S. public, of course, are the two occasions in which the covert campaign escalated into open confrontation: the Bay of Pigs invasion in April 1961, and the Cuban Missile Crisis in October 1962. These events are also well known in Cuba,

Figure 3.1   Billboard near Playa Girón. "Girón: First Defeat of Yankee Imperialism in Latin America"
Source: Photo by Tracey Eaton

but they are known very differently. The word most closely associated with the Bay of Pigs, in the United States, is "fiasco." In Cuba, the victory over the invaders at the beach the Cubans call Playa Girón is celebrated as "the first defeat of imperialism in Latin America" (Figure 3.1). From the U.S. perspective, the installation of Soviet missiles on Cuban soil was an intolerable threat, to U.S. safety and to the balance of power. From the Cuban perspective, the missiles were a defense against another U.S. invasion, and the U.S. insistence that it remain the only nuclear power in the hemisphere just another example of imperial arrogance. The "crisis," from the Cuban perspective, was not the presence of the missiles, but the arbitrary U.S. decision to challenge the Soviets to a nuclear war.

From a larger Latin American perspective, the Bay of Pigs is just one in a long, dreary list of U.S. invasions and occupations of their countries, largely unknown in the United States itself. These include, since 1898, the numerous troop landings in Cuba; the lengthy occupations of Nicaragua, Haiti, and the Dominican Republic; the 1954 overthrow of the Arbenz government in Guatemala; counterinsurgencies and "low intensity conflicts" in Central America in the 1980s; and so on. The only thing that makes the Bay of Pigs unique is that the invasion did not succeed.

Planning for the Bay of Pigs invasion started as early as March 1960, when the Revolution was just over a year old. Many studies have recounted the precise course of events of the invasion. Here, we will try to place it in context by asking: How did the actions of Cuba's revolutionary leaders affect the country's relationship with the United States? How did U.S. actions affect the decisions and direction of the Cuban Revolution? And finally, what changed, and what didn't change, after the Bay of Pigs invasion?

In their Own Words: U.S. Policymakers Respond to Revolution

The longstanding U.S. relationship with, and presence in, Cuba prior to the Revolution, created a series of challenges for the new revolutionary government. The twin goals of nationalism and social justice required a major transformation in Cuba's relationship with the United States. The Revolution sought, and the population clearly supported, political and economic independence from the United States. Economic nationalism, and redistributive social justice, would inevitably involve challenging the U.S. businesses that played such a dominant role in Cuba's economy. How could the Cubans achieve these goals without provoking the kind of sabotage and armed intervention that had overthrown the Arbenz government in Guatemala in 1954? In addition to helping us understand U.S. policy, the words of U.S. officials offer us a unique first-hand view of Cuba during the early years of the Revolution.

U.S. policymakers greeted the Cuban Revolution with a single-minded focus on the interests of U.S. investments in Cuba. The main questions, as far as U.S. policymakers were concerned, were: Would the revolutionary government protect the interests of U.S. businesses in Cuba? How could the United States navigate the new revolutionary context in order to best promote those interests? As Philip W. Bonsal, who was appointed U.S. Ambassador to Cuba immediately after the revolutionary victory, recalled: "In appraisal of the prospects for Cuban–American relations under Castro the extensive private American interests in Cuba were of major significance."[2]

During the first months, policymakers hoped that the new government could be persuaded, or pressured, to maintain a favorable attitude with respect to U.S. investors. They began by seeking the advice of these parties on how to best support their interests. Embassy officials, meeting with American business representatives in Cuba only days after the revolutionary victory, reported that "every man present expressed individually and emphatically, the view that it would be in the interest of the United States and of American business in Cuba for the United States to recognize the provisional government as quickly as possible ... They considered that prompt recognition was necessary to establish the most favorable possible climate in which to carry on business."[3] The following day this advice was carried out, and the United States recognized the revolutionary government.

One of the reasons that U.S. businesses had argued for recognition of Castro, and that the U.S. government went along, was that they could not ignore the overwhelming popular mobilization behind the Revolution. U.S. officials, the Ambassador explained, "had no enthusiasm for Castro, only a determination to be in the best possible position to deal effectively on behalf of American interests with the new ruler whose people appeared united in idolizing him."[4]

The task, then, was to try to guide – or manipulate – the new government into compliance with U.S. business and economic development goals. This could be accomplished, in part, by "strengthening the moderating and stabilizing influences on Castro and the Cuban government."[5] In addition, the United States should "seek to isolate and reduce the influence of the 'radical' element of the 26th of July forces and the Communists" by "maneuvering them into positions where they will be seen to be undercutting Castro's programs."[6]

On May 8th, 1959, Castro made an important statement of the Revolution's goals and policies, in implicit response to U.S. accusations of Communist influence in Cuba. The U.S. Ambassador described a crowd of 600,000 who gathered to hear his speech as overcome with "nearly hysterical adulation" and noted that "this is one man rule with full approval of 'masses.'" The Ambassador summarized Castro's stance: "Revolution neither capitalist, Communist, nor center, but rather step in advance of all. Said current world conflict was between concept which offered people democracy and starved them to death, and concept which offered food but suppressed liberties. Cuban solution was to promote all rights of mankind, including 'social rights.' Only ideas which satisfy both material and spiritual needs of mankind will prosper."[7]

The May 1959 Agrarian Reform, which restricted the size of farms to 3,333 acres, brought the conflict between the Cuban government's goals and the interests of U.S. investors to a head. Land in excess of this size would be expropriated and compensated with 20-year government bonds; the value of the land would be determined by the value that the owners had declared for tax purposes.[8] Many of the properties affected belonged to U.S. individuals or companies.

"I believed both countries would have profited if the Cuban government had given the concerned Americans in Cuba a hearing before decisions were reached on such an important matter," Ambassador Bonsal protested weakly.[9] The State Department concurred that "agrarian reform law causing great consternation in U.S. Government and American sugar circles."[10] Thirty of the 34 U.S.-owned sugar mills sent representatives to meet with the U.S. Ambassador the following day, protesting that their businesses would be severely affected by the reform.[11]

U.S. officials attempted to work with "moderate forces in Cuba which are supporting U.S. efforts to obtain ameliorations of the provisions of the land reform bill which are detrimental to U.S. interests."[12] Bonsal reiterated U.S. interests in repeated meetings with Cuban officials in May and June of 1959: the fear that Cuban sugar exports might decline, leaving the U.S. market undersupplied; and the concern that U.S. property-holders in Cuba be adequately compensated. "I outlined American belief in private enterprise as basis for economic development ... I stressed constructive role of American companies in Cuban economy" Bonsal reported.[13]

The Cubans, however, insisted on their right to determine their own national priorities. "Transforming the system of landholding ... is the indispensable prerequisite in every underdeveloped country for its industrial, political, social, and cultural progress," the Minister of State told Bonsal. "Unless large-scale landholding is abolished," he continued, "Cuba will continue to suffer economic stagnation and an increasing rate of unemployment ... [The agrarian reform] is in the best interests of the Cuban nation, which interest [the government] places above any others." He urged U.S. investors to support Cuba's plans for economic development by investing in industry, which the Cuban government was promoting as a route to national development, and the government to "induce United States investors affected by the Agrarian reform to help further the over-all development of the Cuban economy in accordance with the planned policy that is being carried out. The purpose of this creative policy, the cornerstone of which is Agrarian reform, is to increase productivity, encourage investments, raise the standard of living, and eliminate unemployment, which fully ensures the supplying of Cuban products to American consumers."[14]

Washington was not convinced. After a meeting with several large U.S. landholders on June 24th, the U.S. Secretary of State cabled the ambassador that "you should make every effort persuade GOC [Government of Cuba] avoid precipitate action in carrying out Agrarian Reform Law in its application American properties."[15] Another official concluded bluntly: "With the signature of the Agrarian Reform Law, it seems clear that our original hope was a vain one; Castro's Government is not the kind worth saving."[16]

The Ambassador could not deny that the Cuban population was overwhelmingly supportive of the new government and its reforms. The only opposition came from close supporters of Batista and members of his military, and property-holders whose properties were threatened. In his painstaking search for Communist influence in the new government, he came up empty-handed. Anti-Communists dominated the military, police, and security agencies. There was "no basis" for any of the rumors of Soviet or Chinese advisors. The worst he could say was that Castro's government had a "benevolent tolerance" for Cuba's Communist Party and "has not concentrated on this subject to extent desirable."[17] He elaborated:

> Castro has taken no interest in international situation or in threat of international Communism… I tried to explain significance of support of all peoples of free world in great struggle between freedom and slavery but do not believe he was particularly impressed.[18]

Yet Bonsal continued trying to impress upon the Cubans the importance of private enterprise and foreign investment. In a July 23rd meeting Bonsal tried to impress upon Cuba's Minister of State that "many American private interests in Cuba have made great contributions to the country's economy in the agricultural field; many of our sugar and cattle enterprises have created employment and wealth where previously there was neither population nor production. These companies are entitled to considerate treatment … I referred also to the public utilities companies and to the importance of finding an arrangement which will permit these companies to continue to obtain the capital which they must have in order to meet the requirements of the expanding Cuban economy."[19]

But even Bonsal understood that U.S. economic control in Latin America had not necessarily been beneficial to the people there. "The Castro regime seems to have sprung from a deep and wide-spread dissatisfaction with social and economic conditions as they have been heretofore in Cuba and to respond to an overwhelming demand for change and reform," he wrote. "The universal support it has received from the humble and the lower middle classes is a witness to the strength of this compulsion … If we turn our back on them we risk pushing them into the arms of the Communists."[20]

Also worrisome, the popularity of the Cuban Revolution and its redistributive economic reforms might encourage other Latin American countries to challenge U.S. political and economic domination. A State Department official explained that "there are indications that if the Cuban revolution is successful, other countries in

Latin America and perhaps elsewhere will use it as a model. We should decide if we wish to have the Cuban Revolution succeed."[21] Other U.S. officials concurred with this continental assessment. At the end of 1959 Assistant Secretary of State Roy Rubottom warned that "our attitude to date [could] be considered a sign of weakness and thus give encouragement to communist-nationalist elements elsewhere in Latin America who are trying to advance programs similar to those of Castro. Such programs, if undertaken ... [could expose] United States property owners to treatment similar to that being received in Cuba and, in general, prejudicing the program of economic development espoused by the United States for Latin America which relies so heavily on private capital investment."[22] According to the Secretary of the Treasury, "'large amounts of capital now planned for investment in Latin America' were being held back, because investors were 'waiting to see whether the United States can cope'" with Cuba.[23] U.S. goals in Cuba, as elsewhere in Latin America, Rubottom reiterated, included "receptivity to U.S. and free world capital and increasing trade" and "access by the United States to essential Cuban resources."[24]

Thus the Secretary of State emphasized that "all actions and policies of the United States Government should be designed to encourage within Cuba and elsewhere in Latin America opposition to the extremist, anti-American course of the Castro regime."[25] A secret December 1959 CIA memorandum reiterated that Cuba's Revolution, "if permitted to stand, will encourage similar actions against U.S. holdings in other Latin American countries," and recommended that "'thorough consideration be given to the elimination of Fidel Castro" in order to "accelerate the fall of the present Government." In a hand-written note, the CIA director approved the recommendation.[26]

The 1975 U.S. Senate Committee investigation documented at least eight CIA-sponsored assassination attempts against Fidel Castro between 1960 and 1965, while the Cubans have documented numerous other attempts.[27] CIA officers poisoned a box of Castro's favorite brand of cigars with botulinum toxin, which would cause fatal illness within hours of ingestion. The cigars were delivered to a contact in

February 1961, but apparently never made it into Castro's hands. Other murder weapons that the CIA prepared or obtained and delivered or arranged to have delivered to proposed assassins included lethal pills which a Cuban official was to place in Castro's food, a hypodermic needle filled with deadly insecticide and disguised as a pen, and high-powered rifles. CIA employees tested and perfected all of these poisons. Other ideas which were explored and rejected included planting an exotic seashell rigged to explode in the area where Castro was going skin diving, and presenting him with a contaminated diving suit.[28]

To carry out these murder attempts, the CIA cultivated ties with the U.S. gambling syndicate that operated in Cuba, offering $150,000 for a successful assassination, starting in August 1960.[29] The CIA's syndicate contacts were involved in several different attempts to kill Castro with poison pills from 1960–63. Apparently Castro's internal security forces were able to foil some of these plots.[30]

As U.S. opposition to Castro cemented, his popularity in Cuba remained strong. U.S. policymakers needed to consider, Ambassador Bonsal cautioned, the "continued emotional attachment to Fidel Castro as national symbol by bulk of the Cuban people," as well as "the continued belief by virtually all Cubans in the need for social and economic changes, embodied to date only in Castro's revolutionary program."[31]

Assistant Secretary of State for Inter-American Affairs' Special Assistant Hill mentioned with concern "the impact that real honesty, especially at the working level, has made on the people" and "the fact that a great bulk of the Cubans ... have awakened enthusiastically to the need for social and economic reform."[32] Yet the U.S. goal, he insisted, was precisely the opposite: "we must insure that a successor government comports itself in our interests."[33]

U.S. officials continued to publicly insist on their non-interventionist stance, even as the real policy progressed to invasion, terrorism, and assassination plots. They feigned pained innocence when Castro's charges accurately described what they were doing. U.S. President Eisenhower publicly decried "the tendency of Cuban

Government spokesmen, including Prime Minister Castro, to create the illusion of aggressive acts and conspiratorial activities aimed at the Cuban Government and attributed to United States officials or agencies."[34] While denouncing Cuban paranoia about U.S. intentions and activities, the U.S. government was in fact planning for both the invasion that took place at the Bay of Pigs in April 1961, and the assassination of Fidel Castro.[35] Eisenhower's comment was made over a month after Dulles had approved the CIA recommendation for the "elimination" of Castro, and just a day after the first CIA Special Group meeting to discuss "covert contingency planning to accomplish the fall of the Castro government."[36]

Covert War: Up to the Bay of Pigs

The covert war aimed explicitly "to bring about the replacement of the Castro regime." This "replacement" must take place "in such a manner as to avoid any appearance of U.S. intervention. Essentially the method of accomplishing this end will be induced support, and so far as possible, direct action, both inside and outside of Cuba, by selected groups of Cubans of a sort that they might be expected to and could undertake on their own initiative."[37] The program was practically designed to make the Cuban government suspicious of any organized dissent in their country.

Attacks against Cuba began in late 1959, after U.S. officials had determined that the Castro government was "not the kind worth saving."[38] In January 1960 U.S. officials continued to insist publicly that "the United States is eager to promote better relations with the Castro regime," and emphatically denied Castro's claims that some 30 bombing raids by U.S.-based planes had destroyed 225,000 tons of sugar. They could not deny the evidence, however, when a U.S. plane loaded with explosives crashed over the España sugar mill outside of Havana in February 1960, and Castro appeared on television with the passport of the pilot, U.S. citizen Robert Ellis Frost. The *New York Times* noted regretfully that the incident "was an embarrassment to the United States Government" and "lent considerable weight to numerous past charges by Cuba that planes from this country had been setting fire to sugar cane fields on the island." Maps on the dead pilot's body showed planned routes to other sugar mills which had been bombed in preceding weeks.[39]

U.S. officials also "categorically and emphatically denied" any connection to a bomb blast which killed between 75 and 100 and injured over 300 in early March 1960. The French ship *La Coubre* had sailed from Antwerp loaded with ammunition and hand grenades purchased by the Cubans. The ship exploded in Havana harbor after being unloaded, and Cuban investigations determined that an explosive device had been planted in the shipment before it left Belgium. U.S. officials did, however, acknowledge that such attempts were consistent with U.S. policy.[40]

The economic side of the conflict escalated when Cuba signed a trade deal with the USSR in February, 1960. In exchange for hundreds of thousands of tons of sugar a year, the Soviets would supply Cuba with oil and manufactured goods. In June, U.S. oil companies on the island refused to process the Soviet petroleum – and the Cuban government promptly expropriated them. In July, Eisenhower drastically cut Cuba's sugar quota. In October, Eisenhower declared an economic embargo of the island, and in January of 1961, severed all diplomatic relations.[41]

Meanwhile, on March 17th, 1960, Eisenhower ordered the creation of a Cuban exile army and began the training and planning that climaxed in the Bay of Pigs invasion of April 1961. The CIA chose its long-time officer E. Howard Hunt to organize Cuban exiles, and escorted hand-picked "opposition leaders" from Havana to serve as the new government. Hunt described his role as to "form and guide the Cuban government-in-exile, accompany its members to a liberated Havana, and stay on as a friendly adviser until after the first post-Castro elections."[42] In return for their loyalty, the CIA funded the new Cuban exile organization liberally: Hunt distributed $115,000 a month for salaries and rentals, and the CIA directly provided "arms, boats and communications equipment for infiltration into Cuba" and other Frente Revolucionario Democrático (FRD) expenses.[43]

Various sources in the U.S. government, including different branches of the CIA which were sometimes unaware of what other branches were doing, funneled vast sums of money to different Cuban exile organizations. CIA agent Felix Rodriguez sneaked into Cuba from Key West in early 1961, was met by a party of two dozen Cubans on the coast, transported efficiently to a Havana "safe-house," and spent a month underground in Havana, meeting with the "resistance," traveling, waiting for a weapons shipment which never arrived. His description of the network of safe-houses in Havana and elsewhere, and the various infiltrators hiding there, leaves no doubt as to why Cuban security officials might be concerned about such matters.[44] Rodriguez also claimed CIA responsibility for the fire that destroyed Havana's largest department store, El Encanto, a few weeks before the Bay of Pigs invasion.[45]

Assassination was also contemplated – and perhaps attempted – in conjunction with the Bay of Pigs invasion. E. Howard Hunt recalled that when he proposed assassination as a prelude to invasion, he was assured that this was already in the hands of a "special group."[46] Historian Thomas Paterson notes that "the CIA activated assassination plots in March and April. It seems likely that assassination was part of the general Bay of Pigs plan. [The CIA officer in charge of the invasion Richard M.] Bissell has admitted that he was hopeful 'that Castro would be dead before the landing.'"[47]

The exile army that came to be known as Brigade 2506 trained in south Florida, and at U.S. military and CIA bases in Panama and Guatemala. On April 17th, 1961, the invaders landed on the swampy beach at Playa Girón. CIA intelligence had led them to expect significant support on the ground. Instead, the Cuban military rapidly mobilized to overcome the invaders, and within three days, the invasion was decisively defeated. The Revolution's popularity, both at home and abroad, was strengthened. But so was the Cuban government's suspicion of dissent, at home, and its desire to look abroad for support against a hostile United States. In December 1961, Fidel Castro declared himself a Marxist-Leninist. The Cuban government also turned to the USSR as the best means of deterring or repelling a future U.S. attack. But the conflict between Cuba and the United States was only beginning.

Covert War: After the Bay of Pigs

"As long as Castro thrives, his major threat – the example and stimulus of a working Communist revolution – will persist," one U.S. government report warned after the Bay of Pigs.[48] After the invasion attempt, according to one study, the Kennedy Administration turned to covert action with renewed vigor. "Virtually all agencies of the federal government were enlisted … The State Department, Treasury, FBI, Commerce, Immigration, Customs were brought together in departmental committees to come up with measures that could damage Cuba."[49] As Robert McNamara explained, "we were hysterical about Castro at the time of the Bay of Pigs and thereafter," and there was clear pressure to "do something about Castro."[50]

Shortly after the U.S. defeat the CIA opened a new station on the University of Miami campus to coordinate the secret war.[51] The station's operating budget was over $50 million a year, and it had a permanent staff of over 300 American case officers who oversaw several thousand Cuban agents. It also coordinated international efforts through CIA stations over the world to gather intelligence, convince other countries to break relations with Cuba, and stimulate anti-Castro propaganda, as well as to "persuade, bribe, or blackmail" Cuban officials to defect when they traveled abroad.[52]

What former CIA Deputy Director Ray Cline described as "punitive economic sabotage operations" were the main activities. Agents in Europe sabotaged cargoes and sought to dissuade shippers from going to Cuba. A special staff in Langley, Virginia worked on projects ranging from placing contaminants in Cuban sugar shipments bound for export, to damaging machinery headed for Cuba.

We were really doing almost anything you could dream up. One of our more sophisticated operations was convincing a ball-bearing manufacturer in Frankfurt, Germany, to produce a shipment of ball bearings off center. Another was to get a manufacturer to do the same with some balanced wheel gears...[53]

The station also maintained a clandestine, paramilitary army and navy, training posts and bases, boats, and weapons, paying salaries and providing logistics. One agent claimed that he went on almost weekly missions on the CIA payroll during this period, including "large-scale raids aimed at blowing up oil refineries and chemical plants" as well as dropping off and picking up "teams" of agents along the Cuban coast.[54] Another described missions including attacks on a Texaco oil refinery, factories, and Russian ships docked in Cuban harbors. In one mission, a seven-man team blew up a railroad bridge and watched a train run off the track, and burned down a sugar warehouse.[55]

The U.S. defeat at the Bay of Pigs also led to the establishment of Operation MONGOOSE. Unlike the CIA, which was *supposed* to keep its operations hidden from government officials in order to maintain "plausible deniability," MONGOOSE would be overseen by a newly created Special Group (Augmented) which included Kennedy's top advisors.[56] General Edward Landsdale oversaw Operation MONGOOSE, an administratively separate operation for sabotage and subversion, which accelerated in the summer and fall of 1962. In August of that year the Special Group (Augmented) debated an all-out effort to overthrow Castro, but decided that this "would hurt the U.S. in the eyes of world opinion." General Taylor suggested "that we should consider changing the overall objective from one of overthrowing the Castro regime to one of causing its failure" through economic sabotage.[57] Robert McNamara agreed that the time had come "to take every possible aggressive step in the fields of intelligence, sabotage, and guerrilla action"; by the end of the month, Kennedy's advisors had approved the major attack on Cuba's Matahambre copper mine.[58]

In August 1962 the Cuban exile organization Alpha 66 conducted a raid against a coastal hotel "where Soviet military technicians were known to congregate, killing a score of Russians and Cubans.

Although this particular raid was apparently not sanctioned by the United States," Raymond Garthoff explained, Alpha 66 "was permitted to base itself in Florida." In September a new phase of MONGOOSE began, "calling for more raids into Cuba." Alpha 66 carried out two more raids on September 10th (against British and Cuban cargo ships) and October 7th (on the island). On September 27th another CIA sabotage team was arrested in Cuba. At an October 4th meeting of the Special Group (Augmented) another decision was taken "to step up operations including the dispatch of sabotage teams into Cuba." In the following days three more meetings followed to discuss this, including, Garthoff notes, "one on October 16th in between two meetings in the White House that day on the missiles in Cuba."[59]

The most important attempt was the failed attack at the Matahambre copper mine. A first attempt failed in late 1961 when technical problems prevented the boat carrying the commandos from arriving; the second attempt, in the summer of 1962, was met by a Cuban militia patrol and forced to flee. The third attempt, in October 1962, was also repelled by Cuban troops – on October 22nd, just as President Kennedy was announcing the presence of Soviet missiles on the island, and denying that Cuba could possibly have any need to defend itself from U.S. aggression. One participant in the raid heard Kennedy's speech from his boat off the shores of Pinar del Río, where he was waiting for two missing infiltrators to return.[60]

Though the Cubans were able to prevent the October attack on Matahambre, they could not prevent a November 8th attack which blew up an industrial facility and, according to Castro, killed 400 workers. The team which had carried out this raid was arrested on November 13th. Castro protested in a letter to the U.N. Secretary General: "The capture of the leader of a group of spies trained by the CIA and directed by it, here in Cuba, has shown us how the photographs taken by spying planes serve for guidance in sabotage and in their operations and has also revealed, amongst other things, a desire to cause chaos by provoking the deaths of 400 workers in one of our industries."[61]

On the eve of the Cuban Missile Crisis, MONGOOSE was criticized for its slow progress. At a meeting in October 1962, according to notes taken by Richard Helms, "Robert Kennedy, in expressing the 'general dissatisfaction of the President' with MONGOOSE 'pointed out that [MONGOOSE] had been underway for a year ... that there had been no acts of sabotage and that even the one which had been attempted had failed twice.'" – apparently referring to the attempt at the copper mine. He also stated that President Kennedy "is concerned about progress on the MONGOOSE program and feels that more priority should be given to trying to mount sabotage operations." He urged "massive activity." Roswell Gilpatric confirmed this sense: "The complaint that the Attorney General had ... [was that] the steps taken by the CIA up to that point, [and] their plans were too petty, were too minor, they weren't massive enough, they weren't going to be effective enough."[62]

The Missile Crisis

Many volumes, and even more textbook entries, have been written about the Missile Crisis, or the Crisis de Octubre. Generally, in the United States, they have focused on the decision-making process of a few individuals over the period defined as the "crisis," during which American and Soviet officials played a dangerous game of brinkmanship – as epitomized by Roger Donaldson's film *Thirteen Days*. In this version, the Soviet Union backed down under U.S. strength and insistence.

In the United States, several Cold War assumptions surround the drama of the 13 days, and the early histories of the events. First, older accounts assumed that a relative balance of power existed between the United States and the USSR, and that the siting of the missiles in Cuba created a dangerous shift in this balance of power. Second, older accounts assumed that it was Kennedy's uncompromising strength that convinced the Soviets to back down and agree to remove the missiles. Third, most accounts assumed that Cuba had no need to defend itself against the United States – any missiles must be for the purpose of attack capability.

In the late 1980s the first set of revisionist histories began to be written. The National Security Archive at George Washington University used the Freedom of Information Act –and eventually, a lawsuit against the State Department – to obtain many previously classified documents relating to the crisis.[63] Scholars at Harvard and Brown Universities sponsored a series of conferences that brought together participants from Cuba, the United States, and the USSR to discuss the newly declassified documents, and to try to arrive at a new synthesis. This wave of analysis was decidedly less celebratory than the scholarship of the first decades after the crisis, with the major players in the United States emerging as more fool-hardy than heroic.[64]

The 1990s saw an unprecedented openness for historians of the Missile Crisis, adding to the declassification of U.S. documents the opening of Soviet and Cuban archives.[65] Two major conferences in Havana, on the 30th anniversary of the crisis in 1992, and on the 40th anniversary in 2002, brought together scholars and participants to further debate and clarify some of the major historical questions. Perhaps to the surprise of the earlier generation of Cold War scholars, many of the claims made by the Soviets and the Cubans, previously denied by U.S. sources, turned out to be true. The Cubans did fear another U.S. invasion, and in fact plans for such an invasion were in the works. Soviet nuclear capability was in fact far behind what the United States had developed. U.S. officials knew that placing operational missiles near Soviet borders, in Turkey and Italy, augmented the imbalance. The Soviet purpose of placing missiles in Cuba was to address real threats: to defend Cuba against U.S. attack and to respond to the global strategic and political nuclear advantage held by the United States. The Soviets agreed to withdraw the missiles not because of Kennedy's steely resolve, but because the United States agreed to Soviet demands that it relinquish its plans to invade Cuba – which it did publicly – and that it remove the missiles in Turkey, which it agreed to privately. (Until the release of the declassified documents, U.S. officials roundly denied that any deal had been made with the Soviets.) Khrushchev was shaken, not by Kennedy's strength of will, but by his recklessness and the real threat the U.S. stance posed of nuclear destruction.

Despite U.S. promises, it refused to accept international oversight of its non-intervention pledge, and in fact U.S. attempts to overthrow the Cuban government continued unabated. Only days after promising Khrushchev that the United States would abandon any further attempt to invade the island, the Pentagon was preparing a document to qualify the pledge. "The president had promised to forego only an 'armed seizure by U.S. forces,'" political scientist Lars Schoultz explains, summarizing and quoting the document, "while other actions such as a 'Bay-of-Pigs-type operation' had not been ruled out." Meanwhile Kennedy told his advisors that the promise had been a sham, and that "our objective is to preserve our right to invade Cuba."[66]

Robert S. McNamara summarized the changes in the scholarship after the 2002 conference. "For many years, I considered the Cuban Missile Crisis to be the best-managed foreign policy crisis of the last half-century." Instead, revelations in the documents and at the two conferences revealed a shocking degree of ignorance, miscommunication, bravado, and pure chance in the course of events. McNamara acknowledged that the missiles in no way affected the balance of power. Kennedy, however, felt obligated to respond with force because he was trapped by earlier statements he had made threatening action in the event of such a development. At the 1992 conference Soviet General Anatoly Gribkov revealed that 162 nuclear warheads had been installed in Cuba prior to the U.S. naval blockade, and Fidel Castro declared that Cuba had been prepared to use them, had the United States attacked. In fact, in the very midst of the crisis, MONGOOSE leaders had dispatched three sabotage teams to Cuba, and had 10 more ready to depart.[67] The brink was far closer than either the public at the time, or later historians, had realized.

The crisis, and its resolution, also shook the foundations of Cuba's developing relationship with the Soviet Union. Khrushchev's decision to withdraw the missiles was made without any consultation with the Cubans, who felt that once again, their sovereignty was being made hostage to great power politics. "People went out in the streets singing *congas*," recalled one observer, "chanting 'Niquita, mariquita, lo que se da ¡no se quita!'" [Loosely: "Nikita, faggot, what you give you can't take away!"].[68]

After the Missile Crisis

As Kennedy had privately promised, the U.S. commitment to refrain from invading Cuba was more cosmetic than real. Sabotage operations were temporarily halted, and MONGOOSE was officially disbanded, replaced by an interagency "Cuban Coordinating Committee."[69] But raids, bombings, and sabotage continued and even increased.[70] The assassination of John F. Kennedy caused a momentary paralysis in the secret war. CIA officials involved in the assassination attempts against Castro feared that Cuban forces might have been involved in the Kennedy assassination in retaliation for CIA attacks on Castro; CIA and FBI officials noted worriedly that both Lee Harvey Oswald and Jack Ruby had possible links to mob figures involved in the Castro assassination plots, and to both pro- and anti-Cuban individuals and organizations. The U.S. government had multiple reasons for wanting to put the lid on investigations into Kennedy's assassination, among them, officials' fears that the U.S. dirty war against Castro and Cuba would be brought into the investigation. No government agency wanted to risk what this line of inquiry might reveal. There was too much to cover up.

In addition to the gambling syndicate route, the CIA cultivated contacts with a "highly placed" Cuban government official, Major Rolando Cubela, starting in early 1961.[71] The CIA arranged to have weapons delivered to Cubela in Cuba in 1963 and again in 1964. In addition, CIA agents delivered a "poison pen" to Cubela in Paris on November 22nd, 1963, with instructions to fill it with Blackleaf 40, an easily available insecticide which would be lethal. "It is likely that at the very moment President Kennedy was shot a CIA officer was meeting with a Cuban agent in Paris and giving him an assassination device for use against Castro," the CIA report concluded.[72]

In June of 1965 CIA officials realized that "the circle of Cubans who knew of Cubela's plans and of CIA's association with them was ever-widening." Cubela had become a security risk, and all contacts with his group were broken. Without CIA support, the plot faltered. Cubela and several others involved in the plot were arrested in Havana in March 1966 and sentenced to 25 years in prison.[73]

In April 1964 Johnson called for an end to sabotage raids. Johnson was later quoted as complaining that "we had been operating a damned Murder, Inc., in the Caribbean."[74] Dean Rusk argued that sabotage had a "high noise level" and that it was too difficult to cover up U.S. involvement.[75] The last major CIA-organized raid of the Johnson era was in December 1963, when Cuban exiles mined Cuban waters near a naval base, blowing up a number of boats and killing and injuring several people.[76]

When CIA paramilitary operations were dismantled and shut down, the men the CIA had armed, funded and trained, and the arms the CIA had supplied, did not vanish overnight. "No one in Miami or Langley gave much thought to demobilizing the secret army of exiles," journalist David Corn explains. During the 1960s, 70s and 80s, the hand of these CIA-trained exiles turned up again and again in attacks on Cuba and Cubans, in paramilitary and terrorist attacks in the United States and elsewhere, in drug-running and laundering, in the Watergate burglaries, in the Contra War against Nicaragua, and in supposedly "humanitarian" organizations like Brothers to the Rescue.[77]

The cease and desist order did not apply to economic sabotage, which continued during the 1960s and 70s. The goal of the sabotage was clearly the same as it had been in the early 1960s: to discredit Cuba's experiments with socialism. "We wanted to keep bread out of the stores so people were hungry," a CIA officer assigned to anti-Castro operations told John Marks. "We wanted to keep rationing in effect and keep leather out, so people got only one pair of shoes every 18 months."[78]

The War Continues

The partial hiatus of the mid-1960s did not bring an end to covert actions against Cuba. According to Raymond Garthoff, "One of

Nixon's first acts in office in 1969 was to direct the Central Intelligence Agency (CIA) to intensify its covert operations against Cuba."[79] A brief opening towards Cuba during the Ford years (1974–77) was cut short when Cuba began to send troops to Angola, its first major military engagement in Africa. Jimmy Carter again signaled an opening early in his presidency (1977–81), conditioned on Cuba's withdrawal from Angola. This opening too was derailed as events on the ground provoked Cuba to reverse its gradual withdrawal, and then send troops to Ethiopia as well. (See Chapter 4 for further discussion of Cuba's involvement in Africa.)

U.S. direct intervention in Latin America increased during the Reagan years (1981–89), and Cuba occupied a key role in the development and implementation of the Reagan Doctrine. Reagan emphasized creating, training, arming and supporting irregular forces to fight in Cold War arenas including Afghanistan, where an actual Soviet occupation existed; Angola, where Cuban forces had been helping the Angolans resist South African invasion; and Central America, where Reagan made the alleged presence of Cuban aid and advisors a pretext for the Contra War in Nicaragua and no-questions-asked support for right-wing and military governments in Guatemala and El Salvador. "Using Nicaragua as a base," Reagan warned in 1986, "the Soviets and the Cubans can become the dominant power ... Gathered in Nicaragua already are thousands of Cuban military advisers."[80] In the small Caribbean island of Grenada, the United States invaded in 1983 after a military coup, ostensibly to "rescue" U.S. medical students there, but at least in part because of the presence of Cuban construction workers on a new airport project. It was the first time since the Bay of Pigs that U.S. and Cuban forces actually engaged in combat. Many Cubans believed that a U.S. invasion of Cuba would be next.

Cuban exiles, many with former or continuing CIA contacts, were also behind a long series of terrorist attacks inside the United States, perhaps beginning with a bazooka attack on the United Nations headquarters when Che Guevara was speaking there in 1964, and continuing through the 1980s.[81] The distinction between CIA-sponsored and supposedly independent Cuban exile terrorism against

Cuban targets was always murky. Right-wing Cuban organizations enjoyed the support of local governments in Florida, New York and New Jersey where they operated, and official investigations of their operations were mysteriously bogged down again and again. "In the Dade County police department," wrote *Village Voice* reporter Jeff Stein in 1980, after conducting an investigation of the Cuban exile organization Omega 7, "terrorism experts exchange smiles and look down at their hands when you ask them if the CIA's involved with exile Cuban anti Castro activities. They look to each other to answer first, clear their throats, shift in their seats. The answer is yes." Omega 7 claimed responsibility for over 20 bombings in New York City and New Jersey in the late 1970s, targeting primarily foreign diplomats and Cuban immigrants who did not follow their hard line against the Revolution.[82]

Omega 7 was an offshoot of the umbrella organization CORU (Comando de Organizaciones Revolucionarios Unidos), which also took credit for the October 1976 bombing of Cubana Airlines Flight 455, which killed all 73 passengers. CORU was founded in June 1976 at a meeting in the Dominican Republic, and pulled together members of the Brigade 2506 and numerous other smaller exile organizations. John Dinges and Saul Landau, who researched the organization as part of their investigation into the car-bombing which killed Chilean diplomat Orlando Letelier and Institute for Policy Studies researcher Ronni Moffit in late 1976, interviewed many of those involved regarding the extent of U.S. government involvement with CORU and concluded that CORU operated with at least tacit, and in some cases direct, support from both the CIA and the FBI. "One source, a veteran of the Miami police's fight against terrorism, said, 'The Cubans held the CORU meeting at the request of the CIA. The Cuban groups – the FNLC, Alpha 66, Cuban Power – were running amok in the mid-1970s, and the United States had lost control of them. So the United States backed the meeting to get them all going in the same direction again, under United States control. The basic signal was 'Go ahead and do what you want, *outside* the United States.'"[83]

Terrorist attacks on Cuban targets both inside and outside of the United States mushroomed after the founding of CORU. Besides the 1976 Cubana bombing, these included attacks against other Cuban airline offices and flights and against Cuban diplomats in Latin America, and the murder of former Chilean diplomat Orlando Letelier and his assistant on the streets of Washington, D.C.[84]

In late 1978, a group of Cubans in the United States tried to break the stranglehold of the right wing on Cuban politics by founding the Committee of 75, and publicly supporting improved relations with their homeland. In November of that year, a number of them traveled to Cuba to negotiate with the Castro government regarding the release of political prisoners and permission for exiles to visit the island. The trip was a success in terms of the negotiations: 3,000 political prisoners were released, and tens of thousands of Cuban exiles were allowed to return to visit the island in the months following the Committee of 75 trip. But Omega 7 did not approve. In the year following the trip, two Committee members were assassinated – one in Puerto Rico and one in New Jersey – and others began receiving regular death threats.[85]

The economic embargo imposed in 1960 continued to constitute a pillar of U.S. policy towards Cuba. Although the embargo had significant economic impact on the island, it did not isolate Cuba politically – in fact, it did more to isolate the United States. Year after year, the UN General Assembly voted to condemn the embargo – with almost total unanimity. On occasion countries like El Salvador or Romania would vote with the United States out of political loyalty. The only reliable ally was Israel – which, although it declined to condemn the embargo, itself maintained full economic relations with Cuba, and significant investment there. Numerous scholars, human rights organizations, and international agencies have decried the deleterious effects of the embargo on the well-being of Cuba's population. Their studies suggest that the embargo has, indeed, played a role in undermining the Revolution's economic goals.[86]

A ban on travel by U.S. citizens to Cuba has been in place since the 1960s, though with significant ups and downs, lapsing during the Carter Administration but reinstated by Ronald Reagan in 1980, loosened under Clinton and then tightened again under the second Bush Administration.

When African American journalist William Worthy traveled to Cuba in 1961 without a passport – his had already been revoked when he traveled to China a few years earlier – he was arrested upon re-entry to the United States. "William Worthy isn't worthy to enter our door," folksinger Phil Ochs sang satirically, "Went down to Cuba, he's not American any more. But somehow it is strange to hear the State Department say, 'You are living in the Free World, in the Free World you must stay.'"

4

Emigration and Internationalism

Cubans had been traveling, and moving, to south Florida well before 1959. Cigar makers and their workers sought refuge from the nineteenth-century independence wars by moving their operations to Tampa; by the 1950s, as Alejandro Portes and Alex Stepick note, "for many middle-class Cubans, a South Florida vacation was a yearly ritual; for the wealthy, it could be a daily excursion."[1]

Thus for those Cubans who opposed, were excluded, or found themselves increasingly alienated from the Revolution, emigration was often the first resort. Between 1960 and 1962 200,000 Cubans left, most of them for Miami.[2] In the Revolution's first decade, over half a million Cubans emigrated.[3] By 2004, there were 1.4 million Cubans in the United States, 900,000 of them immigrants and 500,000 born in the United States identifying as Cuban-Americans.[4]

The exodus of such a large portion of the population – 10 percent, by the end of the twentieth century – had complex effects on Cuban society. Most of those who left in the 1960s belonged to the upper classes, and were white. Cuba lost large numbers of doctors, professionals, and businesspeople. This meant, on one hand, that people with the precise skills needed to build a new society were not there to participate. On the other hand, it also contributed to the sense that Cuban society would be rebuilt from the ground up, in completely

A History of the Cuban Revolution. Aviva Chomsky
© 2011 Aviva Chomsky

new ways. The Revolution would train new doctors, professionals, and managers, to reconstruct society in new, revolutionary ways.

In contrast to other revolutionary situations, in which the displaced upper classes stayed in the country and fought to bring back the old order, Cuba's displaced upper classes were simply absent. They still fought to restore their vision for Cuba's future, but they did it from what some Cubans came to call "el exterior" – outside of the country. Castro, historian María Cristina García suggests, was able to "export dissent."[5] Or perhaps the dissenters exported themselves. "Most Cubans who traveled to the U.S. did so under the assumption that their stay would be temporary and they would soon return to their homeland … Most émigrés believed that it was just a matter of time before the United States intervened" to overthrow the revolutionary government.[6] In Cuba, this kind of support for U.S. intervention was derided as *plattismo*, after the long-discredited Platt Amendment.

In some ways, Cuba's experience with emigration in the late twentieth century was typical of Central America and the Caribbean. Most of the Caribbean islands saw 10 percent or even more of their population emigrate during this period. Puerto Rico stood out with 40 percent of its 5 million people leaving for the United States. The Dominican Republic, with approximately 10 million inhabitants, saw 1.1 million emigrate to the United States.

But in many other ways, Cuba's emigration was unique. For most people who want to immigrate to the United States, it's extremely difficult to obtain permission to do so legally. Since 1965, U.S. law has placed a limit of about 20,000 immigrant visas per year on every country. (Before 1965, there was no numerical restriction on immigrants from the Western hemisphere.)

Note that the 20,000 refers to *immigrant* visas. People who want to visit the United States temporarily can apply for other types of visas, like student or tourist visas. Immigration law also creates a special category for *refugees*. Since World War II, the United States has allowed certain people – mostly from Communist countries – to apply for refugee status. The 1962 Migration and Refugee Assistance Act and the 1966 Cuban Adjustment Act allowed virtually all Cubans who tried to come to the United States to obtain refugee status. Over a million Cubans took advantage of this opportunity by the 1990s.

Thus Cubans held a unique status under U.S. immigration law. Many people from other parts of Latin America, even those fleeing war, repression, and persecution on a much greater scale than what Cubans suffered, found it almost impossible to get recognized as refugees. During the bloody decade of the 1980s in Central America, fewer than 5 percent of Salvadorans and Guatemalans fleeing death squads, bombs, and scorched-earth tactics were granted refugee status.

Only Cubans received a warm welcome from the U.S. government that included virtually automatic refugee status, along with special federal programs for jobs, education, and housing. Even Puerto Ricans, who are U.S. citizens, did not receive the special benefits designed for Cubans. Most other Latin Americans encountered harsh immigration restrictions and little access to social programs or benefits.

Most of the Cubans considered themselves, as they were considered by the U.S. government, to be political refugees, fleeing from Communism. Mexicans and Puerto Ricans, in contrast, were considered to be economic migrants – people who came to the United States in search of economic opportunity, rather than for political reasons.

Yet the difference between "political" and "economic" migrants is not as clear-cut as it might appear at first glance. In both capitalist and Communist countries, governments pursued economic policies that had effects on the population and in particular, on the distribution of the country's resources. In Mexico, it was the rural poor who found their economic options choked, and who came to the United States to work, often under miserable conditions, to support their families back home. In Cuba, it was primarily urban professionals who found their economic options cut off by the Revolution. However, as I have argued elsewhere, "U.S. policy was based on the premise that in Communist countries, economic difficulties were the result of government policies, and were therefore political." In the case of a capitalist country like Mexico, however, "U.S. policy was based on the idea that poverty was merely an economic, not a political, problem."[7]

Another unique aspect of the Cuban migration was the arrival of some 14,000 unaccompanied children through a program developed by the U.S. government and the Catholic Church called Operation Peter Pan. "Many parents in Cuba," explains historian María Cristina García, "sent their children ahead to the United States, hoping to be reunited at a later date. Some parents worried about political indoctrination in Cuban schools; others hoped to save their boys from military conscription; and others were motivated by rumors that the government was going to send Cuban children to the Soviet Union and the Eastern bloc for training."[8]

Cuban immigrants were quite different from other Latin American immigrants in terms of their political identities. They began to arrive in the 1960s, just as the two largest Latin American immigrant groups, Mexicans and Puerto Ricans, were beginning to organize and explore what came to be a Third World, anti-colonial identity. The Cuban Revolution itself played an important role in the growth of Chicano and Boricua (Puerto Rican) ethnic identity and consciousness movements. Puerto Rican and Mexican immigrant activists developed an analysis of their people as colonized minorities in the United States, and elaborated an identification with anti-colonial struggles, including Cuba's Revolution. Yet the Cubans who were coming to the United States were those who opposed the Revolution. While the Cuban Revolution, and its protests against U.S. imperialism, found strong echo among Chicano and Boricua (Puerto Rican) activists, Miami's Cubans were working hard to overthrow the island's new political and social order.

Miami

The size, geographical concentration, and racial and social composition of the Cuban exodus meant that both Cuba and Miami – the prime destination for Cubans leaving the island – were transformed. Because the large majority of those leaving, especially in the first two decades of the Revolution, were white, Cuban Miami took on a light complexion, while in Cuba itself, the proportion of whites decreased. And while most Latin American immigrants remained in the lower socioeconomic sectors of U.S. society, Miami Cubans quickly rose to the top.

Alejandro Portes and Alex Stepick note the uniqueness of the changes in Miami: "A large American city [was] transformed so quickly that its natives often chose to emigrate north in search of a more familiar cultural setting." Rather than assimilating, Cuban immigrants established "a parallel social structure." The result was a process of "acculturation in reverse" whereby the Spanish language, and Cuban culture, became dominant.[9]

Miami's landscape was further complicated with the arrival of some 125,000 Cubans during the Mariel boatlift, which began in April 1980 when a small group of Cubans crashed a truck through the gates of the Peruvian Embassy in Havana and asked for asylum. Within days, some 10,000 had gathered there. People's reasons for wanting to leave Cuba, Felix Masud-Piloto explains, included family reunification, "desire for a less regimented life in the United States," desire for access to consumer goods, and political disenchantment – virtually the same reasons that motivated migrants from everywhere in Latin America. However, "these explanations did not convince observers and commentators outside Cuba, who almost invariably chose to interpret the events in strictly political terms." Although the United Nations High Commissioner for Refugees concluded that the Cubans in the Embassy were not refugees but simply people who wanted to emigrate, the U.S. President Carter agreed to "provide an open heart and open arms for the tens of thousands of refugees seeking freedom from Communist domination." Castro, meanwhile, offered to open the Cuban port of Mariel to Miami Cubans who wanted to come and pick up their relatives. Tens of thousands took the two presidents up on their offers.[10] The United States scrambled to respond to the influx, setting up detention and processing centers and pressuring the Cuban government to close the port. In October 1980 Castro did so, and the boatlift ended.

The Mariel migrants were confronted with the social, cultural and political divide between Cubans and other Latino groups in the

United States, and between Cubans in Miami and the changes occurring on the island. Miami's Cubans had tried to recreate, and preserve, the Cuba of the 1950s, before the social changes of the 1960s that swept both Cuba and Latino groups into the United States. "They tried to duplicate the past so exactly," explains María Cristina García, "that Cubans who arrived in Miami during the Mariel boatlift of 1980 often joked that they had entered a time warp and stepped back into the Cuba of the 1950s."[11] And when new Cubans arrived in the 1980s, Miami's Cuban community was not entirely pleased to be confronted with the Cuba that had evolved over two decades of revolution, superimposed onto the Cuba they remembered, and had worked so hard to recreate in Miami. "The established Cuban exile community simply disapproved of the race, ideology, values, and culture of the new exiles, many of whom had grown up with the revolution."[12] Asked whether they experienced discrimination in the United States, 30 percent of those surveyed from the Mariel boatlift believed that Anglos discriminated against them – while 80 percent believed that older-established Cubans did![13]

Most Latin American immigrants in the United States maintain close ties to their homelands, especially in the first generation. These ties include frequent travel back and forth, phone calls, remittances and, towards the end of the twentieth century, videos and internet communications. The hostile relationship between Cuba and the United States meant that these kinds of communications have been much more difficult, and have been subject to arbitrary government policies. Frequently, the decision to leave Cuba for the United States has led to years or even decades of broken family ties. Cuban immigrants created a new version of their old Cuba, in Miami, while Cuba itself was changing rapidly.

American film-maker Estela Bravo, who has lived for many years in Cuba, investigated the impact of the political hostilities on families in her documentary *Miami-Havana*. What she found, on both sides of the border, were family members devastated by the years of separation, and longing to be able to visit.

The film also illustrated the generational split among Cubans in the United States that many studies have commented upon. Older

Cubans clung to what Portes and Stepick call the "moral community" of their Miami culture: "To be a Miami Cuban, it does not suffice to have escaped from the island; one must also espouse points of view repeated ceaselessly by editorialists in Miami's Spanish radio and press" – a "ferocious right-wing frame" that put Miami's Cubans well beyond the mainstream of U.S. politics.[14]

The younger generation, however, does not share the political background of pre-1959 Cuba and the perceived betrayal by the U.S. government during the Bay of Pigs invasion. Some of them grew up in the United States, in the 1960s and beyond, and are more comfortable with the kind of pluralism that dominates the U.S. political mainstream. Others, who grew up in revolutionary Cuba and came to the United States in the 1980s or later, have a more nuanced and realistic view of what the Revolution has meant than do the exiles who see it only as the destruction of their world. As one Mariel informant explained to Portes and Stepick, "These older Cubans are very difficult. If you object to their very narrow and reactionary view of things, they make a scene and accuse you of being with Fidel. They are very dogmatic. I am an educated person and have the right to my own ideas."[15]

Cuba's Global Reach: Beyond the Cold War

While histories of Cuba often portray the island as torn between two superpowers, Cuba's global relations are in fact much more multifaceted and complex. Cuba may have been a battleground in which the United States and the Soviet Union played out aspects of the Cold War. But the Cold War intersected with Cuban nationalism and internationalism in intricate and sometimes surprising ways.

The Cuban Revolution contributed to the growth of a post-Communist "New Left" in the United States, and anti-imperialist movements around the world, that rejected the orthodoxies of the Old (Communist) Left. In supporting anti-colonial revolutions in Africa, Cuba was frequently in the lead, rather than simply following the policies of its supposed sponsor, the USSR. In offering medical and educational aid to other Third World countries, Cuba both mirrored and sometimes surpassed U.S. aid missions. Cuba's role in the Non-Aligned Movement (Fidel Castro was Secretary General from 1979–83) emphasized its often-independent foreign policy and its stature in the Third World.

Marxism's rhetorical commitment to internationalism and worldwide revolution took a variety of forms in Latin America in the twentieth century. During the Popular Front period Communist parties worldwide followed Stalin's lead in allying with what they called "bourgeois political parties" and participating in electoral politics. This meant that many Latin American Marxists opposed armed revolution. While Latin American revolutionaries frequently drew on some aspects of Marxism, they also turned for inspiration to other Latin American traditions, and to national liberation and social justice movements in their own countries' pasts. Latin American history offered a broad spectrum of revolutionary thinkers and movements, ranging from indigenous and slave uprisings against the Spanish to their wars of independence to twentieth-century labor and popular struggles. Latin American revolutionaries developed their own forms of internationalism.

Che Guevara, for example, attributed his revolutionary consciousness to the poverty and exploitation he had seen in his travels through Latin America. In Guatemala in 1954, he witnessed the first U.S. Cold War intervention, when U.S.-trained and backed counterrevolutionary forces overthrew the democratically elected government of Jacobo Arbenz. Anti-Batista publications in Havana identified with the anti-colonial struggle against the French in Algeria in the 1950s. "Since it was not always possible to attack Batista's regime directly, they covered instead the revolutionary struggle in Algeria," one Cuban observer explained.[16]

Cuba and Black Internationalism

Cubans were not the only people to draw a connection between colonial oppression in Africa and in Latin America and the Caribbean.

Black Martinican revolutionary psychiatrist and author Frantz Fanon developed his analysis of colonial oppression while working in Algeria and writing about the Algerian Revolution in the 1950s. Black internationalism – also sometimes called African nationalism – that saw black oppression as part of a global colonial phenomenon and asked blacks worldwide to identify with a common struggle against it, had roots in earlier periods – especially the Garveyite movement of the 1920s and *négritude* in the 1930s. The idea flourished in the 1960s as anti-colonial movements grew across the African continent. Fanon was not the only Caribbean author to identify with a pan-African liberation struggle. C. L. R. James wrote *The Black Jacobins* in 1938, while fellow Trinidadian Eric Williams authored *Capitalism and Slavery* in 1944. Guyanese historian Walter Rodney wrote the anti-colonial classic *How Europe Underdeveloped Africa* in 1972.[17]

Politicized African Americans also made connections to black liberation movements in the Caribbean. Prominent African Americans like Zora Neale Hurston, Kathleen Dunham, and Langston Hughes looked to the Afro-Caribbean in the spirit of solidarity well before the Cuban Revolution. In 1860 20 percent of the black population of Boston hailed from the Caribbean, while 25 percent of New York's blacks were of Caribbean origin during the Harlem Renaissance of the 1920s.[18] Black Caribbean leaders from Marcus Garvey to Claude McKay to Arthur Schomburg played a crucial role in the growth of an Africa-oriented black nationalism in the United States. "Inklings" of the "rich and diverse history of unrecognized linkages between African-Americans and Cubans," remarks Lisa Brock in her introduction to her anthology on the topic, "appear in the biographical footnotes of Langston Hughes, in the liner notes of Dizzy Gillespie records, in the political proclamations of Frederick Douglass, and in bold Havana headlines condemning the treatment of performer Josephine Baker."[19]

Historian Van Gosse looks at black Senator Adam Clayton Powell's embrace of Fidel Castro and the Revolution in early 1959, when white liberals were rapidly distancing themselves from Cuba, as emblematic of much larger sympathies in the black community. "Powell evidently perceived Castro's immense popularity with both African Americans and New York's growing Latino population. In doing so, he anticipated a whole generation of municipal, state and federal black officials from the 1970s on … for whom solidarity with Third World leaders, from Nelson Mandela to Yasir Arafat, was not a threat but a guarantor of popular support." And Powell, Gosse points out, "was actually more conservative regarding Cuba than considerable sectors of the mainstream black community." "Black Americans," Gosse concludes, "felt a strong solidarity with the colonial world, and quite easily recognize a colonial situation and the reality of national liberation." "No one knows the master as well as the servant," Malcolm X explained upon his highly photographed meeting with Fidel.[20]

Manning Marable concurs. "No white political leader," he wrote in 2000, "would ever come as close to receiving this kind of approval from literally every sector of the African American community … Only Nelson Mandela of South Africa surpassed the moral authority and political credibility that Castro could claim within black America."[21]

When Fidel Castro returned to Harlem in 1995 – 35 years after his historic 1960 appearance at the United Nations, when he spurned the upscale hotel assigned to his entourage and lodged instead at Harlem's Hotel Theresa – he was greeted at the Abyssinian Baptist Church by yet another generation of black and Latino leaders: U.S. Congress members Charles Rangel, José Serrano, and Nydia Velásquez, religious leaders Conrad Muhammad and Calvin O. Butts, and scholars and authors Angela Davis, Leonard Jeffries, and John Henrik Clarke, as well as an audience of 1,300 people.[22]

Cuba in Africa and Latin America

In an era of Cold War and superpower politics, Cuba became an important player on its own. The small country took an active role in the Non-Aligned Movement of mostly Third World countries that strove to develop an international voice for former colonies in Africa, Asia, and Latin America outside of the East–West dynamic. As relations with the United State deteriorated, Cuba also became an early challenger to some international institutions under U.S. control, like the World Bank and the newly founded Inter-American Development Bank. Although the United States successfully pushed for Cuba's expulsion from the Organization of American States in 1962, many Latin American countries opposed the move. "La OEA es cosa de risa," sang Carlos Puebla in a popular tune of the day. "How can I not laugh at the OAS?"

These breaks did not mean that Cuba became isolated. Rather, it developed an extremely activist foreign policy. Its military activities around the world placed it second only to the United States, and ahead of the USSR, the supposed second superpower.[23] Its civilian aid programs became the largest in the world, surpassing even international organizations like the United Nations or the World Health Organization. By 2006, Cuba had sent almost 400,000 soldiers and about 70,000 aid workers on missions abroad.[24] As Cuban-American political scientist Jorge Domínguez wrote in 1978, "Cuba is a small country, but it has a big country's foreign policy."[25]

Several different scholars, in the United States, in Cuba, and beyond, have found different ways to explain the size – and the nature – of Cuba's foreign policy. Jorge Domínguez argued that it was a form of realpolitik. As an isolated, small country, Cuba needed to create allies. Third World revolutionary movements were Cuba's natural partners; it was in Cuba's interest to help them succeed. Cuba's goal, as Domínguez's book's title suggests, was *To Make a World Safe for Revolution*.

Piero Gleijeses disagrees. Far from realpolitik, he argues, Cuba's foreign policies were motivated by revolutionary idealism. Cuba incurred huge risks with its activities in Africa. In directly challenging the United States in places like Angola, Cuba jeopardized relations not only with the United States but also with Western Europe and the Organization of American States. At certain points it even risked alienating the USSR. "Castro sent troops," Gleijeses concludes, "because he was committed to racial justice." "For no other country in modern times has idealism been such a key component of its foreign policy."[26]

Carlos Moore takes precisely the opposite view. Focusing on Cuba's involvement in Africa, he argues that foreign policy served to promote the illusion of commitment to black liberation, covering up the reality of racial inequality at home. It was a cynical, practically Machiavellian policy.[27]

The largest Cuban commitment in the 1970s and 80s was in Angola, where the leftist MPLA liberation movement won independence from Portugal in 1975. Cuba sent a force of some 36,000 to help the MPLA repel a South African military invasion encouraged by the United States, and the neighboring struggle of Namibia for independence from South Africa. Cuban military presence in Angola grew to some 52,000 troops by 1988. The Cubans also sent some 16,000 troops to support Ethiopia in early 1978, when the country was invaded by Somalia. Cuban forces helped protect Mozambican ports and oil facilities from attacks by South African-supported rebels in the late 1970s and through the 1980s. And Cuba established smaller military missions (numbering in the hundreds of troops) in the Republic of the Congo, Guinea, Guinea-Bissau, and Benin.[28]

In Latin America, Cuba has lent varying degrees of support to revolutionary movements and leftist governments. In late 1960, after the Río Treaty member states, under U.S. urging, passed the Declaration of San José implicitly condemning Cuba's Revolution, Cuba responded with the First Declaration of Havana announcing its support for hemisphere-wide revolution. Che Guevara's attempt to foment revolution in Bolivia in the mid-1960s was a disaster, ending with his capture and murder by Bolivian forces aided by the CIA in 1967. But Cuba found a strong ally in Chile's socialist President Salvador Allende when he was elected in 1970.

The Sandinista Revolution in Nicaragua owed much to the Cubans. "The Cuban Revolution of 1959 was the critical turning point in [Nicaraguan revolutionary leader Carlos] Fonseca's political evolution," writes his biographer, "opening up the possibility of a deep-going social revolution in his own country, turning him to a study of Sandino's history, and leading directly to the formation of the FSLN."[29] It was in Havana that Fonseca first learned about Augusto César Sandino's uprising against the U.S. occupation of Nicaragua in the 1920s, and began to write and organize, becoming the major theoretician behind the founding of the FSLN in 1962. Nicaraguan priest and liberation theologian Ernesto Cardenal published *En Cuba* describing his experiences there in 1970.

While U.S. policymakers and media have often portrayed the Cubans as acting as proxies for the USSR, most serious scholars tell a different story. "Fidel Castro is nobody's puppet," Jorge Domínguez concluded in 1989. "Cuba led the USSR in fashioning policies toward Central America, inducing the Soviets to behave in ways they might otherwise not have behaved … Cuba has served as a broker and advocate for other governments, especially Grenada's, in their relations with the Soviet Union."[30] Likewise Piero Gleijeses's definitive accounts of Cuba's involvement in Africa conclude that it was the Cubans who dragged an unwilling USSR into support for the Africans.

"The aid Cuba gave Algeria in 1961–2 had nothing to do with the East–West conflict," stated Gleijeses flatly. "Its roots predated Castro's victory in 1959 and lay in the Cubans' widespread identification with the struggle of the Algerian people." Independent Algeria's new President, Ahmed Ben Bella, visited Cuba soon after taking office in 1962. "The two youngest revolutions of the world met, compared their problems and together envisioned the future," Ben Bella explained.[31]

Moscow, seeking detente with the United States in the 1970s, had little enthusiasm for African entanglements. As the CIA concluded in 1976, "Cuba is not involved in Africa solely or even primarily because of its relationship with the Soviet Union. Rather, Havana's African policy reflects its activist revolutionary ethos and its determination to expand its own political influence in the Third World at the expense of the West (read U.S.)."[32]

Civilian Aid Missions

Although Cuba's military involvement has received more attention, another side of Cuban involvement in Africa and Latin America has been the flood of Cuban aid workers, teachers, and doctors, on the continent. Cuba, political scientist Julie Feinsilver notes, has created the largest civilian aid program in the world – not only in comparison to its size and resources, but even in absolute numbers. From 1963, when the first 56 Cuban health workers traveled to work in Algeria, through 1991, Cuba sent some 30,000 health workers abroad, including 10,000 physicians. In 1984, Castro announced an initiative to train 10,000 new doctors specifically to enhance its program of medical aid. At the end of 2005, Cuba had medical missions in 68 countries.[33] Cubans made up the largest contingent of doctors rushed to Kashmir after the 2005 earthquake. Over 300 Cuban doctors were already working in Haiti when the earthquake devastated Port au Prince in early 2010, and more were quickly flown in. "It doesn't matter if things seem impossible," one of them told the *Miami Herald*. "One has to keep up the fight."[34]

Cuba also implemented a massive training program for health professionals from the Third World – all provided free of cost to participants. Between 1961 and 2001, some 40,000 students, primarily from Asia and Africa, traveled to Cuba for training. In 1998, Cuba established the Latin American Medical School (Escuela Latino-Americana de Medicina, or ELAM) specifically for African and Latin American students. In exchange for full scholarships, students agree to serve for five years in underserved communities in their homelands. In 2005–6, there were over 10,000 students enrolled in the school, from 27 countries.[35]

"Rather than a fifth column promoting socialist ideology," Julie Feinsilver argues, "these doctors provide a serious threat to the status quo by their example of serving the poor in areas in which no local doctor would work, by making house calls a routine part of their medical practice and by being available free of charge 24/7, thus changing the nature of doctor–patient relations. As a result, they have forced the re-examination of societal values and the structure and functioning of the health systems and the medical profession within the countries to which they were sent and where they continue to practice. This is the current Cuban threat."[36]

If, as Van Gosse argued, the Cuban Revolution offered the world an example of a revolution that could break with Soviet dogmas, and so opened up the possibility for a whole new way of imagining revolutionary change, the Sandinistas were perhaps the first successful revolution to flourish from the seeds it planted. The New Left in the United States too owed much to Cuba's challenge to the rigidities and atrocities that had disillusioned many radicals in the United States with the Soviet model. By example, by military involvement (in Africa), by medical, technical, and educational aid throughout the Third World, the Cuban Revolution has had an outsized impact on progressive, leftist, and revolutionary movements throughout its 50 years.

5
Art, Culture, and Revolution

From the music of Pablo Milanés and Silvio Rodríguez to the films of Tomás Gutiérrez Alea to the National Ballet to the many research institutes created by the Revolution, Cuba has fostered the creation and dissemination of art at the same time that it has frowned on cultural production "outside the revolution" (as Fidel Castro described it in his "Words to Intellectuals"). Literature, especially, has flourished outside of Cuba as much as inside, with first-generation exiles like Reinaldo Arenas and second-generation like Achy Obejas and Cristina García. In the 1990s and first years of the twenty-first century, both film and music engaged with and challenged the new realities of the post-Soviet period.

Cultural production flourishes, historians tell us, through contact, interaction, and cross-fertilization. Perhaps for this reason, the Caribbean, a global crossroads since 1492 has, despite its small size and its poverty, offered a wealth of cultural riches to the world. Caribbean musical styles, from reggae to salsa, have had an especially large global impact. Cuba was the birthplace of magical realism, the literary style later associated with Nobel-Prize winning Colombian novelist Gabriel García Márquez. World History as a discipline grew from the revolutionary works of Caribbean scholars like C. L. R. James, Eric Williams, and Walter Rodney, who argued for the impor-

A History of the Cuban Revolution. Aviva Chomsky
© 2011 Aviva Chomsky

tance of studying the colonies to understand global developments. The Caribbean fostered early forms of pan-African identity, like those espoused by Marcus Garvey to Frantz Fanon.

Those who have studied revolutionary culture in Cuba have done so from various perspectives. Some, like Richard Fagen and Julie Marie Bunck, have focused on culture as the basis of everyday life, in Bunck's words, "the fundamental beliefs, opinions, and values of a given society."[1] Others have noted the extraordinary expansion of cultural opportunity, including the literacy campaign and the expansion of schooling at all levels, and the proliferation of cultural institutions like libraries, museums, publishing, theaters, local, regional and national places and spaces for producing and participating in cultural activities – the democratization of culture. Sujatha Fernandes focused on current forms of popular culture like film and rap music, suggesting that "the arts have taken on a vital role in formulating, articulating, and making sense of everyday life."[2] Finally, critics like David Craven and Roberto González Echevarría have examined Cuban artistic production itself under the Revolution, ranging from literature to visual and performance arts.

Virtually everybody who studies culture in Cuba confronts the apparent paradox in revolutionary cultural policies and developments. On one hand, the Revolution has fostered, democratized, and contributed to all areas of culture in ways unprecedented in Latin American history. On the other hand, the Revolution has controlled, censored and restricted cultural production to the extent that numerous authors have chosen exile, and many Cubans complain about the limits on what they can read, listen to, see, or do. Since the advent of the internet, this contradiction may have become even more acute.

Those who have studied Cuban culture also differ as to how much cultural change actually occurred, at the popular level, and to what extent the Revolution succeeded in fostering a vibrant production in the arts. Interestingly, Fagen, who was generally sympathetic to the goals of cultural transformation, saw a significant measure of change in the 1960s; Bunck, writing two decades later and who is quite leery of the goals, believes that little change occurred. What Bunck derides as the imposition of "correct ideological thinking" Fagen describes as a "culture-transforming process."[3]

As of 1985, Bunck argues, "the government's policies had utterly failed to mold Che's 'new man' ... Cubans were not thinking and acting as right-minded Marxist-Leninist citizens."[4]

During the first decade of the Revolution, Fagen examined three processes that he saw as key to the Revolution's attempt to create a new political culture: the literacy campaign; the Committees for the Defense of the Revolution (CDRs); and the Schools of Revolutionary Instruction (EIRs). The literacy campaign was a year-long process in 1961; the EIRs functioned from 1960 to 1967; and the CDRs, also created in 1960, continue to function to this day. In all three examples, the revolutionary leadership designed projects specifically aimed at creating the "new man" through mobilization and participation.

These programs were part and parcel of the dramatic structural changes of the early years of the Revolution. Mobilization and education were integral to creating a more equal society, to economic development, and to defense against foreign aggression and domestic subversion. "In the Cuban view," Fagen concludes, "the developmental problems faced by the poorer nations cannot be solved by the conventional application of conventional technology. In fact, national development is not in the first instance a technical or even an economic problem. It is a political problem: its causes are political and its solutions must be political."[5]

Cultural transformation also had a strong *rural* component. Just as the guerrillas in the sierra had developed their revolutionary ideology through their intimate contact with the realities of rural life, so must urban Cubans as a whole raise their consciousness of their country's social and political reality by coming to know the rural areas. Urban Cubans went to the countryside to transform rural culture by teaching peasants to read, but also to transform themselves. It was to be a revolutionary education for both parties.

During the 1970s, the period of institutionalization and a return to material incentives, there was also a certain retreat from the utopian goals of cultural transformation. The re-introduction of material incentives, and the return to legalizing small businesses and even, after 1980, farmers markets, symbolized a scaling down of the ambition of entirely remaking Cuban society and its members.

But if the ideology of the "new man" became less salient, the growth of cultural activity did not. "In 1959, Cuba published less than one million books a year," David Craven points out. "By 1980 it published over fifty million books a year, all of which were sold below production costs, with school textbooks being free to all students … In 1962, the National Council on Culture sponsored events attended by four million spectators, or almost half the population. During 1975, the Cuban government sponsored events in the arts that were attended by 67 million spectators, almost seven times the national population."[6]

Of course cultural change is difficult to measure. One set of data that we can use to add to the discussion is surveys of popular opinion. A survey carried out in the spring of 1960 found an astonishing 86 percent of the population claiming to support the revolutionary government, with 43 percent showing "fervent" support.[7] These figures surely illustrate the degree to which the Revolution, and the popular mobilizations succeeded in capturing the imaginations of ordinary Cubans, indicating just the kind of cultural change that the Revolution sought to create. Over time, however, the overlap between cultural change and explicit support for the government probably became less obvious. If education, participation, and raised political consciousness were central to the revolutionary project of cultural transformation, then a vigorous debate about political and social realities could be seen as evidence of the project's success.

As we have seen above, one arena for such a debate is among intellectuals, in universities and research institutions. But intellectuals have always participated in this kind of conversation – it is their bread and butter. What about the rest of society, the ordinary people whose lives, ideas, and beliefs the Revolution sought to so radically transform?

Both Fagen and Bunck look at the creation and transformation of culture from the top down. Sujatha Fernandes, in contrast, argues that the Cuban state is "not a repressive centralized apparatus that enforces its dictates on citizens from the top down" but rather "a permeable entity that both shapes and is constituted by the activities of various social actors." "Artistic public spheres" are one of the means by which ordinary Cubans participate, debate, and critique political and social realities.[8] Fernandes's approach transcends the dichotomy that emerges when comparing Fagen to Bunck. For the latter two authors, the Cuban population's options are limited to accepting, or rejecting, attempts at cultural transformation from above. In Fernandes's account, the population is an active participant in an ongoing process of cultural creation, along with the state.

We should note, though, that Fernandes is studying popular culture in the Special Period. There have been few attempts to really investigate the nature and role of popular culture in Cuba between 1959 and the 1990s.

Fernandes argues that the Special Period, with the loss of the Soviet Union as an economic support and an ideological mooring, led to increased space for rethinking of culture from the bottom up. In this respect, a parallel process was going on in the popular arena as in the intellectual world.

Literature

According to literary scholar Roberto González Echevarría, "The Cuban Revolution is the dividing line in contemporary Latin American literature, a literature of before the revolution and one of after the revolution." In fact, he argues, "it is difficult to conceive of the Boom of the Latin American novel" if not for the Cuban Revolution. The heightened U.S. interest in Latin America sparked by the Revolution not only gave rise to the growth of Latin American Studies in the U.S. academy as discussed earlier, it also led to a proliferation of opportunities for Latin American authors in the United States, just as Cuba was pouring resources into creating its own literary institutions. The result was an unprecedented cornucopia for Latin American authors.[9]

Probably Cuba's most influential writer has been Alejo Carpentier, whose prolific career spanned the pre- and post-revolutionary periods until his death in 1980. Author of numerous works that have been widely translated, Carpentier also introduced the concept of "magical realism" into Latin American literature. In his prologue to his 1949 novel *El reino de este mundo* [*The Kingdom of this World*] Carpentier coined the phrase "lo real maravilloso americano" – the marvelous real of the Americas. European artists and writers, he argued, had to reach into fantasy to invent the marvelous or magical. In the Americas, there was no need to resort to fantasy. "It had to be an American painter – the Cuban, Wilfredo Lam – who taught us the magic of tropical vegetation, the unbridled creativity of our natural forms with all their metamorphoses and symbioses ..."[10] Europeans struggled to invent novels of chivalry, while "the only honest-to-goodness book of chivalry that has ever been written" was conquistador Bernal Díaz del Castillo's factual account of the conquest of Mexico. "Without realizing it, Bernal Díaz bested the brave deeds of Amadís of Gaul, Belianis of Greece, and Florismarte of Hircania. He had discovered a world of monarchs crowned with the plumes of green birds, vegetation dating back to the origins of the earth, foods never before tasted, drinks extracted from cacti and palm trees ... In such a world, events tend to develop their own style, their own unique trajectories."[11]

The Revolution's investment in literature and culture could be said to span everything from the literacy campaign and the overwhelming emphasis on education, creating the most literate population in the Americas, to the creation of institutes like the Casa de las Américas and the Casa del Caribe, publishing houses, and prizes, to the rediscovery and publication of Cuba's literary history. The Revolution clearly made the promotion of literature a priority. While other revolutions have given rise to a literature of war, or of social change, González Echevarría suggests, "the literature of the Cuban Revolution has been the one created by the sense of self-questioning made possible by the countless Cuban texts put in the hands of the new writers; the literature that has delved into the opened archives of Cuban memory in search of records to assemble them for the first time; the literature that has read and reread the record relentlessly, constructing a literary past to make it available to this generation of Cuban readers and writers."[12] The project included the creation of a publishing industry and huge print runs of classics beginning with 100,000 copies of *Don Quijote* that would "find its way to every corner of the island." A comparable edition of García Márquez's *One Hundred Years of Solitude* in 1968 likewise sold out.[13] And a fortieth anniversary edition of García Márquez's work – the fourth Cuban edition – was the most popular book among the four million for sale at the Seventeenth Annual Havana Book Fair in 2007.[14]

Cuban literary greats like Carpentier (1904–80) and Nicolás Guillén (1902–89) played key roles in leading these efforts at cultural recuperation. Other major Cuban authors who were close to the revolutionary project include Roberto Fernández Retamar (b. 1930), Pablo Armando Fernández (b. 1930), Miguel Barnet (b. 1940), Reynaldo González (b. 1940), and Nancy Morejón (b. 1944). Others, like José Lezama Lima (1910–76) stayed in Cuba, but had more conflictive relations with the revolutionary government.

The challenges and contradictions inherent in the idea of creating a new, authentic, and revolutionary culture are perhaps exemplified in the case of the magazine *Lunes de Revolución*, a literary supplement to the July 26th Movement's daily newspaper *Revolución*. Edited by renowned Cuban authors Guillermo Cabrera Infante and Pablo Armando Fernández, *Lunes* began publishing in March 1959 and at its height had a circulation of 250,000, becoming "the most widely-read and important literary supplement in Cuba's history, and in that of the Western world," according to William Luis.[15] Daring, avant-garde, and revolutionary, *Lunes* published Cuban, Latin American, and world authors, and also coordinated programming on its own television channel.

Over the course of 1960, Cuba's Communist Party, which represented some of the most socially and culturally conservative voices in the July 26th coalition, became more prominent in the revolutionary government. *Lunes*, in contrast, was in the hands of a group of "young free thinkers not aligned with any political tendency." A brewing conflict between Party members rising in the country's cultural institutions and the magazine exploded over the film *P.M.* The documentary depicted Havana's night life, with an emphasis on drinking, bars, and African music and dance. While not seen by its *Lunes*-affiliated producers as being in any way critical of or opposed to the Revolution, it did depict revolutionary Cuba in ways that contradicted the more puritanical Communist vision of proper morality and behavior. In June 1961, shortly after the Bay of Pigs invasion and the heightened demand for national unity and revolutionary closing of ranks, as well as the revolutionary leadership's warming relationship with the PSP and the Soviet Union, the magazine was forced to close its doors. "In one brief moment, the members of the literary supplement and the newspaper had been transformed from representatives of the Revolution into its enemies."[16]

Other Cuban writers suffered the same fate. One of the country's best-known poets, Heberto Padilla, objected to the demands on Cuba's intellectuals in his poem "In Hard Times." "During hard times," he wrote, referring to the official insistence that outside attack, and the danger of subversion, required heightened loyalty, "they" asked the writer to devote every part of his body to the cause. "They explained to him later that all these donations would be useless unless he also surrender his tongue," the poem continues.[17] When first published in 1968, his collection in which this poem appeared won Cuba's highest poetry prize. Three years later, however, Padilla was arrested. After a month he reappeared, to read a public confession of his counter-revolutionary errors.

Intellectuals worldwide, including some of the Revolution's most outspoken supporters, were outraged. Jean-Paul Sartre, Simone de Beauvoir, Italo Calvino, Gabriel García Márquez, and many others signed an open letter of protest. Some, like Sartre and de Beauvoir, became permanently disillusioned with the Revolution. Others, like García Márquez, maintained their support despite their criticism of the Padilla Affair. The Affair marked the beginning of the "quinquenio gris" or "gray five years." Padilla remained in Cuba for another nine years, although he did not publish again until he was allowed to leave and made his new home in the United States in 1980.

Cuban detective writer Leonardo Padura (b. 1955) perhaps exemplifies a new generation of Cuban authors. U.S. detective fiction in translation was immensely popular in Cuba prior to the Revolution. The first wave of post-revolutionary detective stories tried to recreate the genre to meet revolutionary goals: the villains were representatives of the old, corrupt order, while the heroes worked collectively and were motivated by revolutionary values. Little of literary worth came out of this overtly didactic phase.

Padura's writings, published in the 1990s, offer a new, and much more sophisticated, engagement with Cuban realities through the medium of the detective story. His protagonist, Mario Conde, is something of an anti-hero, frustrated both in his personal life and in his assessment of the state of his country. One of his close friends lost a leg fighting in Angola; another is an apparently successful doctor who decides to emigrate. The novels reveal frustrations not only with the material scarcities still – and newly – insurmountable decades into the Revolution, but also with the hierarchical, sometimes corrupt, and overly regimented nature of life. "We are a generation that obeyed orders," the would-be-émigré doctor complains, "but nobody ever thought of asking us what we wanted."[18]

Cuban literature also flourished in the United States. Some Cuban authors chose exile over the course of the revolutionary decades, like Reinaldo Arenas (1943–90, left Cuba in 1980), Lino Novás Calvo (1903–83, left Cuba in 1960), and Heberto Padilla (1932–2000, left Cuba in 1980). Others, like Edmundo Desnoes (b. 1930, left Cuba in 1979), and perhaps Antonio Benítez-Rojo (1931–2005, left Cuba in 1980), left Cuba without necessarily viewing their choice as a political exile – they simply chose to live and work elsewhere. And a new generation of Cuban American authors emerged from those brought to the United States as young children in the years following the Revolution, like Roberto G. Fernández (b. 1951), Cristina García (b. 1958), and Achy Obejas (b. 1956), or those born in the United States, like Ana Menéndez (b. 1970). While they are in some ways children of the Revolution, they are also heirs to earlier generations of Cuban immigrant writers, like Oscar Hijuelos, born in New York in 1951 to Cuban immigrant parents. Other Cuban émigrés like

Guillermo Cabrera Infante (1929–2005, left Cuba in1965) and Zoé Valdés (b. 1959) have made their homes in Europe.

Conversely, writers from elsewhere in Latin America have sought temporary or permanent refuge in Cuba. Uruguayan author Daniel Chavarría (b. 1933) made Cuba his permanent home, while Mario Benedetti passed part of his exile, also from Uruguay, there. Others like Colombia's Gabriel García Márquez maintained close ties there.

Cuba's Revolution, and its literature and institutions, also served as an inspiration to the Latin American genre of *testimonio* or testimony in the 1980s. Miguel Barnet's *Biografía de un cimarrón*, published in 1966, was probably the seminal work of the genre. The Casa de las Américas Prize, and the fostering of the genre and its practitioners there, nourished the environment that gave birth to classic works like *I, Rigoberta Menchu*. Venezuelan anthropologist Elisabeth Burgos-Debray had met with Guatemalan revolutionaries at the Tricontinental Conference in Havana in 1966; they later brought Rigoberta to meet with her in Paris, where the two collaborated on the testimony.[19] The book won the Casa de las Américas Prize in 1983, catapulting it to international recognition. Salvadoran revolutionary poet Roque Dalton spent time in exile in Cuba, as did the subject of the celebrated testimony that he later authored, Salvadoran Communist leader Miguel Mármol.

In terms of literary criticism, González Echevarría notes that "the less academic and more popular a work, the more militant it is."[20] In this respect, literary criticism mirrored nonfiction and scholarly writing in general. Cuba's daily newspapers drummed a relentlessly celebratory party line about current events, even while more specialized publications took a much more sober and in-depth view of matters.

Except for in the case of testimony, revolutionary Cuba's impact on the Latin American literary world probably had as much to do with the institutions it created than with the actual literary production since the Revolution. In the areas of film, music, and visual and especially poster art, in contrast, revolutionary Cuba's innovations and works had a dramatic impact both domestically and internationally.

Figure 5.1   ICAIC headquarters, Havana, 2008
Source: Photo by Aviva Chomsky

Film

The Cuban film institute, ICAIC (the Instituto Cubano de Arte e Industria Cinematográficos or Cuban Institute of Cinematographic Arts and Industry), was created in March 1959, only months after the revolutionary government came to power (Figure 5.1). ICAIC, David Craven suggests, "was a haven for the most flexible and open-minded figures within the Cuban government."[21] Indeed, along with music, Cuban film has probably been the most vigorously socially engaged and critic of the arts.

Directors affiliated with ICAIC like Tomás Gutiérrez Alea, Humberto Solás, Pastor Vega, Sara Gómez, Julio García Espinosa,

Sergio Giral, and others have produced an astonishing number, variety, and quality of films over the decades of the Revolution. Some delved into Cuba's history, exploring new angles and interpretations in light of contemporary scholarship and events. Sergio Giral's *El otro Francisco* (1975) reinterpreted a celebrated nineteenth-century Cuban abolitionist novel, *Francisco*. The novel, in the genre of *Uncle Tom's Cabin*, offered a somewhat romanticized and melodramatic approach to the evils of slavery, with the slaves as humble victims, slave-owners as cruel individuals, and abolitionists as humanitarians. The film gives us "the other Francisco" – a slave who is a multidimensional rebel – and a slave system and abolitionist movement that are imbedded in their time and place, the colonial sugar economy. Tomás Gutiérrez Alea also turned to nineteenth-century slave society in *La última cena* (1976), the story of a slave-owner who tries to reenact the Last Supper with his chosen slaves. The 1791 Haitian Revolution and the 1959 Cuban Revolution resonate in the background of the drama and again, a rebel challenges the structural and ideological realities of the slave system. These, and other films, developed the genre of historical film in explicit dialogue with the present.

Other films engaged directly with contemporary realities. Gutiérrez Alea's *Memorias del subdesarrollo* (1968), based on Edmundo Desnoes's novel originally titled *Inconsolable Memories* in English, delves into the life and psyche of an alienated, almost paralyzed, bourgeois intellectual who remains in Cuba after the Revolution, observing the departure of his family and colleagues, the profound changes occurring in society, and the panic of the Missile Crisis with a detached sort of fatalism. The film turned the attention of the world to Cuban cinema. "The reviews published throughout the world following the film's release offer the same laudatory epithets whether they come from New York, Paris, London, or Montevideo. The words 'remarkable,' 'extraordinary,' 'outstanding,' 'perfect' were all applied to the film. 'One of the best films of all times,' David Elliott wrote in 1978 in the *Chicago Sun-Times*, while Arthur Cooper stated in *Newsweek* that '*Memorias del subdesarrollo* is undoubtedly a masterpiece, a complex, ironical and extraordinarily clever film.'" "What is still fascinating today about this film, and what presumably fascinated audiences at the time," Nancy Berthier concluded recently, "is the way Gutiérrez Alea, by means of profoundly original aesthetics, put the issue of the relationship between the intellectual, or quite simply the individual, with the surrounding society in terms of a fundamental dilemma. To choose to be solitary, or in solidarity, to live in distance or fusion?"[22]

Pastor Vega's *Portrait of Teresa* (1979) aimed at "planting a little bomb in every living room" with its sensitive portrayal of a woman struggling with the "triple day" of caring for husband and children, work in a textile factory, and her union's demands on her talents as a dancer and organizer. Her husband grows increasingly angry with what he sees as her failure as a wife and mother, while Teresa is torn between the camaraderie and self-fulfillment of the dance troupe and her anguished cry that "the day only has 24 hours!" The film was released a few years after the passage of the 1975 Family Code that legislated women's equality in the home as well as in the workplace.

Teresa, like many films that followed in the 1980s, looked at how the ideals of the Revolution translated into the realities of everyday life. For all of its successes in creating opportunities for education and meaningful work, health care, and adequate nutrition, the Revolution did not bring anything close to First World prosperity. *Portrait of Teresa* unflinchingly depicts overcrowded busses, unappetizing school lunches, unreliable water and electricity, and broken television sets.

Even in ICAIC there were limits, however. Sergio Giral's 1981 *Techo de vidrio* or *Glass Ceiling*, which depicted corruption and racism in contemporary Cuba, was not distributed on the island. In the mid-1980s, Giral described *Techo de vidrio* as "a failed film. I tried to make a film about contemporary topics, in a more or less critical tone, but I wasn't pleased with the results. It is very difficult for us to broach and elaborate on contemporary topics," he explained.[23] After relocating to Miami in 1991, Giral spoke more harshly about the fate of *Techo*: "It's clear that political-ideological censorship was always present ... My film, 'Techo de vidrio,' was censored from the onset and ended up in the memory hole."[24]

Techo was in some ways a casualty of the political climate of the 1970s. ICAIC was reorganized in 1982 under the direction of veteran filmmaker Julio García Espinosa, leading to some decentralization and experimentation with new genres, including comedies like Juan Carlos Tabío's *Se permuta* (1984) and *Plaff* (1988). *Se permuta* used Cuba's housing scarcity – and housing policy – as a backdrop to a domestic comedy. As in other areas of the economy, there is no "free market" in real estate in Cuba. Residents are allowed to move if they can find someone willing to exchange homes, which has led to a complex, eBay-style system of advertising house swaps. Likewise *Plaff* poked fun at the bureaucracies and material hardships of everyday life.

While the above-mentioned films incorporated critiques of contemporary realities, the cultural and political establishment raised no objections. The reception of *Alicia en el pueblo de Maravillas* – *Alice in Wondertown* – when it was first shown in 1989 was quite different. *Alicia* was another comedy that parodied Cuba's bureaucracies and inefficiencies. But in the political and economic context of the collapse of the Soviet bloc and the vast uncertainty facing Cuba – *Miami Herald* columnist Andrés Oppenheimer was predicting "Castro's final hour" – the ax came down on *Alicia*. Only a few days after the film was released, and won an award at the Berlin Film Festival, it was banned in Cuba. Even more dramatically, the Cuban Film Institute was informed that it would become one of the many victims of the economic crisis, and be merged with the film and television division of the Armed Forces. The Institute saw this as a death blow to the autonomy and creativity of the country's entire film industry.

After loud and intense protest, the government backed down – partially. The Institute was restored, but its head, García Espinosa, was replaced with his predecessor, Alfredo Guevara. And *Alicia* remained banned, a victim as much of the historical moment in which it appeared as of the longstanding contradiction between the liberatory and the repressive strains in Cuban cultural policy.

Sergio Giral described *María Antonia*, released in 1990 and the last film he made on the island, as his best work. Like his earlier historical films, *María Antonia* delved into Afro-Cuban culture – the Yoruba-based *santería* – and harsh realities of poverty and racism. Although based on a 1968 play and set in the 1950s, it clearly critiqued contemporary realities as well, especially in the final scene where the poverty and racial inequalities of the past are transposed into the present.

Although Giral subsequently left Cuba for Miami, other historic and new directors continued to push Cuba's film industry in new directions in the 1990s, with films like Gutiérrez Alea's *Strawberry and Chocolate* and *Guatnanamera* (1995) and Fernando Pérez's *La vida es silbar* (*Life is to Whistle*, 1998) enjoying acclaim both on the island and abroad. The economic crisis of the 1990s meant that Cuban filmmakers had to turn abroad for funding, which brought both new challenges and new opportunities.

Music

Cuba's musical heritage is vast, as are its contributions to world music. In the United States, Cuban music probably had its largest impact through its influence on the development of the genres of jazz in the first half of the twentieth century, and salsa in the second.

Some aspects of Cuban music were affected or transformed by the Revolution, while in others, the island's musical traditions simply continued their own trajectories. Singer-songwriters like Carlos Puebla, Silvio Rodríguez and Pablo Milanés became the musical face of the Cuban Revolution in much of the Spanish-speaking world during the 1970s and 80s and beyond. Traditional Cuban *son* music underwent an international revival in the 1990s with the release of "The Buena Vista Social Club" CD in 1997, and the film in 1999. Newer variations on the traditional forms, ranging from rap to reggaeton, also flourished in the 1990s and into the new century.

Puebla is best known for his topical songs, commenting on the political and social realities especially during the early years of the Revolution. His best-known song is probably "Hasta Siempre, Comandante," written in 1965 when Che left Cuba to spread the Revolution elsewhere in Africa and Latin America. "Your revolutionary love is taking you to new places, where they await the strength of your arms in liberation," he sang. "Here we are left with the clear, intimate transparence of your beloved presence."

The "New Song" movement in Latin America, and its Cuban version, the "Nueva Trova," aimed to challenge the commercial and foreign domination of the airwaves with authentically local and meaningful music. From Chile to Mexico, musicians turned to indigenous and local musical roots and developed a music that engaged with, rather than served to escape from, Latin American realities. The protest music movement in the United States in the 1960s and 70s, with artists like Bob Dylan and Joan Baez, emerged from the same kind of artistic desire for a music that was relevant, topical, and grew from indigenous roots.

Milanés and Puebla relied mostly on traditional Cuban musical forms. Rodríguez took experimentation with the traditional forms to its greatest heights, both musically and poetically. Some of his most moving songs explored the bounds of the personal and the political, with magical imagery, emotion, and political commentary fused into haunting melodies. Lost blue unicorns are found in the mountains of El Salvador, while children find the strength to face the future even without the Three Kings. "I was born to dream the sun, and to say things that awaken love," he writes, in a song that evokes a nightmare of bombs and chaos.

Both Milanés and Rodríguez kept up their pace of creative production and political engagement into the 1990s. (Puebla died in 1989 after a long illness.) "How seductive questioning is," Rodríguez wrote in "Disillusionment" in 1989. "Disillusionment – a brilliant fashion show. It opened a business, rediscovered leisure. Like tourism, it invented the abyss. It touched the diamond and turned it to coal." Milanés, who is openly bisexual and in fact was imprisoned at the end of the 1960s, recorded "The Original Sin" in 1994, describing a love between two men. "We are not God," he warned. "Let's not get it wrong again," referring to Cuba's long-standing and various forms of discrimination against homosexuality.

In the 1990s there was a flowering of Cuban rap music, ranging from commercially oriented and fairly apolitical groups to more edgy, underground groups. "At first the state promoted commercially oriented rap as a way of diluting rap's radical potential," Fernandes explains, but soon it "turned to praising the underground groups for their rejection of commercialism." In the latter position, Cuba's government followed other leftist governments in Latin America that "build alliances with the hip-hop movement" in order to take advantage of "the role that hip-hop can play in engaging black youth."[25]

One Cuban critic suggested that Cuba's revolutionary context meant that Cuban rappers played an entirely different role in society than elsewhere because of "the emancipatory vision that these people share with the Cuban Revolution, its forms of struggle, its acts of resistance; as its characteristic cultural *cimarronaje* at work from the time of the Haitian Revolution until Cuban Culture and History today."[26] Thus "while Cuban rappers build networks with U.S. rappers based on race and marginality that transcend national affiliations, they simultaneously generate a critique of global capitalism that allows them to collaborate with the Cuban state."[27]

Annelise Wunderlich believes that the increased salience of racial inequality in the Special Period is one of the reasons the Black Pride message in U.S. hip hop has reached such a receptive audience in Cuba. The Cuban rappers she studied "look up to Malcom X, Mumia Abu-Jamal, Nelson Mandela, and other black icons," and they sought out exiled Black Liberation Army member Nehanda Abiodun to teach them about black history. Meanwhile, "Cuban hip hop has become the darling of the American underground rap scene. Socially conscious rappers … have come to the island in search of what many consider the pure essence of hip hop."[28]

Sport

The revolutionary government made sport central to its domestic and foreign policy. Sport was integral to education and to equalizing opportunity in society. It was also a key element of Cuba's international projection. In some ways, the success of the socialist Revolution was pegged to the success of its athletes. Athletic achievements would illustrate the potentials unleashed and fostered by socialism. Athletes, write Paula Pettavino and Geralyn Pye in their study of sport in Cuba, serve as "revolutionary role models and as sources of national pride."[29]

The Cuban government initiated a national sports program in 1961, using the slogan "el deporte es salud" – sport is health. Physical education programs were implemented in all schools – beginning with preschool – under the auspices of the new Institute for Sports, Physical Education, and Recreation (INDER). Specialized sports schools were established at the secondary school level for children who showed particular talent, where, in addition to the normal curriculum, teens were offered special facilities and training. From there students could move on to attend higher education in Sports Training to prepare for international competitions. In the early grades, physical education focuses on movement and gymnastics; in the upper grades, team sports become central.

Community-based sport is another pillar of Cuban sport policy. Access to sports was democratized as the exclusive pre-revolutionary private sports clubs were opened to the public. Sporting events were also made free, and participation in sport was guaranteed as a right in the 1976 Constitution. Cubans of all ages are encouraged to participate in exercise through their family doctors (particularly the approximately 30 percent of the population that suffers from hypertension) and through elder programs.

Cuban athletes were soon bringing home significant numbers of Olympic medals, increasing from none in the 1950s to dozens in the 1992, 1996, 2000, 2004, and 2008 games. Cuban runner Alberto Juantorena, who won a historic Olympic double (400m and 800m) in 1976 and went on to become President of the Cuban Athletics Federation and Vice Minister of Sport, exemplified the nationalistic and revolutionary emphasis placed on sports competition in Cuba when asked how winning the medals changed his life: "My main point in this regard was to compete for my country and my people and to receive the support of the entire Cuban society, to carry my flag in whatever competition I was in, the Olympic Games, Pan-American Games. Then I received support from the Government to compete for my country, and to represent Cuba in competition."[30]

Sport suffered during the Special Period as cutbacks undermined athletic programs, and Cuban athletes faced the increasing lure of defection. Some 50 members of the 1993 Cuban delegation to the Central American and Caribbean Games in Puerto Rico chose to stay there. Baseball heroes Liván and Orlando "El Duque" Hernández were among two dozen or so players recruited by Cuban American agent Joe Cubas. "I'm an enemy of the Cuban government," Cubas bragged. When Cuban baseball teams travelled, Cubas would be there dangling lucrative offers.[31]

Many of the players recruited by Cubas were frank about their decision to leave. "The government doesn't want there to be any stars in Cuba. They want everyone to be equal. They want Linares, who is the best player in Cuba to be the same as any ordinary man that you don't know, even though he is a star in Cuba. They want him to have the same house, the same living conditions. They want everyone to have the same resources. But sometimes one needs things, things that the government doesn't give you. So you say, 'If I'm a great player here, why can't I also play in the Major Leagues.' Understand? You decide to leave the country to resolve your family's financial problems," said Angel López. "In Cuba we won three straight championships. And we didn't get things, presents, incentives. They would treat you to a beer, they'd pay for a night at the hotel with your family, but nothing more. One would ask for things that one needed and they would deceive you. Time passed and it was always the same, the same. And people started to get upset. And they were saying 'in the big leagues you get this, and this, and this.' And Arrojo was the first to defect. Upon seeing his success, we've all started to make our own decisions. That's the way life is," added Jorge Díaz.[32]

As in other areas, the Special Period began by causing hardship for almost everybody, but the economic changes introduced to ameliorate it inevitably moved the country away from its emphasis on equality. By the end of the 1990s, with defections and cutbacks threatening the Cuban teams' international reputation, the government began to offer significant material incentives to keep players on their teams. Players were offered personal items like equipment and toiletries, as well as cars, houses, and the right to earn money in hard currency.

Dance

Cubans, like all of the people of the Caribbean (and most of the rest of the world, but *especially* the Caribbean), were dancing well before the Revolution. But dance, like everything else, was socially divided. The upper classes scorned local, traditional, and popular dancing, preferring European forms. "A privileged class that appreciated good ballet ... brought the biggest stars of the day to Cuba," and their children could study the dance at the Escuela Pro Arte Musical in Havana.[33] Meanwhile African-based dance forms like the *rumba* flourished among the popular classes, but were disdained and persecuted by polite society.

The revolutionary government set about to democratize access to formerly "high" culture, and to elevate and promote Cuban cultural forms formerly viewed as "low." The Conjunto Folklórico Nacional (National Folkloric Group) was founded in 1962 to "contribute to the rescue and recovery of our dance and musical roots."[34] As ethnomusicologist Yvonne Daniel explains, "Cuba's revolution in 1959 served to distinguish and further separate differing African religious practices, as the new nation looked inward for its identity. During the early days of restructuring a new society, African religions were highlighted as proof of Cuba's Afro-Latin, rather than simply Hispanic, identity. While actual religious behavior was repressed within Cuba's early communist/atheistic ideology, cultural representations from its African religious history were promoted as such in educational and tourist settings."[35]

Reporter Ana Campoy interviewed Fernando Alonso, husband and professional partner of celebrated ballerina Alicia Alonso. Early in 1959, she recounts, the Revolution "knocked on the Alonsos' door ... In walked Fidel Castro and one of his collaborators. Sitting on the edge of the bed, they talked with Fernando about world and local politics for hours, until Fidel said, 'I came here to talk about ballet.' 'I always have time to talk about ballet,' Fernando recalls saying. 'How much money do you need for the ballet company to start up again?' Fidel asked. 'I don't know, *Comandante*, 100,000 dollars,' answered Fernando. Fidel, Fernando says, gave them 200,000. 'The revolution was a beautiful thing in the beginning,' Fernando says."[36]

The National Ballet Company performed revolutionary ballets, and they performed them everywhere: "on makeshift platforms set in factories, in schools, and in countryside cane fields." Today, "ballet followers more resemble a sports crowd than the aristocratic elite who first brought the dance for to Cuba," Campoy explains. "Fans yell and roar in the middle of a performance. Dancers have to stop in the middle of their routines to bow because the applause drowns the orchestra. Bouquets are thrown left and right to the favorite dancer of the moment, and when fans disagree, they come to blows."[37]

As in the case of sport, access to ballet training was universalized, and children with talent were recruited into special schools for advanced training. Also like sport, Cuban ballet soared into the international scene.

Political Culture

Cuban intellectuals have been involved in a lively debate, especially since the 1990s, about the nature and meaning of democracy. While calling for a deepening and expansion of democracy in their country, they are careful to distinguish their own from U.S. conceptions of formal democracy.

Two Cuban scholars explain that "the construction of democracy in Cuba is not an exercise in constitutional engineering ... but an all-encompassing project of social justice, development, national independence, and participatory opening."[38] Another Cuban academic explains: "elections are not synonymous with democracy but represent only one aspect of democracy. The West has tried for decades to reduce democracy to the exercise of voting every four years. To me, democracy is the daily input of the population on matters that affect their lives and not simply the casting of a ballot for a menu of candidates backed by powerful forces."[39] Improving democracy, argues another Cuban analyst, should "not be only, nor even principally, about multiparty systems, periodic supervised elections, or other common topics in the regional discourse about democracy, but rather about popular participation, social justice, equity, national development and other elements that are of greater importance for the construction of stable democratic regimes and the growth of societies where human rights are more fully respected."[40] Cuban scholars point to institutions like the elected Popular Power assemblies, participation in mass organizations, and institutional channels for discussion and debate of policies and laws as the forums for direct democracy in Cuba.[41]

Cubans also emphasize that U.S. aggression has served to limit democratic possibilities in their country. In particular, the reality of U.S. interference has contributed to government sanctions against independent political organizing: "A scenario of negotiation and lessening tensions between the United States and Cuba could allow the Cuban political system to overcome these restrictions. If the United States would renounce its internal political activities in Cuba, this would mean that Cuba could allow a loyal opposition to develop."[42]

Cuban analysts, however, are by no means uncritical of their country's political and economic institutions. There is an important current of opinion within Cuba that, while still rejecting U.S. conceptions of liberal democracy, coincides with liberal conceptions in some areas such as calling for a free and critical press, and greater tolerance of differing political positions. "Democratization must inevitably include the strengthening of the spaces for participation that allow the common citizen to influence decisions that affect their lives, to take part in debates regarding national directions, to have an effective control over their representatives, and have access to the necessary and relevant information. In sum: to move from being a mere consumer of policies to being an active producer of policy."[43] Cuban scholars clearly distinguish between criticism from the right, which rejects the socialist experience entirely, "basing their criticism on supposed universal values of the model of so-called representative democracy, based upon private property, a multi-party system, electoral trafficking [el comercio electoral], and individual freedoms," and those from the left, "which include internal criticisms that party activists, academics, political leaders and the Cuban population have about the Cuban political system" and call for a "more diversified, decentralized and depersonalized power structure" and whose goal is to "preserve revolutionary power and develop a participatory democracy."[44]

Thus there is an important voice among Cuban intellectuals that from a position of support for the Revolution calls for greater political space for debate, a more open and critical press, and greater political participation. Yet their position differs from that of U.S. critics of Cuba in several significant ways. First, they argue that if Cuba has not developed these aspects of democracy, it is precisely *because* of U.S. threats. "The unanimity present in the Cuban media is the reflection of a *siege mentality* conditioned by U.S. pressures, which work against greater pluralism and a broader public debate," argues a Cuban media critic.[45] "Some of the intolerance that you see in Cuba toward the dissenters against the system has to do with the perception that these dissenters are allied with a powerful foreign country," explains another Cuban intellectual. "We are dealing with an undeclared war that the United States is waging against us. So obviously you don't get the kind of tolerant environment you might find in Switzerland ... A relaxation of the way that dissenters against the system are perceived would require a relaxation in the international environment so that we could accommodate dissenting views against the system in a different way."[46]

Moreover, Cuban critics tend to draw a clear distinction between the issue of political openness, debate, and participation, and the idea of a multi-party system. While they see limitations on the former as the unfortunate result of historical and international factors, the absence of the latter is not seen with regret. "On many occasions multi-party systems are identified with pluralism. But that is not necessarily the case; sometimes multi-party systems are precisely the way to *deny* pluralism. In Cuba during the 1900s, we had plenty of political parties but no democracy. For us, the multi-party system consistently denied the possibility of an alternative road for the country," explains Juan Antonio Blanco.[47] Luis Suárez Salazar argues that "actually existing democracy" in Latin America and the Caribbean is a "democracy of 'apartheid.'" "The contribution of a popular democracy is to construct a representative system in a different manner than the liberal bourgeois democracies do. Our representative system does not have to be constructed on the basis of a multi-party system that has historically been a failure in Cuba." Nonetheless, Suárez is critical of the limitations on popular mobilization and participation in Cuba, and calls especially for a greater "ability of popular representatives at all levels to *make well-thought-out decisions* (and evaluate their results) regarding all of the issues which affect the citizenry."[48] Likewise, Haroldo Dilla argues that Cuba needs "a more pluralist approach to politics, in accordance with the sociological, cultural, ideological, etc. diversity of the country" – but with the recognition that "pluralism cannot be reduced to the organization of several political parties. In fact, 'actually existing' multi-party systems have shown a tenacious incapacity to reflect the diversity that exists in society, diversity which in large part has tended to be expressed outside of the formal party system."[49]

Hugo Azcuy explained the difference in the Cuban view of "pluralism" from that in the United States this way: "In Cuban political culture today, identity includes social values that go beyond national traits. It would be incomprehensible to conceive of Cuban society as a mosaic of separate compartments, of unconnected sectors that have nothing in common except the fact that they coexist side by side. Cuban identity comes from a strong sense of community, forged in almost four decades of sacrifice and dangers, particularly because of having to confront external enemies that are hostile to the revolution … In this context, pluralism does not mean moving towards fragmentation and rupture of Cuban society."[50]

Note that Azcuy does not reject the notion of pluralism in Cuban society. In fact, he argues that political developments in Cuba during the 1980s and into the 1990s went precisely in the direction of recognizing and accommodating pluralism.

The need for a more pluralistic expression of Cuban society has been accentuated in the recent years of the crisis, but its antecedents are in the second half of the 1980s, when people began to publicly question the copying of the Soviet institutional and ideological model that began in the 1970s. In 1990 there was an important public debate, which even had a mass character, about the need to introduce changes at the root of the institutional system. Among the most important steps in this process were the new space given to private, non-profit associations, and also to religious organizations.

In the space of a few years, since 1985, when the Law of Associations was passed, and since 1987, when the Civil Code was passed, more than 2,000 associations and civil organizations were created, including the majority of those which function today as non-governmental organizations. These include a wide spectrum of cultural, scientific, sports, and environmental groups, etc.

This pluralism represents a recognition that the diversity of Cuban society, which has always existed, cannot go on being expressed exclusively within the old mass organizations.[51]

Cuban intellectuals' analyses of politics in the United States and Cuba are important to understand in several respects. First, they present a nuanced view of the political system that U.S. analysts tend to promote as a universal ideal. It is clear that for many Cuban thinkers, multi-party democracy is only one form among many forms of democracy, and not necessarily the most attractive one. Second, reading Cuban authors' analyses of their own political system encourages U.S. audiences to acknowledge that Cuba's political system cannot be described simply and statically, as it generally is in U.S. political discourse, as a "dictatorship." Cuban citizens nominate candidates and vote in secret ballot elections; they participate in mass organizations; they participate in neighborhood, workplace, and municipal assemblies where real problems are discussed and debated, and decisions are made. What's more, the political system has evolved considerably over the course of the Revolution, and includes aspects that encourage and open spaces for political participation as well as aspects that discourage and close it off.

The discussions about democracy taking place in Cuba show that Cuban social scientists are not – as they are often portrayed abroad – merely regurgitators of an official, party-determined ideological line. Outsiders often assume that all domestic critics of Cuba's political system – especially those calling for greater democracy – are dissidents. But there exists a voice in Cuban intellectual life that seeks change from within, seeking to slowly open space for dialogue and debate by their own work.

Food

Food is a central, perhaps the most central, aspect of culture. At the very least, it is an aspect of culture that every member of a society partakes in, every day of their lives. And food is another aspect of culture that the Revolution vowed to transform.

What Cubans eat is, like other aspects of Cuban culture, a product of transculturation. The staples of the Cuban diet are rice, beans, meat, and *viandas*, a category which includes starchy root vegetables and plantains. The origins of the rice are African and Chinese; the beans, South American; the meat, primarily beef, pork, or chicken, is European; while the *viandas* are either native to the Americas, like *malanga* and *boniato*, or introduced from South Asia through Africa, in the case of the plantain. Cubans also drink prodigious amounts of coffee (native to Africa, but brought to the Caribbean by Europeans) and rum (a byproduct of sugar, also introduced to the island by the Spanish).

By the 1950s urban Cubans tended to enjoy a diet heavily influenced by U.S. processed and packaged foods, while the rural poor made do with small amounts of rice, beans and *viandas* or, when even those were unaffordable, sugar-water. Except for *viandas*, much of what Cubans ate was imported, since two-thirds of the island's farmland was not cultivated – much of it used for pasture – and of the land that was under cultivation, over half was devoted to sugar.[52]

The Revolution initially focused on the issue of distribution. The Agrarian Reform and the other social reforms and programs of the first years of the Revolution aimed, primarily, at redistributing the country's resources. As the country's poor majority increased its share of the wealth, it spent its money, first and foremost, on food. Demand rapidly outpaced supply. To prevent price increases that would just exclude the poor again, the government first imposed price controls, and soon, began rationing. In a situation of scarcity, it seemed to be the only way to ensure equitable distribution.

By 1980 locally produced and rationed goods were increasingly supplemented by processed foods from the eastern bloc, with a distinct Eastern European flavor: cheeses, hams and sausages, yogurt, wine, Soviet and Bulgarian canned goods and preserves. The parallel market functioned until the Rectification Campaign in 1986. "My oldest son was born in 1980, and grew up full of Eastern Europe," a colleague explained. "My younger son didn't – he was born in 1986!"[53]

Until the Special Period, the distribution system – along with other changes that increased food availability on and off the ration – contributed to a drastic shift in Cuba's health profile. Instead of the malnutrition that had plagued the poor prior to the Revolution, the most common diet-related diseases became obesity, hypertension, heart disease, and diabetes. An informant explained to one health researcher what Cubans like to eat: "Meat!! We like to eat pork. Beans and rice of course. But here we cook the beans and rice with lard and oil also. Everything has to be fried – chicken, plantains, malanga, and potatoes. We eat lots of food with flour – bread, spaghetti, pizza, crackers … We use lots of salt and sugar in our food. And we don't eat many vegetables or fruits. And then there is the alcohol and the sodas."[54]

Nutritionist Medea Benjamin and her colleagues noted that culture and politics interfered with any attempt to promote a less fatty and more plant-based diet. "Government leaders themselves are not totally convinced that the diet needs changing," they explain. "Many of the officials we interviewed [in the early 1980s] seemed to accept uncritically the 'modern' western diet as superior. Take the question of animal versus vegetable protein. We discussed this in our interview with Vice President Rodriguez, and while he recognized that animal protein may not be better nutritionally or economically, he saw it as associated with development. 'We don't support the idea that has been tossed around in international circles that developed countries are going to have animal protein while developing countries get vegetable protein,' he told us."[55]

6

Cuba Diversa

Like all modern former slave societies, Cuba has been deeply divided by race and gender. The Revolution made eliminating racial and gender inequality a centerpiece of its goals, yet its approach was very different from that pursued in the United States in the 1960s and beyond. In the United States, organizations from below pressed for legal and social changes to create equal opportunity. In Cuba, legal changes came from above, while independent organizations aimed at pushing for social change were frowned upon. Black nationalist organizations, most whites and many blacks agreed, had no place in Cuba. Neither did feminist organizations. Women would be mobilized in the state-sponsored mass organization, the Federation of Cuban Women, while blacks were simply Cubans, requiring no special organizations once racial equality was legislated.

Cuba achieved unparalleled success in equalizing access to education and health care. Women were massively incorporated into the workforce, and many aspects of women's traditional domestic tasks were socialized. But neither racial nor gender inequality disappeared. In the case of sexual orientation, the revolutionary leadership made no claim to pursue equality. Homosexuals were excluded, and at times openly persecuted, until the 1990s.

A History of the Cuban Revolution. Aviva Chomsky
© 2011 Aviva Chomsky

Race

By early 1959, the revolutionary leadership had clearly established that overcoming racial discrimination and racial inequality would be a fundamental goal. Afro-Cuban lawyer Juan René Betancourt urged the Revolution to avoid the "mistakes" of 1895, and argued that "there would not be a 'real revolution' in Cuba if the question of racial equality was either ignored or silenced." In a major March 1959 speech, Castro identified the "battle to end racial discrimination in the workplace" as one of the four major economic issues facing the Revolution.[1]

The revolutionary government moved quickly to outlaw racial discrimination. Four years after *Brown v. Board of Education* ruled segregated schools unlawful in the United States, and a year before the Congress of Racial Equality began its campaign to desegregate lunch counters in the southern United States, Cuba banned all public and private forms of racial exclusion.

Other early reforms that were not specifically focused on race also addressed the country's racial inequalities. Because Afro-Cubans were disproportionately poor, they benefited disproportionately from the economic reforms that redistributed the country's resources. Likewise, because Cubans of color were barely represented among the country's elites, few were threatened by the redistributions, and few participated in the exodus of the professional classes to Miami between 1959 and 1962. The white exodus created a Cuba that was progressively darker hued, and more racially equal.

Afro-Cuban scholar Pedro Serviat heralded the Revolution's structural approach to overcoming racial inequality in his 1986 book *El problema negro en Cuba y su solución definitiva – The Black Problem in Cuba and its Definitive Solution*. Even as the book appeared, though, the Third Congress of Cuba's Communist Party was acknowledging that in fact there had been no "definitive solution" as it called for measures to increase the presence of women and blacks in the Party's leadership.

As Serviat explained revolutionary policy in the first decades:

The main gain was to guarantee the right to work for all citizens under equal conditions. This was achieved with some concrete measures. The Revolution opened secretarial schools, with priority for former domestics, the majority black. Many of them later went on to work in banks as secretaries, clerks, etc. The opening of catering, management and foreign service schools enabled thousands of black and white citizens of humble origin to train in various fields... The beaches, sports and recreational centers were nationalized... The Revolution put culture at the service of the people; revindicated Cuban national culture; encouraged popular values in young people, irrespective of race or sex; helped to promote values previously discriminated against such as those of African origin practiced by slaves, blacks and free coloreds; promoted mass study of the popular arts; and, it goes without saying, set up a socialist education system, one for the whole island, for all citizens, male and female, blacks, whites, workers and peasants. In Cuba there is no longer any private education, which was a source of racial discrimination... Another measure taken was to permit the entry of black men and women into certain sports such as fencing, gymnastics, swimming, tennis, shooting, horse riding and rowing, previously prohibited to blacks... With the elimination of discrimination, housing in places once exclusive to the white aristocracy went to black and white families.[2]

The commitment to dismantling racial inequality may have prioritized legal and structural reforms, but it did not end there. Government policies and programs also attempted to challenge the negative attitudes towards black cultural forms that permeated Cuban society. The Institute of Ethnology and Folklore was founded in 1961 to study and promote Afro-Cuban art forms, and starting in 1962 the state sponsored Festivals of Popular Culture that likewise offered a venue for public performance.[3] To some, however, the folklorization of black culture under the Revolution smacked more of paternalism than of equality.

Cuban history, as well as revolutionary ideology, contributed to the belief that the primary route to racial equality lay in transforming the socioeconomic structures that sustained inequality, and eliminating racial discrimination in the country's laws and institutions. After all, as José Martí had proclaimed, "to be Cuban is more than being white, more than being black, more than being mulatto." The Partido

Independiente de Color had tried organizing on the basis of race back in the 1910s. The vicious response in 1912 contributed to silencing that approach for many decades. Cubans of all colors seemed publicly in agreement after 1959: there was no need to create specifically black organizations to advance black interests, and there was no need to delve into the cultural foundations of racism. There was certainly no place for the kind of black nationalism that developed in the United States in the 1960s. In fact, this route would challenge many Cubans' understanding of their history and the fundamentally colorblind nature of Cuban nationality. Furthermore, the continuing U.S. threat contributed to an environment in which calls to national unity often silenced challenges and dissent in the area of racial politics as well as others.

For many African Americans, the Cuban Revolution represented a challenge to white supremacy as embodied in a centuries-old colonial order. In a study of how the black press in the United States responded to the Revolution, Van Gosse concludes that black journalists were "responding to grassroots pro-Castro sentiments in urban black communities across the United States ... The desire to represent the Cubans' point of view, implicitly challenging the perspective of the white press, reflected an impulse toward Third World solidarity that in 1959, at the height of the decolonization drive in Africa and elsewhere, ran deep in black America. Cuba and Castro ... indicated the ways in which the nascent anti-imperialism of African-Americans would surface powerfully a few years later, during the era of 'Black Power,' the Black Panther Party, and the multiracial movement against the war in Vietnam."[4]

Black nationalists in the United States, though, had varying experiences in, and reactions to, revolutionary Cuba. To some, the Revolution's insistence on Cuba's inherent racial harmony was anything but benign. "Communism," wrote John Clytus after a visit to the island, "with its benevolent method of ending the racial problem by condensing all races into one-big-happy-human-race, would bring down the final curtain on black consciousness."[5]

When Black Panther activist Bill Brent hijacked a plane to Cuba to ask for political asylum after a shoot-out with the San Francisco police, he expected to be greeted as a revolutionary comrade-in-arms.

"I had been hoping to become part of the beauty of the Cuban Revolution," he wrote later.[6] Instead, Cuban authorities took him immediately to a jail cell. "I came here asking for asylum because I believe in revolution," he told his interrogators. "The police in my country had declared all-out war on the political group I belonged to. We were fighting against our government the same way you people fought against Batista's."[7] Brent later learned that, in the context of internal divisions in the Black Panther Party, Eldridge Cleaver had told Cuban authorities that Brent was a U.S. spy, which accounted for his lengthy incarceration upon arrival in Cuba. Nevertheless, it was also clear that his Cuban interrogators were not impressed with his revolutionary pronouncements. Once released from jail, he was sent to what he called a halfway house with other political exiles from the United States. While the conditions were privileged, in material terms, they were also isolated from the rest of Cuban society. "The government preferred not to include us in a regular work plan," he realized later. "We were foreigners and our ideas about revolution were vague, naive, and romantic."[8]

The account he heard of Eldridge Cleaver's time in Cuba was also illuminating. "Eldridge Cleaver had come to Cuba from Canada by boat. The Cubans took him in, gave him a house and a car, and let him shop in special stores. He had access to the best restaurants, bars, and nightclubs in Havana. His house was always filled with young Cubans who admired him as a high official of the Black Panther Party. He got away with a lot of things here for a while, but when he started organizing a Panther chapter in Havana, the shit hit the fan."[9]

Mark Sawyer surveys the various black nationalists from the United States who spent time in Cuba and their wide variety of reactions to the Revolution and its approach to racial issues. "Cuba played a central role in defining revolutionary and cultural nationalism in opposition to each other in the 1960s and 1970s," he concludes.[10]

Merely declaring an end to racial discrimination does not in itself bring about a transformation of deeply imbedded structural inequalities, as the experience of the United States has shown. Decades after school segregation and other forms of racial discrimination were outlawed in the United States, both de facto segregation and other forms of inequality continue to flourish. In 2007, 40 percent of African American children attended schools that are 90–100 percent black.[11] But Cuba's legislation of racial equality took place in the context of a massive socioeconomic transformation. How successful was it?

Cuban American historian Alejandro de la Fuente took a comprehensive look at the Revolution's successes – and failures – with respect to racial inequality. In a number of key socioeconomic areas, Cuba presents a dramatic contrast with the United States and Brazil, two other countries with large populations of African descent. In life expectancy, educational achievement, and professional opportunity, the gap between the races shrank or disappeared in Cuba, while remaining seemingly insurmountable in the United States and Brazil. These achievements correlate with the priority the Revolution placed on improving and equalizing access to health care and education – and its overall success in these areas.

In other areas, the Revolution was less successful both in improving people's lives overall, and in narrowing the racial disparities it had inherited. De la Fuente noted two in particular: housing and criminality. With respect to housing, he noted that the improvement in the island's housing stock had remained a trouble area for the Revolution over its many decades. Not only was the housing supply chronically inadequate, there was also little change in the geographical and residential racial demographics of the island. "The government's failure to meet housing demands allowed for the survival and reproduction of traditional residential patterns which combined race with poverty and marginalization," he wrote.[12]

While the residential disparities might be explained as an inheritance of pre-revolutionary patterns, the second racial gap that de la Fuente uncovered was both more complex and more troubling. Just like in the United States and Brazil, blacks in Cuba were incarcerated at significantly higher rates than whites. De la Fuente notes that for the particularly racialized criminal category of "social dangerousness" – a vaguely defined category – 78 percent of those arrested were people of color (blacks and mulattoes) in a 1987 study.

"Social dangerousness" charges included violations like drug and alcohol use and vagrancy. "Such a lax, broad definition of antisocial behavior created enough room for racialized notions of proper conduct to be enforced more freely than under the specific provisions of the penal code," de la Fuente concludes.[13]

Disproportionate arrest rates for blacks, especially for young black men, make revolutionary Cuba look much like the United States and Brazil and seem to undermine the Revolution's claims to have eliminated racial inequality. De la Fuente suggests two ways of explaining the apparent contradictions. One, structural changes that have reduced socioeconomic inequality do not necessarily or immediately bring about corresponding shifts in social attitudes. Deeply imbedded cultural beliefs about race may be more resistant to change than are infant mortality rates and economic and educational opportunity. Or they might require different kinds of methods for change.

Second, he notes that despite increased economic opportunity for blacks in many areas, the historical legacy of residential segregation was not overcome. Thus "the chance for young blacks to grow up in these poorer areas remained significantly greater than for whites. Likewise, the chances for young blacks to be socialized in what Cuban criminologists referred to as the criminal micro-environment were also significantly larger."[14]

The second conclusion is in some ways the more optimistic of the two. It suggests that government spending and activism can indeed bring about fundamental social change even in such apparently obstinate social areas like racial inequality. The former possibility, that racial attitudes are durable even in the face of structural change, offers a less hopeful vision for the possibilities of social change. History does not offer us many counter-examples.

Other authors – Carlos Moore and Mark Q. Sawyer, in particular – offer an even more pessimistic account. Cuban exile Carlos Moore complained of Fidel Castro's "icy silence on anything remotely touching the plight of Black Cuba."[15] Both authors argue that an attempt to privilege nationality and class, to disdain racial consciousness and to avoid directly confronting racism per se characterized the

Cuban Revolution and limited its ability to shake the country's racial divisions. Sawyer calls Cuba's racial ideology one of "inclusionary discrimination" that "encourages the ongoing marginalization of Afro-Cubans in Cuban social, economic and political life."[16] As in the early national period, state claims and a national ideology of racial inclusiveness allowed powerholders to marginalize and prohibit black organizations, movements, and claims for rights.

For Moore, official antipathy towards and repression of explicitly black political consciousness and organizing undermined any supposed attempts at creating racial equality. "It was out of the question for Blacks themselves to define the content of their own oppression, or define the terms of their ethnic emancipation," Moore writes. "The Castro leadership would resist and even repress attempts by black dissenters to force the issue into the open."[17]

De la Fuente and Sawyer give more credit to the state projects that "created significant opportunities in other areas of social, political and economic life for blacks."[18] They also agree, however, that despite these successes, a complex combination of factors led racial inequality to resurface in even more virulent form in the Special Period, as I will discuss in the next chapter.

Gender

The Revolution's push to overcome gender inequalities in some ways paralleled, and in other ways differed from, its approach to racial inequality. Structural reforms were key: creating economic opportunity for women, especially poor women, and socializing many of the domestic tasks that fell disproportionately on women. But the revolutionary leadership also saw sexist beliefs and ideologies as more of a problem than it did in the case of race. Women were encouraged to form their own organization, the Federation of Cuban Women, under the auspices of the Communist Party, and identify and challenge the problems that faced them specifically as women.

As in the case of race, the structural changes did significantly improve the situation of many Cuban women. In addition, ongoing, explicit campaigns targeted sexist attitudes and gender inequalities. The FMC, like other mass organizations such as the CDRs, really played a dual role as both a bottom-up and a top-down organization. On one hand, it was a vehicle for women to gather, organize, and articulate and press for their interests as women. On the other, it served as a means for the government to mobilize women in support of its goals. To the extent that the government's goals expressed the goals of women, the dual role worked. Some critics, though, argued that "The FMC's principal task ... was to defend a Revolution whose interests were defined by a male elite. The FMC and Cuban women in general participated very little in the making of policies that governed their lives and the lives of their children and families. When it came to power, the ideas, perspectives, and experiences of Cuban women simply did not count."[19]

"The FMC never embraced a feminist ideology," U.S. feminist Margaret Randall explains. "On the contrary, its upper echelons, like the revolutionary leadership overall, made it clear that decolonization was the priority and they considered feminism an imported bourgeois notion that would ultimately divide the working class ... Feminists from the developed countries were seen as dangerous, at the very least out of touch with Cuban reality and perhaps intentionally disruptive."[20]

Two key elements of the Revolution's gender policies were the incorporation of women into the workforce, and the 1975 Family Code that mandated equality between men and women. The Code gave men and women equal rights and responsibilities in the public sphere, but also in marriage and family matters. Perhaps most controversially, it stipulated that both partners in a marriage had both the responsibility and the right to contribute equally to supporting the family and that, in the case that only one partner engaged in paid employment, this did not relieve him or her from "the obligations of cooperating with the housework and child-care."[21]

In the 1950s, women constituted 13 percent of Cuba's working population. A quarter of these working women were domestic workers; most others were teachers, social workers, or nurses. By 1980, women comprised 30 percent of Cuban workers; by 1990, they were 40 percent.[22] None of these were domestic workers, the category having been outlawed. When anthropologist Helen Safa interviewed Cuban women workers in the early 1990s, she found that over 90 percent "feel that work has had a positive impact on them, that it has made them feel more independent, experienced, and capable."[23]

The health revolution, and its emphasis on maternal and child health, dramatically improved the lives of women. In the 1950s, only half of the births in Cuba took place in a hospital. With an infant mortality rate of 60 out of 1,000 and a maternal mortality rate of 120 out of 100,000, childbearing was a risky business. By the 1990s, over 99 percent of births were taking place in a hospital, and the infant mortality rate had been reduced to 10 per 1,000 – at a par with the far richer United States. Contraception and abortion became widely available.

As educational and work opportunities – and demands – increased for women, so did conflicts between their traditional domestic roles and their work lives. Women had long held the primary responsibility childcare, cooking, and maintaining the home. In the film *A Portrait of Teresa*, the protagonist's mother sighs when her daughter complains about her competing responsibilities. "Women will always be women, and men will always be men," the mother informs her daughter. "Even Fidel can't change that."

One revolutionary solution was to socialize some of women's traditional activities. Day care was dramatically expanded, and came to incorporate educational and health roles as well, at a low cost. Neighborhood centers were open from 7 am to 7 pm, and provided meals and medical check-ups. But the demand for day care greatly outpaced the government's ability to supply it. In the 1980s and 1990s, Cuba had over a million women workers – and only 100,000 day-care slots.[24]

Providing food for their families was also traditionally a woman's role. The rationing system and ongoing scarcities meant that obtaining food was often a laborious task, requiring hours of waiting in multiple lines. Cuban families, explain Benjamin and her colleagues, "buy their rationed goods in four places: the *bodega*, or grocery store, for the monthly 'food basket'; the *carnicería*, or butcher shop, for

meat and chicken; the *puesto*, or vegetable stand, for fruits and vegetables in season; and the *lechería*, or dairy store, for bottled milk.
Not only do they shop in four stores, but they often stand in line at
each one. This was a serious problem during the 1960s and early
1970s, and women often gave up their jobs so they could queue for
food."[25]

Workplaces and schools began to provide lunch, the main meal of
the day, in an effort to equalize access and diminish some of the
burden on women. The government also introduced "Plan Jaba" or
the Shopping Bag Plan in 1971. In families where all of the adults
worked, they would receive a special stamp in their ration book
allowing a family member to simply drop off their shopping bag on
the way to work, and pick it up, filled, at the end of the day – thus
avoiding the long line.

As in the case of race, the economic crisis of the 1990s recreated
some of the pre-revolutionary inequalities that the revolution had
worked so hard to overcome (see Chapter 7).

Sexuality

The Revolution made an early and explicit commitment to eliminating race and gender inequality. There was no such commitment in
the area of sexual orientation. On the contrary. In the first decade of
the Revolution the (heterosexual) nuclear family was clearly defined
as the essential unit of society, and non-heterosexual activity and
relationships explicitly proscribed.

As numerous studies of sexuality and sexual orientation in Latin
America have shown, the dichotomy currently common in the United
States and Europe between "heterosexual" and "homosexual" is a
cultural construction. In other cultural and historical contexts, different categories and distinctions prevail. While same-sex sexual
activity has existed in all times and places, the idea that individuals
possess a "sexual orientation" towards members of the same, or the
opposite, sex, is culturally and historically specific. In Europe and
the United States, it dates to the late nineteenth century. Prior to this

time, while the existence of same-sex sexual activity was widely recognized, it was not seen as constituting an identity or a sexual orientation. Identifying sexual orientation as such, in fact, was part of pathologizing it.[26]

In Cuba prior to the Revolution, Ian Lumsden explains in *Machos, Maricones and Gays: Cuba and Homosexuality*, the categories "macho" and "maricón" distinguished men based on their identification with traditional, stereotypically male or "macho" forms of public behavior (and implied sexual practices), rather than on their choice of sexual partners. A man could be "macho" and have sexual relations with other men, as long as he maintained the dominant or active role in the partnership. "Maricón" is a generally derogatory term for a man "whose comportment appeared effeminate and deviated from stereotypical masculinity."[27] Levels of stigma and prejudice against those identified as *maricones* was perhaps comparable to the stigma against homosexuals in the United States, but this prejudice could not accurately be described as "homophobia" since the very category "homosexual" – meaning a person with a sexual orientation towards those of the same sex – was not a meaningful category in the Cuban context.

Roger Lancaster describes a comparable system of beliefs and ideas in Nicaragua, where the term "cochón" parallels the use of "maricón" in Cuba. "The term marks and delimits a set of sexual practices that partially overlaps but is clearly not identical to our notion of the homosexual. The term specifies only certain practices in certain contexts. Some acts that we would describe as homosexual bear neither stigma nor an accompanying identity of any special sort whatsoever."[28]

These traditional ideas and categories grew out of Cuba's Spanish and African (and probably also indigenous, though the evidence in this regard is more murky) heritage. In the nineteenth and twentieth centuries, they were also influenced by the increasing presence of people and institutions from the United States. Imperialism, many authors have argued, is inherently gendered and sexualized. Edward Said offered the insight that Orientalism – the study of what Europeans defined as "the Orient" in the eighteenth and nineteenth centuries – was part and parcel of European imperial endeavors. The Orient was depicted as fundamentally Other, passive, and feminized, await-ing European penetration. Later authors have built on these ideas and extended them to other parts of the world. In the case of Cuba, manly notions of conquest defined the relationship between the United States and Cuba from the start. Moreover during the mid-twentieth century, Cuba's place as a site for tourism, pleasure, and sin was highly sexualized. It was no wonder, as Ian Lekus has argued, that "the revolutionary government made eradicating this [sexualized] colonial economy a priority ... Given the especially sexualized nature of Cuba's past relationship with the United States ... sexual reform became all the more important to symbolizing the revolution's rejec-tion of Yanqui domination."[29]

This sexual reform did not incorporate ideas about gay rights, however. The gay rights movement of the 1960s and 70s was chal-lenging norms of prejudice and exclusion in the United States, and in fact offering new ways of defining gay identity, just as the close connection between Cuba and the United States was broken. Meanwhile, new elements shaped by Communist ideology and by Soviet sexology as well as Cuba's own form of revolutionary machismo contributed to both official and unofficial repression against sexual non-conformity during the first decades of the Cuban Revolution.

Repression of homosexuality reached its highest point during the first decade of the Revolution. The battlefield mentality of the Revolution was exacerbated by the unremitting threats from the United States, and the overwhelming challenge of recreating the economy. In 1963, the government instituted a military draft for men aged between 16 and 45. The draft also became a means of separating out those who the authorities considered potentially subversive or oth-erwise unfit for military service. By 1965, those thus identified were being sent to newly established "Military Units to Aid Production" or UMAPs – something between a concentration camp, a prison labor facility, and a rehabilitation program.

Men who were openly homosexual fit squarely into that category. "Nothing prevents a homosexual from professing revolutionary ide-ology and, consequently, exhibiting a correct political position," Fidel Castro told Lee Lockwood in 1965. "And yet," he went on, "we would never come to believe that a homosexual could embody the conditions and requirements of conduct that would enable us to consider him a true Revolutionary, a true Communist militant. A deviation of that nature clashes with the concept we have of what a militant Communist must be."[30]

Rehabilitation programs were not new to the Cuban Revolution. Even the Literacy Campaign was, in its conception, a kind of rehabilitation. Starting in 1960, the Ana Betancourt Schools for Peasant Women – directed by psychiatrist Elsa Gutiérrez – brought close to 100,000 women from rural areas to Havana for a year of training in a trade, as well as political education, cultural activities, and health care. When they returned home, their families "found the young women transformed – healthy, their teeth fixed, their dysentery cured. Back in their small towns the *Anitas* helped to establish local sewing and dressmaking programs. Some founded FMC delegations. Vilma Espín later observed that the *Anitas* became 'the first political leaders in the countryside.'"[31] Domestic workers too were offered schooling and opportunities to move out of domestic service, which was seen as a linchpin of Cuba's entrenched social inequality that the Revolution was aimed at overturning. When prostitution was outlawed in 1961, prostitutes too were offered rehabilitation and schooling, and the chance to participate productively in the new society.

The UMAPs were created in 1965 to "rehabilitate" men who were considered unfit for military service. "Between 1965 and 1967 the UMAP became a catch-all for delinquents who had been denounced by their neighbors or the CDRs. These military units took in any person who failed to conduct himself in accordance with the official definition of proper behavior. The UMAP housed persons rounded up as vagrants, counterrevolutionaries, and so-called deviants: homosexuals, juvenile delinquents, and religious followers, including Catholics, Baptists, and Jehovah's Witnesses."[32]

Both nationally and internationally, people – including many supporters of the Revolution – protested the UMAPs, and they were terminated between 1967 and 1969. Many of the protests were based not on a positive view of gay rights, but rather against the cruelty and brutality of the camps.

The idea that homosexuality was a psychiatric disorder, and could be caused by contact with adult homosexuals (and conversely, "cured" by exposure to appropriately masculine adult men), continued to characterize Cuba's policies through the 1970s. (This idea was not unique to Cuba, of course. In the United States, the debate about homosexual teachers in the classroom is far from closed.)

It was not until the 1980s that U.S.-style ideas about gay identity and gay liberation began to take root in Cuba. Concurrently, both Western and Soviet scientific thought retreated from the criminalization and stigmatization of homosexuality. Going along with international trends, homosexual acts were decriminalized in Cuba in 1979, although statutes prohibiting "public flaunting" of homosexuality remained on the books. Gay identity continues to evolve in Cuba today and, especially in urban areas, is far more engaged with U.S. and European gay movements than in the past.

Tomás Gutiérrez Alea's 1994 film *Strawberry and Chocolate* could be seen as emblematic of the political and social openings of the Special Period. Set in 1979 – well after the closing of the UMAP, but just at the end of the *quinquenio gris*, the five-year period during the 1970s during which the space for political and intellectual debate was probably at its nadir – the film traces an unlikely friendship between Diego, a supporter of the Revolution who refuses to conform to any of its orthodoxies, and David, a Young Communist League member. Diego diverges from a revolutionary hard line in almost every area: he's a religious believer, a free-thinking artist and bibliophile, openly homosexual, and declines to mobilize for voluntary work and other revolutionary activities. David is outraged, intrigued, and suspicious when Diego tries to pick him up in the popular Coppelia ice cream parlor in downtown Havana – and offers him a book by then-banned Peruvian author Mario Vargas Llosa. Over time, David's mind is expanded beyond the naive revolutionary jargon he espoused at the start of the film, while he struggles to convince Diego that the Revolution is more than its mistakes, and that it's up to them, as true revolutionaries, to push for greater openness. Clearly a critique of the narrowness of permissible thought and behavior during this period, the film attracted enormous audiences and discussion when it opened in Cuba in 1994.

Some foreign analysts critiqued the film as disingenuous. The 1979 setting, they argued, allowed the film to both avoid addressing the period of greatest repression against homosexuality in the 1960s, while also implying that repression and discrimination were things of the past. Others, however, saw the film as an enormous contribution to bringing into the open a critique of revolutionary dogma, with regard to sexuality but also to literature, the arts, and the freedom of thought and action that Diego's character represents. The closed-minded nature of the Cuban bureaucracy, the film makes clear, forced Diego into exile. "We need more Communists like you," Diego tells David wryly.

Almost all of the sources cited above, like most studies of homosexuality in Cuba, focus on males. Lesbianism remains understudied and often close to invisible. A very few documentaries, novels, and academic studies have begun to address lesbian history and life in Cuba, including Sonja de Vries's documentary film *Gay Cuba* (1995) and émigré novelist Zoé Valdés's *Dear First Love*.[33]

There are perhaps some parallels in the way Cuban authorities, and many ordinary Cubans, responded to U.S. activists in the gay and lesbian movement, and to those in the Black Power movement. Cuban revolutionaries were resentful of North Americans imposing their own values and analysis on the Cuban reality, and, in particular, suspicious that critiques of the Revolution were fostered by, or at the very least played into the hands of, the imperial project of destroying the Revolution. Their vision of national liberation did not encompass U.S.-style identity politics. At the same time, the ideals of the Revolution and the concept of national unity excluded or ignored some Cuban realities and diversity as well.

Religion

Religious diversity has also characterized Cuba's history. The Catholic Church has deep roots in Cuba's colonial history, yet has always played an ambivalent role. Catholicism itself is broad enough to encompass a huge diversity of political and social positions over five centuries in the Americas. Some Catholic theologians defended

Spanish racial superiority and colonial rule, while others challenged it. Catholic missionaries defended, and participated in, the enslavement of Africans and indigenous people, while others fought against the slave systems. In the twentieth century, Latin American bishops elaborated a Theology of Liberation that challenged the Church to take a "preferential option for the poor" and to struggle with the poor for their liberation – including in Marxist-oriented revolutionary movements. Priests like Camilo Torres in Colombia died in battle after taking up arms in late twentieth-century revolutions; others, like Monsignor Oscar Romero in El Salvador, were murdered by right-wing death squads. Romero was killed after calling upon soldiers to refuse to follow orders that contradicted their consciences.

Catholicism was not the only religious tradition in Cuba. Pre-existing indigenous religions left their mark on the ways that spiritual beliefs and religious life evolved in Cuba. Even in the late twentieth century, anthropologist José Barreiro found Taíno religious beliefs surrounding medicine, burials, dances, agricultural cycles, and other customs to be alive and well in some areas in eastern Cuba.[34]

The different African peoples forcibly transported to Cuba from the sixteenth to the nineteenth centuries brought their own religious traditions. These were then transformed and recreated in Cuba, especially during the nineteenth century when the slave trade reached its zenith. Santería, Palo Monte, and Abakuá are three religious traditions that grew in Cuba among Africans from the Yoruba (southwestern Nigeria), Congo, and Igbo/Calabar (southeastern Nigeria) regions from which large numbers of slaves were brought to Cuba.[35] These religions thrived and evolved, frequently in secrecy, under conditions of slavery. Santería especially adopted Catholic saints into its cosmology, and in turn permeated popular Catholicism.

Cuba's religious diversity was further enhanced by some 100,000 Chinese who were brought as indentured sugar plantation workers in the mid-nineteenth century, Christian and Muslim Arab immigrants in the late nineteenth and early twentieth centuries, and a wave of Jewish immigrants from Europe around the same time. After the U.S. occupation in 1898 Protestant missionaries also flocked to the island, establishing churches, schools, and seminaries.[36]

Fidel Castro was educated by Jesuits; revolutionary leader Frank País was the son of a Baptist pastor and himself a teacher in a Baptist school. But early revolutionary policies reflected a suspicion of organized religion, for several reasons. Most of Cuba's Catholic priests were foreign – Spanish – and conservative. Their churches and their schools served Cuba's elites. When the government abolished private schools in its push to create equal access for all, Catholic and Protestant schools were among those closed.[37] Many Spanish priests were deported, accused of supporting the counter-revolution. After Castro declared himself to be a Marxist and the Revolution a Communist revolution, religious practice was officially frowned upon. The 1976 Constitution declared Cuba an atheist state and the Communist Party banned religious believers from membership. At the same time, though, it guaranteed "freedom of conscience and the right of everyone to profess any religious belief."[38]

Afro-Cuban religions, which had less institutionalized presence, were less affected by governmental restrictions. They were associated historically with the oppressed and their struggle against colonial oppression, and corresponded more easily – though not perfectly – with the ideologies and policies of the revolutionary government.[39]

Protestantism in Cuba was historically linked with U.S. involvement there. Most of the Church leadership was from the United States, and services were often held in English. Still, it too had a mixed heritage. U.S. Protestantism's links to abolitionism in the nineteenth century and the Civil Rights movement in the twentieth meant that it incorporated spaces for revolutionary thought. Black Protestantism in both the United States and the English-speaking Caribbean was infused with African cultural forms and tied to black liberation in ways that had important resonances in Cuba. West Indian migrant workers in Cuba brought their own strains of often African-inflected Protestantism.

Most U.S. and Cuban Protestant pastors left for Miami in the early 1960s. Some Cuban Protestants, however, especially among the Eastern Baptists, saw no conflict between their religion and the Revolution. Reverend Raúl Suárez, a young Baptist minister in eastern Cuba, joined in the defense effort during the exile invasion at the Bay of Pigs in 1961. He went on to take a position as the Vice Rector of the Baptist Seminary in Havana, where he had himself studied, and, in 1971, as Pastor of the Ebenezer Baptist Church – named after the Reverend Martin Luther King, Jr.'s congregation in Atlanta – in the heavily Afro-Cuban Havana neighborhood of Marianao. In the 1980s he became Executive Secretary of the Cuban Ecumenical Council.[40]

In 1984 the Cuban Council of Churches (CCC) invited a delegation of African American religious leaders, including the Reverend Jesse Jackson, to Cuba. Jackson and others met with Fidel Castro – successfully negotiating the release of several dozen political prisoners. In 1987 the CCC, under the leadership of Raúl Suárez, founded the Centro Memorial Martin Luther King, Jr. in Havana.[41]

Cuba's Catholic Church was somewhat isolated from the winds of Liberation Theology that emanated from Rome, and later from meetings of Latin American bishops in Puebla, Mexico and Medellín, Colombia in the late 1960s and early 1970s. But by the 1980s these winds were reaching Cuba, primarily through the Central American revolutions in Nicaragua and El Salvador. In 1986 Brazilian Liberation Theologian Frei Betto published a long interview with Castro, *Fidel and Religion*, in which Castro emphasized the correspondence between Marxist and Christian thought. As in other areas, the Special Period brought some significant openings towards religion, which will be discussed in the next chapters.

7

The "Special Period": Socialism on One Island

Some things changed drastically with the fall of the Soviet bloc, which eliminated the trade and aid relationships that had sustained Cuba's economy for three decades. To survive in the new international context the Cuban government implemented dramatic economic reforms including opening to foreign investment, allowing some forms of private enterprise, facilitating remittances, and promoting tourism. It nevertheless maintained a commitment to preserving some of the key gains of the Revolution, especially the health and education systems. The generation that came of age during the Special Period tended to be less impressed with the Revolution's achievements, and more cynical about its contradictions. Social inequalities increased, and phenomena associated with pre-revolutionary poverty like prostitution and begging reappeared. While the United States, and especially the older generation of Cubans in the United States, remained obsessed with Fidel Castro, his serious illness in 2006 did not lead to the overthrow of the Revolution, but rather to an orderly transfer of authority to his brother Raúl.

A History of the Cuban Revolution. Aviva Chomsky
© 2011 Aviva Chomsky

1993–95: Rapid-Fire Reforms

When I arrived in Cuba for the first time in January 1995, economic contradictions abounded. Brand new farmers markets offered abundant fresh produce – but most Cubans couldn't afford it. It was illegal to rent an apartment to foreigners – but everybody did it. Cubans carried ration cards that entitled them to food and other necessities at heavily subsidized prices – but what the card guaranteed often wasn't available. Dollar stores offered luxury items – and products that most people considered necessities, like cooking oil and toilet paper – to foreigners and to the few fortunate Cubans who had access to dollars (Figure 7.1). Until just over a year before, Cubans could have been arrested for possessing dollars. Was capitalism coming to Cuba in the wake of the loss of Soviet trade and aid?

The dollar stores looked a little bit like supermarkets in the First World – but only a little bit. Some shelves were empty. Some shelves

Figure 7.1   A dollar store in Havana, 2008
Source: Photo by Aviva Chomsky

held long rows of a single brand of a single item. There was no competition or advertising. All of the stores were owned by the state. Large signs promoted their purpose: "Captación de divisas" – the capture or collection of [foreign] currency. The stores were part of a larger project to bring hard currency into the country, and into the socialist system.

These government-run stores symbolized the contradictions of Cuba's tentative, partial opening to capitalism in the 1990s. The stores sold luxury items and even basics that were not available in the peso economy. The profits from the stores were to be used to fund state services for the benefit of all, but the system put the government in the paradoxical position of fostering inequality to subsidize equality.

The same thing happened with sectors like tourism, foreign investment, and private businesses. By allowing these activities, regulating them, and taking some of the profits in the form of markups, fees and taxes, the government hoped to be able to sustain its strong social safety network.[1] But all of these initiatives brought with them materialism, consumption, and inequality.

Dollarization meant that Cubans abroad could now send money to their relatives on the island, and Cuba could join the ranks of poor countries that rely heavily on remittances. On a global scale, the $20 billion annually transferred from wealthy to poor countries via remittances (as of 2000) is larger than what's transferred in foreign aid or investment, and for many poor countries, remittances are their largest source of foreign currency.[2]

Legalizing the dollar in the summer of 1993 was only the first in a series of economic reforms or openings that brought capital – and capitalism – into the country. In many ways Cuba's economic reforms of the 1990s resembled the Structural Adjustment Programs or SAPs implemented by other Third World countries under World Bank and International Monetary Fund auspices as a condition for new loans. Government spending and services were cut, and some state industries were opened to the private sector. In some ways, the reforms were even harsher in Cuba, because they were carried out without the international loans to cushion their effects. Cuban sociologist Haroldo Dilla noted wryly that "Cubans are beginning to experience

Figure 7.2   A farmers market in Havana, 2000
Source: Photo by Jackie McCabe

the displeasures and pleasures of now being actually, and not only symbolically, Latin Americans."[3]

State farms were converted into cooperatives (UBPCs) in September 1993. By the end of 1996, the percentage of farms under state control had dropped from 82 percent to 24.4 percent.[4] Economic decision making was decentralized. Farmers markets, where producers could sell directly to the public, were reinstituted in October 1994 (see Figure 7.2). (The first experiment with farmers markets was from 1980–85, but they were closed during the Rectification period.)

Subsequent reforms opened Cuba to foreign investment and joint ventures, allowed Cubans to work for foreign entities, promoted tourism, and legalized certain forms of self-employment. Foreign and joint ventures were especially sought in the mining (nickel), energy (oil and gas) and tourism sectors, while free trade zones were established to attract foreign manufacturers. Artisans markets where producers could sell directly to the public were opened. The "dash of capitalism" that Benjamin *et al.* had identified in the early 1980s was becoming a torrent. In 2000, 22 percent of Cuba's workers were employed in the non-state sector – either through self-employment, or working for foreign enterprises.[5] Self-employment reached a high of 156,600 workers in 1999, until new policies started to rein in some of these opportunities.[6]

As part of the campaign for foreign exchange, the Cuban government started to encourage emigrants to visit. It relaxed visa restrictions for Cuban Americans, and allowed them, for the first time, to stay with relatives rather than in hotels. The number of return visits skyrocketed, from only 7000 in 1990 to over 80,000 a year between 1994 and 2001.[7]

The government offered a basic rationale for all of the rapid-fire economic changes between 1993 and 1995 and the apparent contradictions they brought with them. Faced with the loss of its Soviet-bloc trade and aid, the Cuban economy had gone into a tailspin after 1989. For decades Cuba had been sustained and cushioned by aid, trade, and in particular, the "fair trade" that the Soviets carried out with Cuba. Rather than paying "market" prices for Cuba's sugar – which had decreased precipitously as beet sugar and corn syrup provided lower-cost alternatives – the USSR paid prices that actually reflected what it cost to produce Cuban sugar. And Cuba's economy was utterly dependent on imports – especially fuel – that it bought using these earnings. Now the system had collapsed. The new policies, while painful and contradictory, were the only way to compensate for the loss in Soviet economic support and both revive the economy and maintain the social services that had become the trademark of the Revolution.

Social Impact of the Market Reforms

The reforms succeeded in bringing economic growth, but they also brought inequality. Government control of the economy had allowed for an extraordinarily egalitarian distribution of the country's wealth. Prior to 1989 Cuba's salary spread had ranged from about 80–90 pesos a month for the lowest paid worker, to about 450–500 pesos a month for a high government official – that is, a ratio of about 5 to 1. Now, the gap between those who had access to dollars and the private economy, and those who continued to subsist on their state salaries, grew astronomically. One economist estimated that the ratio was 829 to 1 in 1995, and 12,500 to 1 in 2001.[8]

Cuban jokes reflected the economic distortions. A woman brought her husband, a renowned brain surgeon, into the psychiatric ward. "He's hallucinating! He thinks that he got a job as a taxi driver and we've become rich!" By 2000, about half of Cuba's population had access to dollars, either through remittances, through their employment, or through self-employment.[9]

Global economic inequalities have led to a generalized phenomenon of "brain drain," in which highly skilled and educated workers leave the Third World for the First, where they can enjoy greater opportunities and attractive lifestyles. In Cuba, the Special Period led to what one analyst called a "domestic brain drain."[10] Highly trained workers left skilled positions in the state sector for unskilled work that paid more. Education itself became less important. The government could no longer guarantee employment, even to young people who graduated with fine credentials. Before the 1990s, almost everybody who graduated received a job placement with their diploma. In 2001, only 72 percent did.[11]

Another disincentive was that professional jobs were no longer a guarantee of material security. Like the brain surgeon in the joke, many educated Cubans abandoned or supplemented their professions and went to work for dollars. Government restrictions tried to limit the drain by prohibiting certain groups of professionals – like doctors – from working in the private economy. But this policy, in turn, discouraged many ambitious young people from seeking education. Higher education was supposed to lead to greater opportunity – now it looked like more education was going to limit a young person's opportunity. Opportunities for higher education also shrank, as university slots were reduced to accommodate the lack of available jobs for college graduates. In 1980, 17 percent of the school-age population had gone on to pursue higher education, while in 1990, the figure was 21 percent. In 1997, only 12 percent did. "One of Latin America's most educated populations became 'deschooled' as well as 'deskilled'," Susan Eckstein concluded. Several thousand school-age children (ages 5–11) "worked" in the old section of Havana, either begging or offering minor goods and services to tourists.[12]

The money that Miami Cubans sent to their relatives on the island created other contradictions. Overall, Miami Cubans came from the wealthier, and whiter, sectors of pre-revolutionary Cuban society. Although the Miami Cuban community had diversified since the Mariel boat lift in 1980, the earlier, whiter arrivals were still economically better off. They also tended to be more politically anti-revolutionary. Their relatives in Cuba, who had long tried to downplay any connection to the former elites and the Miami exile community, suddenly found that these old relationships were an advantage instead of a disadvantage.

Cubans in the 1990s talked about what they called the "triple blockade." First was the U.S. economic embargo, which had been in place since the early 1960s and was strengthened during the economic crisis of the 1990s with the Torricelli bill in 1992 and the Helms–Burton Act in 1996. Second was the disappearance of the Soviet bloc. Finally, the third blockade was the internal blockade: the bureaucracies, rules, and lack of imagination that made economic change a lumbering and difficult process.

Limits to Capitalism

Not all of the changes in the Special Period went in the direction of capitalism. As Susan Eckstein usefully pointed out, some Special Period reforms were aimed at maintaining and even strengthening the socialist sector. In most of Latin America, the debt crisis of the 1980s led to "structural adjustment" programs that included privatizations, cutbacks in government spending, and incentives to foreign investors. Cuba was already way ahead of the rest of Latin America in social spending: in 1990, Cuba spent 20 percent of its GDP on social services, including health care, social security, and education

– twice the 10 percent that other Latin American countries spent.[13] But as Cuban economist Pedro Monreal explained in 2002:

> [Cuban] government policies to deal with the crisis were markedly different from the pattern of economic adjustment that other countries have adopted. Essential social services such as education and health care were provided universally and at no cost even in the worst moments of the crisis. Subsidized food – although in relatively reduced amounts – guaranteed a minimum level of nutrition, while other important social programs were designed to support particular social groups. Adherence to norms of fairness and social justice was the hallmark of Cuban adjustment policies during the 1990s.[14]

Julie Feinsilver notes that during the economic crisis "Cuba continuously increased its spending on domestic health as a percentage of total government spending in order to shield the most vulnerable population from the worst effects of the crisis."[15] Not only did health spending increase; so did spending on social security and education. Even during the worst years of the crisis, these areas grew both in absolute terms and as proportion of GDP. In 1998, 32 percent of the GDP was spent on social services – still the highest in Latin America.[16] While the lack of hard currency meant that these peso expenditures couldn't resolve shortages of medicines, materials, and infrastructure, Miren Uriarte emphasized that the government's continuing commitment to its social welfare role distinguished Cuba's path from other experiments with structural adjustment. She noted three areas in particular: "commitment to equity in access by maintaining all services free of charge … commitment to universal access," and that "the government's role as the main actor in this sphere remained unchanged."[17] (See Figure 7.3.)

Monreal, Uriarte and Feinsilver view the cautious nature and pace of reforms in a positive light. To other analysts, Cuba's failure to implement a "shock treatment" approach to economic reform meant that Castro was trying to sustain a "power reserve" for hardliners. "Behind the pretense of market reforms, the Cuban government ended up magnifying the power of the state to decide who can benefit

Figure 7.3   A *bodega* in Havana, 2009
Source: Photo by Arnold Weissberg

from market activities and by how much," wrote political scientist Javier Corrales.[18]

While foreign investors have been invited into Cuba, the state maintains certain controls that go well beyond what companies face in other countries. For example, the state oversees the hiring of employees. Foreign companies pay their workers' wages in dollars directly to the government, which then transfers the money to the workers in pesos. The government argues that this system enables it to use the valuable foreign currency to sustain its social programs, rather than having it all go into the pockets of the few workers lucky enough to get those jobs. As Corrales points out, however, the system violates International Labor Organization regulations that prohibit the confiscation of wages.[19]

Even though salaries came through the government, in pesos, employment in the foreign sector brought benefits for workers. Employers often supplemented wages with perks like food items and sundries difficult to obtain in the peso economy, as well as with more expensive gifts and dollars.[20] In some key sectors like mining and construction, employers could make supplemental payments legally in dollars or convertible pesos. Many foreign employers in other sectors unofficially paid workers part of their salary in dollars.[21] Foreign sector employment also, unlike self-employment, included state benefits like unemployment insurance and pension.

Starting in 1994, the government began to pay hard currency bonuses to state workers in key industries including tourism, mining, electricity, ports, and tobacco. About a quarter of Cuba's workers were receiving these cash bonuses in 2000, and even more were receiving in-kind benefits.[22] Foreign enterprises offered the same kinds of perks, in even larger sums.[23]

While most Cuban analysts, as well as U.S. scholars like Eckstein and Feinsilver, emphasize the continuing commitment to socialism despite Cuba's reforms, Corrales draws the opposite conclusion. "It is not socialist ... because the state is now the guarantor, in fact, the generator, of enormous inequalities: the state determines who has access to the thriving state-external sector; everyone else is either a loser or a mere survivor. The state is thus directly responsible for the rise of inequality in Cuba." The current system does not distribute society's good equally or fairly; rather it serves to benefit "a small winning coalition."[24]

Charting New Territory

Another set of reforms harked away from Soviet-style centralism and industrialization – Eckstein called them "precapitalist," although some of them might just as usefully be termed "post-capitalist/post-socialist" or "post-industrial." Government strategists tried to make the best out of fuel scarcities, promoting green agriculture and bicycle use. They also tried to find different ways forward, taking advantage of Cuba's greatest strength, its highly educated population. The government promoted biotechnology, health tourism, educational tourism, and the export of doctors.

Although Cuba's system of land tenure was changed in the 1990s, the agrarian reforms of the 1960s were not exactly reversed. In terms of peasant access to land, the 1993 reform actually put more land into the hands of small farmers, by dismantling the state farms and turning them into cooperatives or small plots. The Cuban state also continued to provide easy access to credit and to technical assistance – benefits that structural adjustment programs generally restricted.

Other inputs became a lot harder to come by, especially those that Cuba had to import with hard currency like pesticides, fertilizers, fuel, and farm equipment.[25] Cuban scientists and agricultural economists argued that this was Cuba's chance to become a world leader in green agriculture, and many outside experts agreed.[26] Cuban farmers, though, were not always happy to be asked to experiment with organic and low-technology solutions. Nevertheless, Laura Enríquez found that more people were moving into agriculture – "repeasantization," she called it – and that these old and new peasants actually fared somewhat better than the urban population during the economic crisis.[27]

A renewed emphasis on the environment went beyond agriculture. The relationship of environmental consciousness and environmental protection to economic growth and development is not an obvious one. Most environmentalists argue that both capitalist and socialist models of industrialization and economic progress have been based on plundering the natural environment. Much environmental destruction in the Third World has been the result of colonial and neo-colonial plantation agriculture and extractive economies. But socialist Cuba's agricultural and industrial systems exhibited much of the same environmental recklessness as those in the capitalist world.[28]

Yet many, in the Third World and the First, argue that environmental consciousness is a luxury, and that economic development necessary for the survival of the world's poor must come first. "It is particularly rare for governments anywhere to propose, adopt, or enforce stricter environmental requirements during times of economic crisis," Daniel Whittle and Orlando Rey Santos point out.[29]

Nevertheless, Cuba's 1992 Constitutional amendments incorporated new environmental concerns. Chapter 1, Article 27, regarding "the state, the environment, and natural resources" recognizes "the close links they have with sustainable economic and social development to make human life more rational and to ensure the survival, well-being and security of present and future generations" and mandates that "it is the duty of citizens to contribute to the protection of the waters, atmosphere, the conservation of the soil, flora, fauna and nature's entire rich potential." The new Constitution was followed by a formal adoption of the 1992 Rio Summit principles on the environment, the establishment of a Ministry of Science, Technology and the Environment in 1994, and the passage of a plethora of laws to implement new forms of new environmental protection.

On paper, Cuba's new environmental legislation is impressive. The challenges, as Whittle and Rey Santos point out, lie in the competing interests of economic development and environmental protection, and in the fact that given the state's role in the Cuban economy, the government is essentially regulating itself.[30] Yet Whittle and Rey Santos, as well as other analysts, see encouraging signs that the will to enforce the laws is solid.[31]

Contradictions: Inequality and *Jineterismo*

There were a number of ways in which the economic openings, while ostensibly racially neutral, in fact tended to the advantage of lighter-skinned Cubans. Despite the relative socioeconomic equality that the Revolution had brought about among the races, there were global, structural, historical, and ideological factors that came to the fore in different ways during the Special Period and resulted in some older patterns of racial inequality resurfacing.

The legalization of the dollar, in 1993, benefited those with relatives in Miami. Cubans joked that to survive the Special Period, you need to have "fe" – Spanish for "faith," but playing on the acronym for "familia en el exterior" – family abroad, to send you money. Because of pre-revolutionary racial inequalities, whiter Cubans were far more likely than Cubans of color to have relatives abroad, especially relatives who were part of the first generation of exiles who had prospered in the United States. A late 1990s study showed that 96 percent of Cubans in Miami still classified themselves as "white."[32] So lighter-skinned Cubans benefited disproportionately from remittances.

Lighter-skinned Cubans also benefited, in subtle and not-so-subtle ways, from the hiring preferences of the tourism industry. European and Canadian investors brought with them their own racial preconceptions, and their imaginings about what the tourists who used their hotels and resorts would prefer. Cuban government officials, who played an important role in hiring, also carried racial stereotypes, and beliefs about what the foreigners would prefer. Often the euphemism "buena presencia" or "good appearance" – which implied characteristics associated with whiteness – was used as an explicit or implicit job qualification. All of these global and local racial prejudices contributed to a preference for lighter-skinned employees, especially in positions of authority or in dealing with the public, which were also some of the better-paying positions in the foreign sector.[33] A survey in Havana in 2000 confirmed that lighter-skinned Cubans were more likely to be paid in dollars, and to receive more dollars, than their darker-skinned counterparts.[34]

In the newly opened economy, privilege begat privilege. Vestiges of pre-revolutionary privilege – like a large house, or a car – now brought access to the tourist economy. Access to dollars opened new paths to investment and self-employment. Lack of initial access meant continuing, and compounded, exclusion. So social and racial inequalities tended to reproduce themselves and grow.

The tourist sector played on domestic and foreign racial stereotypes in other ways also. Afro-Cuban culture became one more tourist attraction. Few foreign tourists went to Cuba to see the racially diverse National Ballet Company. Many, though, eagerly sought out the opportunity to see Afro-Cuban dance performances or Afro-Cuban religious ceremonies. In some respects these foreign desires, and the Cuban government's programs to fulfill them, benefited black Cubans who obtained employment and funding in this sector. But performing one's ethnicity for tourists also carries a psychic and cultural cost.

In some ways all Cubans paid the psychic or cultural cost of per-forming their society for tourists. The Revolution itself became a tourist attraction, with Che t-shirts and key-chains hot items.

Another psychic or cultural cost was in what some critics called "tourism apartheid." New hotels catering to foreigners were not only prohibitively expensive, they were positively off-limits to Cubans. The government assumed, with some justification, that foreign tour-ists would prefer to avoid haggling and hassling by Cubans eager for dollars. It also made half-hearted attempts to promote more socially acceptable forms of tourism – family tourism, educational tourism, health tourism – rather than the "vice" tourism based on gambling, liquor and prostitution, that had historically characterized the island's industry. But government attempts to protect tourists from Cuban hustlers created painful contradictions. Cubans could be criminal-ized just for associating with foreigners or entering the newly reno-vated spaces created to please tourists.

Jineterismo – a range of legal, semi-legal and illegal activities servic-ing the tourist economy – became rampant. While overt prostitution was illegal, it was often officially tolerated, though occasional crack-downs occurred. But many Cubans engaged in dating, companion-ship, and other relationships with foreigners that blurred the lines between prostitution and other types of casual or even serious rela-tionships. A "Zippy" cartoon from 1995 parodied two foreigners' encounter with a scantily-dressed Cuban woman who accosts them calling "Hola, boys! You're cute! Would you like to buy me dinner?" In the last frame, Griffy sits with Zippy over drinks, commenting "That was **not** what I expected! She **did** just want to discuss **Hemingway** & go **shopping**! Plus, she had a **degree** in **engineering**!"

But in the area of gender, too, the Special Period seemed to reawaken some very old patterns that the Revolution had sought to transform. Political scientist Mala Htun summarized the situation by saying "as the struggle for survival has grown more acute, latent social differences have been manipulated into justifications for unequal opportunities."[35] "Because women are generally responsible for the well-being of the home and the family economy," explains Julie Shayne, "they are forced into the position of making ends meet." She quotes cinematographer Belkis Vega in a 1999 interview:

This special period has weakened… the struggle of women's revital-
ization. If [feminism] gets weakened because women are exhausted
from the struggle of trying to survive… other struggles become secondary, because the struggle is one for food, of "How do I feed my
family?" "How do I keep my house?" "How do I manage to provide
my children with shoes and clothing?" And that takes a front stage
role… The work takes up so much time that all you want at the end
of the day is to watch a soap opera to disconnect, to evade things so
you can sleep.[36]

The influx of the tourist industry and the dollars it brings has also
offered different opportunities to men and women. The industry
advertises the country's women with seductive and demeaning
images. And although both males and females have been drawn into
the prostitution industry, the largest numbers have been among
young women, especially women of color.

Cuban American Coco Fusco describes the *jineteras* she interviewed in the mid-1990s as "sophisticated traffickers in fantasy." One
of the women, describing how the neighbors viewed her business,
replied "They see the *gallego* (Spaniard) coming in with a girl, and
they don't see him. They see a chicken, rice, beans – a full fridge."[37]
While emphasizing the women's agency, she also concluded that "I
felt I was watching the saddest part of Cuban socialism's last chapter
– living proof of the island's own nihilistic version of a Generation
X without any dreams of a future beyond the next purchase."[38]

The derogatory term *jinetera* [prostitute] and, by association, *jine-
tero*, came to refer to anybody who received some kind of benefit
from association with foreigners. It could be the licensed taxi driver
or the professional who moonlighted without a license; it could be
the unofficial tour guide who found foreigners a room or a meal. But
the term carried with it a weight of illegitimacy. Even if the activity
was perfectly legal, calling it *jineterismo* implied that it was selling
oneself for the almighty dollar. Some Cubans opined that the country
itself was selling out its ideals for dollars.

But the line between *jineterismo* and the free market is a murky
one. After all, performing services or providing goods in exchange
for pay is inherent in the capitalist system. What looked like *jineterismo* in Cuba could be called simply the law of supply and demand

in a capitalist country. Even academics, in the capitalist world, are quite accustomed to designing research projects based on where grant money exists, while publishing houses select manuscripts based on some kind of judgment of what will sell.

Opting to Leave: The 1994 Exodus

The United States greeted Cuba's economic crisis with a surge of publications predicting "Castro's Final Hour." Meanwhile President Clinton tightened the embargo in 1992 with the Torricelli legislation.

In the summer of 1994 the economic crisis was at its worst. The full effects of the Special Period hung oppressively over the country. Food was scarce. As the burning summer wore on, electricity cuts stilled the fans that most Cubans relied on. Meanwhile most of the population looked on as the lucky few who had access to dollars, and the newly opened dollar stores, exhibited their purchases. In August, something snapped.

In 1984 the United States had agreed to grant up to 20,000 visas a year to Cubans who wanted to immigrate. (The ceiling was raised to 27,000 in 1990.) But the Interests Section in Havana made it very difficult to obtain these visas – in 1993, for example, only 2700 were granted.[39] The double standard made it almost impossible for Cubans to obtain a visa by following legal channels – but rewarded those who simply took off for the United States by sea with no documents.

As the economic crisis hit, in 1991, Bay of Pigs veteran José Basulto, a wanted criminal in Cuba for his participation in an array of terrorist attacks – including one attempt to assassinate Castro – founded a new Miami organization, Brothers to the Rescue. Its stated goal was to patrol the waters between Cuba and Florida, picking up rafters fleeing the island, and counting on their official welcome into the United States.

Cuba claimed humanitarian reasons for trying to prevent illegal exit by sea, insisting that U.S. policies privileging those who arrived without formal permission encouraged the risky voyages that had resulted in many deaths. The Cuban Coast Guard returned those it was able to intercept in Cuban waters. Smugglers, and those who endangered the lives of children, were generally prosecuted. Brothers to the Rescue, the Cubans argued, only further encouraged the dangerous practice.

In this context, as the hot summer of 1994 wore on, a few Cubans resorted to desperate acts – stealing or hijacking ships – to leave bound for Florida. In accordance with U.S. policy, they were welcomed, if they could make it out of Cuban waters. In mid-July, a Cuban navy ship rammed a stolen tugboat, drowning 41 would-be migrants aboard. In early August, a naval officer was killed during a hijack attempt. The temperature, and the tensions, rose inexorably. Riots shook downtown Havana. Then, on August 11, Castro decided to call the bluff of the United States. Cubans wishing to leave by sea, he announced, would no longer be intercepted. The coast was open for departure.

Hundreds of Cubans poured out to sea in the following week. Florida's governor protested that the state could not handle the influx. On August 18, U.S. President Bill Clinton announced the unprecedented: that Cubans attempting to reach the United States without permission would no longer be welcomed. Rather, they would be sent to the U.S. military base in Guantánamo. "In a stroke, Clinton turned Cubans into the legal equivalent of Haitians," the *Washington Post* noted in wonderment.[40] By the end of 1994 some 50,000 refugees were housed there, at a cost of $500,000 to $1 million a day.[41] But when Cubans saw that their guarantee of automatic entry into the United States had evaporated, the numbers leaving declined precipitously.

Most of the Cubans sent to Guantánamo were eventually admitted to the United States. But Clinton was also forced to acknowledge the noxious effects of the U.S. policy, in effect since the 1966 Cuban Adjustment Act (CAA). In May of 1995, he announced the new "Wet Foot, Dry Foot" policy. Cubans picked up at sea would, like would-be immigrants without visas from anywhere else in the world, be returned home. Those who managed to arrive on land – whether from the Straits, or through Mexico – with "dry feet," would still be granted the preferential treatment and almost automatic refugee status conferred by the CAA. He also agreed to facilitate the visa-granting process, to encourage Cubans to enter legally. Cuba, for its part, agreed to restore its policy of intercepting unauthorized rafters.

Brothers to the Rescue, deprived of its raison-d'être but still in possession of numerous aircraft, revived the 1960s tactic of Havana flyovers, dropping leaflets calling on the Cuban population to rebel. The Cuban government protested regularly to the United States about violations of its airspace and, in early 1996, shot down a small plane, killing its pilot. The Cubans claimed that the plane was inside Cuban airspace, which Brothers to the Rescue denied. The ensuing outrage encouraged the U.S. Congress to pass the Helms–Burton legislation, tightening and expanding the U.S. embargo against Cuba. Relations further soured in 1998, when U.S. authorities arrested five Cuban intelligence agents who had infiltrated organizations like Brothers to the Rescue and Alpha 66. The Cubans argued that the agents were not spying on the United States, but rather on terrorist organizations planning attacks on their country. They had even shared information with the FBI. But the Cuban Five remained in jail as of early 2010, becoming something of an international cause célèbre.[42]

While sea departures decreased drastically after the accords, they did not cease entirely. A new smuggling industry emerged, with professional smugglers charging thousands of dollars to bring Cubans to the shores of Florida. One of the most notorious cases was that of a six-year-old boy named Elián González. Although his divorced parents shared custody of him in his hometown of Cárdenas, Cuba, his mother and her boyfriend absconded with the boy on a small boat bound for Miami in late 1999. Only Elián survived the journey. He was picked up by fishermen, turned over to the Coast Guard, and eventually to his Miami relatives. While the Miami family enveloped him in their midst, his Cuban family, including his father and two grandmothers, demanded his return. Miami's Cuban community mobilized passionately, and the world watched as an AP photographer captured an image of federal agents seizing the child from the arms of his relatives to return him to his Cuban family.

Other Cubans came through Mexico. While Mexicans and other Latin Americans risked death trying to evade the Border Patrol in the desert, as author Tom Miller pointed out, "if you're Cuban and arrive illegally, even brought in by a professional smuggler, you are rewarded with a fast-track to residency and citizenship." Cubans "don't need to wade the Rio Grande or walk the Sonoran Desert – they can simply stroll up to any port of entry along the 2000-mile border and say to the U.S. immigration inspector, '*Soy cubano. ¿me permite entrar?*' I'm Cuban, mind if I come in? And the answer is almost always, 'come on in!'"[43]

Debate and its Limits during the 1990s

I was not the only U.S. traveler to comment on the process of change in Cuba in the 1990s. Just as Congress was tightening the trade embargo, the Clinton Administration moved to allow educational, religious, and human rights groups to travel to the island. Curiosity about the revolutionary – or some thought, post-revolutionary – process in Cuba grew. Simultaneously, the Cuban government reached out to foreign tourists and scholars. A parade of travelers, journalists, and students from the United States visited Cuba in the 1990s and wrote about what they saw. Cuban travel literature became a booming genre. By the year 2000, some 35,000 to 40,000 people from the United States had visited Cuba under the newly relaxed travel restrictions, and 750 U.S. colleges and universities had obtained licenses for academic exchanges there.[44] The boom continued until the Bush Administration severely cut back permitted travel to Cuba in 2003 and 2004.

Within Cuba, social scientists debated Cuba's economic prospects, both inside and outside of the government. While the daily newspapers continued to offer relentlessly optimistic accounts of economy and society, scholarly journals plunged into criticism and debate. Cubans also engaged with foreign scholars, traveled abroad, and published co-authored essays and books with their foreign colleagues.[45] The space for debate "within the Revolution" grew.

Cuba's new 1992 Constitution formalized this growing political openness. Cuban sociologist Haroldo Dilla summarized some of the changes that were particularly significant in terms of political freedoms: "the proclamation of the nondenominational character of the state and the prohibition of any form of discrimination against religious believers, the suppression of allusions to democratic centralism and unity of power, the suppression of the strictly class-based definition of the social foundation of the state, and the establishment of direct elections for parliamentary seats." He noted, however, that the impact of the change in the parliamentary electoral system was limited by the subsequent electoral law that allowed only one candidate per seat.[46]

Dilla led the way in examining how the growing incapacity of the state to provide services and products contributed to the formation and strengthening of civil society. People improvised systems and organizations to fulfill needs formerly fulfilled by the government and its organizations. The 1992 Constitution provides that the government "recognizes, protects and supports social mass organizations … that originated from the historical class struggle of our people and that represent specific interests of our citizens and incorporate them in the tasks of building, consolidating and defending socialist society." The Cuban Law of Associations governs nongovernmental organizations (NGOs), both guaranteeing their right to exist, and mandating their obligation to "coordinate" and "collaborate" with the government and its official organizations.[47] The number of NGOs mushroomed in the early 1990s.

The limits to the new space for NGOs were revealed in March of 1996, when Raúl Castro made a televised speech attacking scholars who he claimed had sold themselves to the enemy, accepting foreign funding, privileges, and travel in exchange for writings tailored to outside goals. In particular, he mentioned the Centro de Estudios sobre América (CEA), a prominent Havana think tank that had produced a good deal of significant and challenging work on Cuba's economic and political direction.[48]

The CEA case reveals the subtle and complex ways that intellectual freedom is managed in Cuba. Some restrictions are enforced in harsh and overt ways, well documented and known on the outside. But prison sentences are reserved for Cubans accused and convicted of conspiring with outside forces (i.e., the United States) for the overthrow of the Cuban government. In the CEA case, nobody was formally charged or judicially punished. The head of the Center, who had encouraged much of the innovative work there, was demoted, replaced by a Communist Party hardliner. Several others also lost their positions, and a number of researchers chose to leave. Most of them found new homes in other Cuban research facilities, but a few of them left the country.

Another Cuban organization that pressed the limits during the Special Period was Magín. Magín was begun in 1993 by a small group of professionals distressed with the continuing gender inequality and, in particular, the ways that women's bodies were being used to sell the island to tourists. "They were outraged by images of seductive mulatas, their full buttocks barely covered by bikini thongs, and full-breasted sex objects beckoning from beneath the ever-present royal palm."[49] Despite the suspicion of the FMC, Magín members published, held workshops, and met with international feminist groups. But the FMC undercut Magín members' invitation to the 1995 World Conference on Women in Beijing, insisting that the FMC had filled all of the slots available for Cuba's delegation. When Magín applied for NGO status under Cuban law in 1996, the Party's Central Committee refused, as if, long-time Revolution supporter Margaret Randall suggested, "they were afraid these women might be duped into making contacts or doing work which inadvertently played into the enemy's hands." Randall wrote acerbically that "trusting the insights and intelligence of its own best citizens rather than relying on such insulting excuses might have pushed true revolution forward."[50]

The climate for debate and criticism in Cuba was not improved by President Clinton's vaunted "Track Two" policy for eliminating the Castro government. The first track was the longstanding negative policy of opposing the Revolution. Track Two would add a positive side of trying to promote U.S. goals by reaching out to potential or actual Cuban dissidents, trying to foster academic and other non-governmental contacts that would lure Cubans into the

U.S. or "pro-democracy" camp. While the Cuban government welcomed the increased travel to Cuba that Track Two engendered – it complemented Cuba's own strategy of increasing tourism and fostering opposition to U.S. policies among those who had traveled to the island – Track Two's focus on cultivating dissidence from within only increased the government's suspicion of Cubans who seemed too close to foreigners.

Some leading intellectuals affiliated to the Party challenged Raúl's 1996 speech by speaking out in defense of academic freedom and critical thought. Abel Prieto, the President of Cuba's Artists and Writers Union (UNEAC) and a Politburo member, announced that "critical art" is "indispensable" for the Revolution, and characterized Raúl's speech as a "self-criticism" since it was directed at Party organs. "There will be no new censorship, nor will we return to the 1970s with their socialist realism, nor witch-hunts" Prieto announced. "Critical art and political debate are indispensable to maintain the cohesion of Cuban intellectuals around the revolution" he continued.[51]

Alfredo Guevara, the head of Cuba's film institute (ICAIC), also implicitly responded to Raúl's speech in his eulogy of Tomás Gutiérrez Alea, the director of "Strawberry and Chocolate" – a film that explicitly criticized the closed intellectual atmosphere of the 1970s. "He was a difficult revolutionary, and that made him even more of a revolutionary," Guevara stated. "Simpletons are not revolutionaries, even less those who believe they are."[52]

Minister of Culture Armando Hart also made statements mitigating – or elaborating upon – Raúl's words at the presentation of the next issue of *Contracorriente*, stating that the Ministry of Culture must "provide a space for dialogue on the complexities of society."[53]

A new issue of *Temas*, a journal that CEA members had collaborated closely with, also came out undisturbed after Raúl's speech. The issue included the essay by CEA researcher Hugo Azcuy – who suffered a fatal heart attack the day after the speech was made – on the nature of "civil society" in Cuba. The free publication of *Temas* led some to believe that Raúl's speech should not be seen as a sign of a new intellectual closing in Cuba.

In fact some sources interpreted Raúl's speech as a *call* for critical debate rather than an attempt to silence it. By focusing on aspects of the economic opening that had not been officially acknowledged and discussed openly until now – aspects like prostitution, inequality, and corruption – the speech opened some space for public debate on these issues.[54]

8

Cuba into the Twenty-First Century

Raúl's 1996 speech had criticized the "nouveaux riches" of farmers, self-employed workers, and intermediaries, who had benefited disproportionately from the economic openings, as well as those who were receiving money from abroad. "We have to struggle tenaciously to ensure that they strictly abide by the law and pay the progressive tax on their earnings," he proclaimed. He also acknowledged the surge in unemployment, which added to the inexorable growth of economic inequality.[1]

The speech, and the policies that followed it, signaled a response to popular discontent with some of the economic distortions introduced by the Special Period reforms. The rush towards so-called "free" markets would be reined in. Most analysts see the economic openings slowing or even reversing after the mid-1990s.[2] The Special Period continued into the first decade of the twenty-first century, but shifted into what the Cuban government called *estrategia de perfeccionamiento* – fine-tuning, rather than dramatic experimentation.

Fine-tuning meant trying to address some of the new problems created by the economic opening, as well as the problems that the economic opening itself was trying to resolve. The problems were familiar to anybody living in a capitalist world, but exacerbated by Cuba's overall poverty, and by the extent to which the Revolution's legitimacy was based on overcoming these problems: unemployment,

A History of the Cuban Revolution. Aviva Chomsky
© 2011 Aviva Chomsky

consumerism, social and economic inequality. Many of the post-1996 measures were aimed at restricting aspects of economic opening that had opened the door to these social ills. But since these social ills were in a sense inherent in economic opening itself, the resulting policies continued to create contradictions. Stricter regulation and taxation of small businesses and the self-employed, for example, had the effect of driving some into the black market, and leading others to simply close.

From *Perfeccionamiento* to Recentralization

From 2003 to the present recentralization has predominated. If many of the 1993–96 reforms went in the direction of market opening, the period after 2003 saw an attempt to restrict and turn back some of these reforms. Carmelo Mesa-Lago describes this period as one of "drastic recentralization measures in economic decision making and further reduction of the small private sector."[3] If the reforms slowed after 1996, they positively reversed in late 2005, in what Pérez-López termed "rectification redux."[4] "If defined as a time span of policy experimentation and reform," he writes, "the special period is over."[5]

The architects of the market opening were removed from the Cuban Cabinet. The Minister of Economics and Planning, the Minister of Finance and Prices, and the Minister of Basic Industry, all of whom were involved in the earlier reforms, were all replaced between 2003 and 2004.[6]

One example of recentralization was de-dollarization. In late 2003 the government introduced the "convertible peso." Cubans could still have dollars – but they couldn't spend them. First they would have to change them into convertible pesos, which would from then on be the only currency accepted at Cuba's hard-currency businesses. The dollar stores became "convertible peso stores." In May 2004, prices in the convertible peso stores were raised between 10 and 35 percent, while in June 2004 peso salaries were raised. All of these measures served as a kind of levy on dollar-holders, forcing them to subsidize the peso economy. They could be seen, alternately, as an unjustified punishment for the winners in the new economy, or as an attempt to restore a measure of equity.

"According to official sources," wrote economist Mario González Corzo with some skepticism, "de-dollarization represents an attempt to reduce the existing (income) gaps and inequalities that exist between households functioning in the peso economy and those that somehow earn hard currency and/or receive remittances from abroad."[7]

Another set of regulations attempted to undo the privileges that workers in the tourist economy had accrued. In January 2005, tourist workers were banned from taking gifts, accepting invitations, and accessing a spectrum of other benefits from the foreigners with whom they worked. Mesa-Lago and Díaz-Briquets and Pérez-López called the measures "draconian."[8] At the same time, though, Díaz-Briquets and Pérez-López seemed to concur with the Cuban government that "corruption in state-run companies, particularly those that operate with hard currencies in the tourism sector, seems to be out of control. Among the corrupt practices that are alleged to be common in the tourism industry are accepting commissions from foreign businessmen, nepotism, selling jobs, and misuse of official cars, expense accounts, and travel."[9]

Corrales explained the measures – which also included "penalties on the self-employed, heavy taxation of *paladares* [small private restaurants in people's homes], increased restrictions on foreign direct investment" – as simply a "decision to punish reform winners." While many Latin American countries had slowed or moved away from structural adjustment programs, he noted, few besides Cuba "have had an open policy of penalizing reform winners."[10] The number of self-employed dropped from a high of 208,500 at the end of 1995 to only 149,990 in 2004, and continued to fall as restrictions and taxation on them increased.[11]

Economists committed to the structural adjustment model criticized the brakes put on the market policies at the end of the 1990s. Jorge F. Pérez-López called the new direction "the return of ideology."[12] Corrales complained that "the uneven economic reforms served to mislead – in fact, completely fool – those actors who in the early 1990s were pressuring for deep economic and political opening. The reforms allowed the state to give the impression that the regime was moving toward the market – the type of signal that was necessary to placate the pressures coming from reform advocates – when in fact, the government never intended to follow that path." Cuba's failure to go further meant that what happened in Cuba was "stealth statism" or "the pretense of market reforms."[13]

Archibald Ritter agrees that the Special Period is over, but he does not see this ending as simply a return to the past. Ritter describes the current reformulation – what he calls the "grand design" – in the following terms:

> The central feature of the "grand design" is a new basis for the genera-tion of foreign exchange earnings now emphasizing nickel, medical and educational services, and, in time, perhaps petroleum. It empha-sizes Cuba as a "knowledge economy and society" producing high value services for Latin America and the world. The older economic foundation – remittances, tourism, and lesser merchandise exports – will of course continue, but will be given less emphasis. The new economic master-plan also includes a stronger centralized control of the economy as well as "socialist purification" and a shoring up of the basic infrastructure necessary for sustained economic expansion and prosperity, so far emphasizing the energy sector.[14]

Thus Ritter describes the current situation not as a reversal and an end of reform, but rather a new phase in an ongoing process of eco-nomic experimentation. Some Cuban economists had been arguing since the 1990s that Cuba's advantages, and its future, should rest on its human capital. Rather than competing with other poor countries in a race to the bottom to offer low-wage workers to manufacturing companies, or cheap vacations to foreigners, Cuba should compete in the international playing field with its special strengths: its natural beauty – ecotourism; its doctors and professionals – health tourism, export of doctors, and attracting foreign students; and its skilled and educated workforce – promoting exports in biotechnology, medica-tions, and other high-value products.[15] Much of what Ritter sees happening in the post-2005 reforms seems to lead in this direction.

For example, 2006 was declared the "Year of the Energy Revolution." The "Revolution" had two sides to it: one, to improve Cuba's energy infrastructure in order to resolve the chronic shortages and black-outs that had afflicted the country since the loss of Soviet-supplied petroleum after 1989; and two, to address sustainability by improving energy efficiency and reducing use overall. Like previous campaigns all the way back to the Literacy Campaign of 1961 (the Year of Literacy), the energy campaign called for large-scale popular participation and mobilization in pursuit of major change.[16] Green billboards exhorted Cubans to save energy. The government distributed energy-efficient appliances from light bulbs and pressure cookers to stoves and refrigerators. "President Castro approached the energy situation with a micro-managed and quasi-military campaign ... The advantage of this approach, rooted in a command economy, is that it consisted of rapid though simple actions. However, the weaknesses are also those of the command economy: over-riding of people's decision-making based on their own perceived best interests, aborted gradualist learning-by-doing, and amplification of error."[17]

A visitor described the refrigerator delivery in a Havana neighborhood. "A megaphone woke me, and I went quickly to the door. The entire neighborhood – children, adults and grandparents – was congregated around an old man shouting: '¡Compañeros! ¡Compañeros! We require that all men in the quarter cooperate with the new mission of our Energy Revolution!'... From that moment on, not a single door closed until late in the evening when the task was done."[18]

There were other changes in late 2005 that imposed more controls on the market. On October 17, Havana's gas stations were taken over by specially trained social workers. Gas station operators, Castro charged, had been pilfering supplies and selling gasoline illegally, pocketing the profits. The same day, the military was placed in charge of the Port of Havana – again, to combat corruption. In November, the police raided farmers' markets, targeting farmers who were selling produce without first fulfilling their obligations to the state. Later that month, illegal bicycle taxis were targeted.[19] All of these actions targeted activities that were illegal, but had been widespread and tacitly tolerated.

Scholars and analysts offer four basic models for characterizing the shifts in Cuban economic policy in the 1990s and beyond. Mesa-Lago sees the current phase as a continuation of a cycle that has characterized Cuba's approach since the early days of the Revolution. Pragmatism (1970–86, 1993–96), where economic policies were more market-oriented, followed by periods of idealism (1960–70, 1986–93, 1996–present) where state control, moral incentives, and socialist ideals were emphasized. Eckstein argues, rather, that pragmatism has governed Cuban government policies all along, with idealism being mobilized to justify decisions taken for very pragmatic reasons – often because there were few other options. Corrales sees the post-2000 recentralization as proof that the market reforms were a false promise. Ritter portrays the process as more of a progression, with each new phase growing from new analyses of an evolving reality.

In some ways the debate over whether Cuba's policies are motivated by ideology or by pragmatism is a futile one. In every period, and in every country, a government's goals and beliefs are realized in the real world and within limits and structures beyond its control. No governing body is without an ideology, and no governing body can impose its ideology in a vacuum. Every governing body has adjusted and shifted its programs as circumstances have changed.

Even those who criticize the re-centralization admit that corruption was endemic in the dual economy – in some ways, built into it. "Self-employed workers generally obtain inputs from the black market, which in turn is largely fed by theft from the state sector," Díaz-Briquets and Pérez-López explain. They cite an example raised by Ana Julia Jatar-Hausmann, who describes how Jorge, a self-employed shoemaker, evaded directly answering the question of where he obtained his tools and equipment. "It is, in fact, a silly question," Jatar-Hausmann explains.

> Everybody knows that there are no free markets for any of the instruments used by Jorge; nor are there supplies for most of the products the artisans make. They either take them from their workplaces (in other words, steal them) or they buy them in the black market. Where

do the products in the black market come from? From other workers who do the same thing. Everyone has to steal in Cuba for survival.[20]

The situation is perhaps not all that different from what Benjamin, Collins and Scott found in the 1980s:

Many supporters of the revolution justify their black-market purchases by such arguments as "Everyone else does it," or "Even Ramón buys black market coffee, and he's in the Party." So you get ironic situations: the woman who participates in her street's Committee for the Defense of the Revolution, and spends her weekends practicing in the militia or volunteering to work in the countryside, but buys black-market chicken from the butcher, knowing that it comes from short-weighing her neighbors and probably her own family as well. The black-market forces Cubans to live by a double standard, and this is probably its most pernicious effect.[21]

However, not all agree that increasing enforcement and centralized control is the best remedy for these problems. Díaz-Briquets and Pérez-López argue that transparency, rather than control, is the best antidote. Mesa-Lago points out that recentralizing made state enterprises less efficient, reduced the number of joint ventures, and discouraged investors and tourism. He also notes that the 1986 Rectification campaign, which closed down private markets, in fact led to an increase in black market activity.[22]

While government economic policies play an important role in how the economy fares, it's also important to remember that economics is not an exact science. No economist has yet managed to provide a foolproof solution for the problems of poverty plaguing the Third World, or even the First.

In the first decade of the twenty-first century, the "triple blockade" was exacerbated by a fourth: a series of natural disasters. Cuba was struck with five hurricanes between 2000 and 2005. The last two, Charley and Ivan, in 2004, caused $2.15 billion of damage: "54,325 hectares of crops were damaged; 2.4 million animals had to be moved, which also affected production particularly of pigs and poultry (800,000 chickens died); 5,360 dwellings were destroyed, and 94,896 were damaged."[23] On top of the hurricanes, beginning in 2003 the island was afflicted with the worst drought in over a hundred years, causing, by the end of 2004, another $84 million in losses.[24]

Civil Society into the New Century

Despite the state's ambivalence towards independent organizations, epitomized by the crackdown on CEA and Magín, the late 1990s saw a kind of a boom in different forms of organizations and intellectual and artistic production. Some state-sponsored entities, like research institutions, became independent NGOs. Other NGOs have independent roots, or roots in different religious entities, and operate with state approval. Then there are illegal organizations, that identify clearly with opposition to the Cuban government and have either not sought legal status, or been denied it. Researchers found 350 of these organizations in 1996, and 470 in 2003. "Common threads running through these [latter] organizations," explain Díaz-Briquets and Pérez-López, "are that they are very small, command very few resources, and operate illegally ... members of these organizations risk the possibility of harassment, fines, and arrests at any time for breaking the law."[25]

In the area of gender and sexuality, the new century saw significant advances. The National Center of Sexual Education (CENESEX), founded in the 1970s, had long been a progressive voice in the struggle to "undermine traditional prejudices and taboos about sexuality."[26] Under the direction of Raúl Castro's daughter and noted sexologist Mariela Castro since 2000, the Center has pioneered efforts like a "Diversity is the Norm" campaign, the right to sex-change operations under Cuba's national health system, approved in 2008, and enthusiastic participation in World Anti-Homophobia Day celebrations in 2008 and 2009. As of mid-2010, however, the government had still not implemented proposals for equal marriage rights.

Religious organizations too found new spaces opening at the end of the twentieth century. Cuba's 1992 Constitution removed language defining the state as atheist, redefining the country instead as a secular state, and banning discrimination against religious believers and practitioners. Along with other Special Period developments, these changes led to a kind of boom in religious practice and presence.

The Pope's 1998 visit to Cuba – the first ever – revealed aspects of both a changing Church and a changing Cuba. The Catholic Church gained more autonomy and power as an institution during the Special Period. It was one of the few entities that had the infrastructure and the international connections to address some of the needs created by the economic crisis. In some ways, the economic crisis led to a crisis of faith too, and some turned to the Church for answers.

In 1992 the government approved the establishment of Caritas Cuba. Caritas, an international Catholic relief organization based in Rome, is active around the world – but had been banned in Cuba until then.[27] In 1993 the U.S.-based Catholic Relief Services initiated a project to support Caritas Cuba, and by 2008 had shipped $27 million in relief supplies.[28]

Afro-Cuban religions experienced a different kind of political opening in the 1990s. Because they are not centrally organized and have no institutional hierarchy or data collection, it's harder to measure increases in religious practice. But Santería, in particular, has boomed as a practice and as a tourist attraction. Katherine Hagedorn's study of the Conjunto Folklórico Nacional de Cuba explains how the government founded the group in 1962 as part of an effort to support and validate Afro-Cuban cultural forms. By the 1990s, practitioners realized that Santería could also be a source of income. Some *santeros* turned commercial and sought to sell the Afro-Cuban religious experience to visitors from abroad.[29] Many Cubans resented what one scholar termed "auto-exoticism" or "*jineterismo cultural*" – prostituting one's culture for dollars.[30]

Cuban film flourished in new ways under the economic constraints that began in the 1990s. As the government's ability to fund the film institute frayed, both established and emerging filmmakers were forced to look for sponsors abroad. This new dependence on the market, rather than the state, brought both opportunities and challenges. Sujatha Fernandes points out, for example, that "themes of homosexuality and Afro-Cuban spirituality are seen as particularly appealing to international audiences, given the attractiveness of 'difference' as a marketable commodity."[31] This meant that previously obscured themes could now be explored. But dependence on the market could pose its own demands and limits on artistic freedom and imagination. Nevertheless, joint productions of the 1990s cosponsored by ICAIC and foreign sources, like *Guantanamera* and *La vida es silbar* enjoyed critical acclaim both on and off the island.

Meanwhile, what Ann Marie Stock called "street filmmakers" also emerged in the Special Period. Making use of new cheaper and lighter technology like hand-held video cameras, and pursued by young aspiring filmmakers outside of ICAIC, a whole new genre of Cuban film developed out of adversity. "Out of necessity, working with limited budgets and without industry infrastructure, this generation became adept at *resolviendo* and *inventando*," Stock explains. Most of their films are short, and many are documentaries. Children of the Special Period, the new cineastes "turn their cameras toward the margins, to recover the disenfranchised, those who have been left behind by Cuba's hegemonic socialist project."[32]

Films like Humberto Padrón's *Video de familia* (2001) illustrate some of the artistic and political strengths of the genre. Shot independently, the film was distributed by ICAIC and won numerous awards in Cuba and internationally. The story takes the form of a video postcard, recorded by family members to the son (or brother) who moved to Miami four years earlier. As the camera records, the family conversation explodes in arguments about race, politics, emigration, family relations, everyday life, and the daughter's unexpected revelation of the absent son's homosexuality.

Many of the new Cuban organizations and projects operated within the spaces for civil society delineated by legal guarantees. Some have pressed the limits and sought more fundamental changes in Cuba's laws and social and economic systems. In 1998, the Christian Liberation Movement's Oswaldo Payá founded the Varela Project, collecting signatures, according to Cuban law, for a referendum that proposed some fundamental changes to the Cuban political system. The Project called for a referendum on five issues: freedom of speech and association; freedom of the press; amnesty for political prisoners; the right of Cubans to form companies; and changes to Cuba's electoral laws.[33] The Varela Project explicitly distanced itself from other "dissident" and exile organizations, insisting that it operated within Cuban law and was committed to legal, nonviolent means of change.

In early 2003, increasing dissident activity – some of it linked to the U.S. Interests Section – coincided with a spate of armed attempts to hijack planes or boats to Florida. Several of these were successful, but Cuban officials intercepted an attempt to force a Havana Bay ferry to Miami, arresting the hijackers. Three hijackers were tried and sentenced to death, leading to a round of protest. Meanwhile, 75 members of dissident organizations were also arrested, and sentenced to up to 28 years in prison. An international outcry ensued.

About half of those arrested were associated with the Varela Project. They were accused, and soon convicted, of accepting funds and support from James Cason of the U.S. Interests Section. Cason, the Cuban Foreign Minister explained, had turned the Interests Section into a "headquarters of subversion against Cuba" and was using his diplomatic status as a cover for working to overthrow Cuba's government. Varela Project members were his witting, or unwitting, tools. By working as agents of a foreign government dedicated to the overthrow of Cuba's government, and by collaborating with the implementation of the Helms–Burton Act, they were violating Cuban law.[34] (Most of those who remained imprisoned were freed in July, 2010, in a deal brokered by the Spanish government and the Cuban Catholic Church.)

Disillusionment

Although the results of the economic reforms looked positive in the aggregate, Cuba's people did not benefit equally. A survey in Havana in 2000 showed 77 percent of the population had "insufficient income to cover their daily expenses;"[35] 42 percent of Cubans surveyed in 2007, and 43 percent in 2008, believed that low salaries and the high cost of living were the biggest problems facing their country.[36]

Older generations of Cubans may remember Cuba prior to the Revolution, and the headiness of social change and possibility of the 1960s, or at least the relative material stability of the 1970s and 80s. This background lent the changes of the 1990s and early 2000s a poignancy, or even anguish. For those who came of age in the Special Period of the 1990s, those early decades seem a distant chimera. Both those who lived the experiences, and those who learned about them in school, though, had to face contemporary realities that did not live up to revolutionary dreams. The Revolution was supposed to bring equality – but what was visible in the 1990s and beyond was a growing inequality. The Revolution was supposed to bring an end to national economic dependence and the neocolonial relations that entailed, but the 1990s brought a renewed influx of foreign tourists and foreign investment, now heralded as Cuba's salvation. The Revolution was supposed to create opportunities for Cuba's people by overcoming underdevelopment, but in the 1990s jobs and opportunities seemed to exist only abroad. The 1990s generation was also heavily exposed to a materialism and cynicism in global youth culture that hadn't touched previous generations – both because of changes in the nature of global youth culture, and because new technologies were creating quantum leaps in the global connectedness of youth.

Cuban blogger Yoani Sánchez described a "Generation Y" in her country, referring not only to the U.S. idea of a "Generation X" but also to the popularity of names, like hers, beginning with the letter Y: "Yanisleidi, Yoandri, Yusimí, Yuniesky." (In Cuba, as well as other parts of Latin America and especially the Caribbean, there has been a marked tendency to invent new names as the influence of the Catholic Church and the practice of giving children names from the Bible waned at the end of the twentieth century.) This generation, she writes, was "born in Cuba in the '70s and '80s, marked by schools in the countryside, Russian cartoons, illegal emigration and frustration." Sánchez writes in a voice of sophisticated cynicism that U.S. and European readers have found irresistible, and she has won accolades from *Time Magazine*, *Foreign Policy*, and Barack Obama in the United States, to *El País* in Spain, for her trenchant critiques of everyday life in Special Period Cuba.

Bush-Era Policies

In 2002 Bush appointed James Cason head of the U.S. Interests Section. Cason took an active role in promoting and supporting opposition groups in Cuba. His activities succeeded in raising the international profile of Cuba's opposition. But they also contributed to the March, 2003 wave of arrests. The dissident groups had been infiltrated, and were charged under the 1999 Law for the Protection of Cuban National Independence and the Economy (Ley de Protección de la Independencia Nacional y la Economía de Cuba, Ley 88) with accepting gifts and money from Cason and other organizations, and supplying them with information, for the express purpose of overthrowing Cuba's government.

The trade embargo was loosened in 2000, with the U.S. Congress allowing sales of food and limited amounts of medicine. By 2004 Cuba was the third largest recipient of U.S. food exports, and the United States was Cuba's largest source.[37] The shelves of the dollar stores were filled with U.S. brands. Just as the U.S. government acquiesced to U.S. farmers' demands for access to the Cuban market, however, it made it more difficult for Cuban Americans to visit their relatives in Cuba.

In mid-2004, the United States limited family visits to immediate relatives to once every three years, as well as restricting remittances to immediate family members. The Cuban American community was, unsurprisingly, divided about such measures. Some of the older immigrants had few family ties left in Cuba, and their anti-revolutionary politics remained as virulent as ever. To them, restrictions on family visits seemed like good politics. The post-1980, and especially post-1994 immigrants, though, tended to have closer family ties, and more nuanced politics. Even if they considered themselves opponents of the Cuban government, they saw the restrictions as an attack on the Cuban people, not the regime.

In 2000, candidate Bush received 82 percent of the 450,000 Cuban American votes in Florida. In 2004, after the new restrictions were put into place, polls found his support dipping to between 60 and 70 percent. Among Cubans born in the United States, only 32 percent supported the president. "We older Cubans lived inside the monster, and we know that you have to keep fighting that old dictator. That's what President Bush plans to do," one older Cuban immigrant explained, justifying his support for Bush. "The president is asking us to choose between ideology and family. It's a stupid question. Don't make me choose," countered a younger man, announcing that he, for one, intended to vote for Kerry.[38] Another recent immigrant added, in 2008, "I don't think of the people there as pawns for us to play with ... They include my parents. They include my sister. I truly feel for them. I don't want to hurt the Cuban government if it's going to hurt them."[39]

Cuba, Venezuela, and the ALBA

The election of Hugo Chávez in Venezuela in 1998 significantly changed the dynamic of inter-American relations. Cuba had never been quite as isolated as U.S. policymakers suggested. In the Third World and among non-aligned countries, Cuba was a leader and the United States more often than not isolated; even among U.S. allies, none followed the U.S. lead in cutting off relations with the island. Still, Susan Eckstein could reasonably argue, in a chapter entitled "From Communist Solidarity to Communist Solitary", that, compounding the loss of the Soviet bloc, "Cuba in the early 1990s also faced difficulties with its Latin American neighbors. Cuba lost regional allies when a U.S. intervention ousted Panama's Gen. Manuel Noriega in December 1989 and when the Sandinistas were defeated in the February 1990 Nicaraguan elections."[40] Just over a decade later, it was clearly the United States that had become isolated in the hemisphere, with leftist parties winning elections from Chile, Brazil and Argentina to Nicaragua, and Venezuela's Hugo Chávez claiming the mantle of continuing the Cuban example. Venezuela also had something the Cubans desperately needed: oil.

Chávez signed an initial five-year agreement to sell oil to Cuba at controlled prices – in part in exchange for medical and other services

– in 2000. The deal was expended in December, 2004, when Chávez and Castro launched the Bolivarian Alternative for Latin America and the Caribbean (Alternativa Bolivariana para América Latina y el Caribe), an alternative, socialist model for economic integration in the Americas. The ALBA offered a direct challenge to the neoliberal, capitalist integration proposed by President Bush in the Free Trade Area of the Americas or FTAA. The initial accord was a petroleum-for-doctors agreement between Cuba and Venezuela: in exchange for close to 100,000 barrels of subsidized petroleum a day, Cuba would provide 30,000 health professionals for Venezuela's Barrio Adentro program, and train tens of thousands of Venezuelans in Cuba's medical schools and in Venezuela. Barrio Adentro follows the Cuban model of providing comprehensive health services, at no cost, in poor and marginal neighborhoods. In 2006 the program was expanded to include Bolivia, where Venezuela funded a Cuban program to send doctors and develop medical facilities.[41] By 2007, one analyst suggested that Venezuela was "approaching the role of great subsidizer that the Soviet Union had played in 1960–2000."[42]

Cuba after Fidel

In the summer of 2006, a 79-year-old Fidel Castro announced that, due to illness, he was temporarily ceding the presidency to the First Vice President of the country, his brother Raúl. In February of 2008, he declared that he would not seek re-election when his term expired a few days later. The National Assembly unanimously chose Raúl Castro to succeed Fidel as President.

In Raúl Castro's first few months in office he proposed various economic steps that excited much commentary both at home and abroad. One set of reforms sought to stimulate agricultural production by offering incentives to small farmers, including leasing state land to private farmers, and raising state prices for agricultural goods. Access to computers, video recorders, and cell phones, previously restricted, was opened, and Cubans were granted entry to tourist hotels. Raúl called on Cubans to openly discuss the country's political and economic problems. "Fidel cannot be replaced unless all of us replace him together," he told Havana university students, signaling what many Cubans saw as a shift to a less personalistic and more collective style of leadership.[43] He also announced that a Party Congress would be held in 2009 – the first since 1997, and the sixth since 1959. "If Fidel were still President and he was the one announcing the congress, I think most people would yawn," said one Cuba watcher. "But for Raul, it's saying, 'By the end of next year we're going to face the music and put forth a record.'"[44]

Ten U.S. Presidents, beginning with Dwight D. Eisenhower, had sought to remove Fidel Castro from office and overturn the Cuban Revolution. Only months after Fidel ceded the presidency, Barack Obama was elected President of the United States, promising "change."

Even Cuban Americans – traditionally the group most resistant to any opening towards Cuba – were changing. A poll conducted a month after Obama's election showed that 55 percent of Cubans in south Florida supported ending the embargo, and 65 percent wanted to see diplomatic relations re-established.[45] This brought them close to the U.S. population as a whole, which by a 71 percent margin believed that diplomatic relations should be restored.[46]

At the Americas Summit in Trinidad only a few months into his term of office, Obama reiterated that "the United States seeks a new beginning with Cuba." His announcement that he was lifting Bush-era restrictions on Cuban American travel to the island and remittances, and was ready to discuss restoring direct mail and a new accord on migration, was welcomed by many Cubans and Cuban Americans. This did not, however, constitute a new beginning. Although his administration was more flexible about granting travel permits, Obama did not restore the educational travel possibilities that had been implemented by Clinton and continued into the first years of the Bush Administration. While Raúl Castro called for talks between the two governments on all topics, with no preconditions, the Obama administration continued to insist that dialogue would be limited unless Cuba carried out internal reforms.

Meanwhile, the global economic downturn and falling prices for Cuban exports compounded natural disasters – two major hurricanes in 2008 – to make 2009 a bleak year economically for Cuba. A survey in March of 2009 concluded that "Cubans struggle to survive from day to day ... They are particularly concerned about food shortages and rising prices, and worry that hurricane damage and the global financial crisis will make their situation worse. Many respondents fear that Cuba might be entering another 'Special Period'."[47] A Cuban economic official concurred that Cuba was going through a "very deep and difficult crisis."[48]

By the end of 2009 hopes on both sides of the border for an end to the hostilities were also dimmed. The United States refused to even acknowledge Cuba's key demands that it release the "Cuban Five" imprisoned intelligence officers, that it end the blockade, and cease its attempts, covert and otherwise, to interfere in Cuba's internal affairs. "The Obama honeymoon here is over," declared the *New York Times's* Marc Lacey from Havana at the end of the year, referring to statements by Raúl Castro and others accusing the United States of "open and undercover subversion against Cuba."[49]

Conclusion

Two competing visions of Cuba seem to hold sway over the U.S. imagination. One is the Caribbean vision, of Cuba as a tourist destination, hot, colorful, beach-ringed, with plenty of music, drink, and sex. People in this Cuba are happy and carefree. The other is the Soviet vision, of Cuba as a dingy, gray, repressed police state, where citizens live in dreary fear.

Both visions are figments of a foreign imagination, Cubas invented by the worldviews of foreigners. The real Cuba is, like every country, diverse and complex. Its history over the past 50 years of the Revolution is also diverse and complex, and anything but static.

On my most recent visit to the island, in the summer of 2008, I was struck by three things in particular.

Since all of my personal experience in Cuba has been since the economic crisis that began in 1991, I always ask people "how is the situation?" This time the first answer people gave was about transportation: it's gotten much better. New Chinese buses were comfortable and reliable. It may seem trivial – but it has made a huge difference in daily life in Havana, a sprawling city in which almost everyone needs to commute.

On a more somber note, people hinted that both the health and the education systems, so long held up as the greatest successes of the Revolution, were faltering. As the state became less able to guarantee meaningful work, or even subsistence, to the more highly educated, both students and teachers were abandoning the goal of education and dropping out. A new program was trying to crash-train teachers and place them quickly in the schools, but their qualifications were weak, further undermining the system.

Health care too was suffering. Family doctors' offices were going unstaffed as tens of thousands of doctors were exported to Venezuela and elsewhere to bring back desperately needed foreign exchange. In April 2008, Raúl Castro announced reforms that would consolidate the system, closing understaffed offices and making the remaining offices responsible for more people, and sending more medical students into family doctor residencies.

In an August, 2009 report, Amnesty International documented other obstacles facing Cuba's health system. Key among them was the U.S. embargo. "The restrictions imposed on trade and financing, with their extraterritorial aspects, severely limit Cuba's capacity to import medicines, medical equipment, and the latest technologies, some of which are essential for treating life-threatening diseases and maintaining Cuba's public health programmes," Amnesty concluded.[1]

Also disturbing were the comments of some old friends, a couple in their early sixties. They are professionals, free thinkers shaped by and deeply committed to the Revolution, both working in fields that kept them engaged with constantly rethinking how to bring about social justice and economic development. Their only daughter, also highly educated and motivated, had married since the last time I saw them. She met her husband, a Spaniard, through her work when he was on business in Havana. They, and their new baby, now live in Spain.

"We call ourselves the generation of orphan parents," my friend sighed. "All of our friends are in the same predicament. Their children worked hard, got educated – and now there is no opportunity for them here. What would my daughter's life have been, if she'd stayed? The daily struggle, waiting for us to die so they could have our apartment?"

I do not wish to sum up the Cuban revolutionary experience or cast an overarching judgment on it. The Revolution has been wildly audacious, experimental, and diverse. It has evolved under often adverse circumstances. It created unprecedented socioeconomic equality, and showed the world that it is indeed possible for a poor, Third World country to feed, educate, and provide health care for its population. It fostered astonishing artistic and intellectual creativity, while also creating stifling bureaucracies and limits on freedoms that many in the United States take for granted. It also showed just how extraordinarily difficult it is to overcome economic underdevelopment.

The history of the Cuban Revolution is still unfolding, and the most educated predictions have proven wrong again and again. I left Cuba in August, 2008 both optimistic and pessimistic, and mostly, curious, about what would happen in the coming years.

One of the best things about studying the past, or a different country or culture, is how it can enable you to see things about your own reality in a different light. Usually we take our own historical context for granted. Until we are brought face to face with other possibilities, it's hard for us to even imagine that they exist. If we want to imagine a better world for all of us, I can think of no better place to start than by studying the Cuban Revolution.

Notes

Introduction

1 Gallup, "Favorability: People in the News," www.gallup.com/poll/1618/Favorability-People-News.aspx. Results from August 2006.

2 Examples include historian Thomas M. Leonard, *Fidel Castro: A Biography*; historian Robert E. Quirk, *Fidel Castro*; political scientist John Gerassi, *Fidel Castro: A Biography*; journalists Georgie Ann Geyer, *The Untold Story of Fidel Castro*; Volker Skierka, *Fidel Castro: A Biography*; and Tad Szluc, *Fidel: A Critical Portrait*. In addition see British diplomat Leycester Coltman, *The Real Fidel Castro*; physician Peter G. Bourne, *A Biography of Fidel Castro*; Nestor Kohan and Nahuel Scherma, *A Graphic Novel Life of Fidel Castro*; and Ignacio Ramonet, *Fidel Castro: My Life: A Spoken Autobiography*.

3 Manifesto of the Junta Cubana de Renovación Nacional, cited in Pérez, *Cuba: Between Reform and Revolution*, p. 236.

4 Kozol, *Children of the Revolution*, p. 171.

5 Telegram from the Embassy in Cuba to the Department of State, September 4, 1959. *FRUS 1958–60*, VI, p. 596.

6 Rubottom, January 14, 1960, *FRUS 1958–60*, VI, p. 743.

7 "President Bush Discusses Cuba Policy," October 24, 2007, www.whitehouse.gov/news/releases/2007/10/20071024-6.html.

8 Remarks of Senator Barack Obama: Renewing U.S. Leadership in the Americas. May 23, 2008, www.barackobama.com/2008/05/23/remarks_of_senator_barack_obam_68.php.

9 See Winn, *Victims of the Chilean Miracle* and Davis, *Victims of the Miracle*.

10 Adorno, "Havana and Macondo," p. 376.

11 Black, "Introduction: Understanding the Persistence of Inequity," p. 3.

12 Fagen, "Latin America and the Cold War," p. 6. See also Fagen, "Studying Latin American Politics."

13 Smith, "Memoirs from LASA's 14th President," p. 20.

14 Smith, "Memoirs from LASA's 14th President," pp. 20, 21.

15 Smith, "Memoirs from LASA's 14th President," pp. 20, 21.

16 Pérez-Stable, "Review: The Field of Cuban Studies," p. 250; Kirk and McKenna, "Trying to Address the Cuban Paradox."

17 Pérez, "History, Historiography, and Cuban Studies," p. 66.

18 Vilas, "Is Socialism still an Alternative for the Third World?"

19 Vilas, "Is Socialism still an Alternative for the Third World?"

20 Speech by Fidel Castro Ruz, President of the Council of State and the Council of Ministers of the Republic of Cuba, at the Opening Session of the Group of 77 South Summit Conference, Havana, April 12, 2000, www.g77.org/summit/ ceniai.inf.cu/f120400i.html.

21 World Public Opinion, "Cubans Show Little Satisfaction with Opportunities and Individual Freedom," January 10, 2007, www.worldpublicopinion.org/pipa/articles/ brlatinamericara/300.php?lb=brla&pnt=300&nid=&id=. See also Gallup News Service, "Just One in Four Urban Cubans Satisfied with Personal Freedoms," December 18, 2006, www.gallup.com/poll/25915/Just-One-Four-Urban-Cubans-Satisfied-Personal-Freedoms.aspx.

22 International Republican Institute, "Cuban Public Opinion Survey," September 5–October 4, 2007, www.iri.org/lac/cuba/pdfs/2007-10-18-Cuba.pdf.

23 World Public Opinion, "Latin American Publics are Skeptical about U.S. – But Not about Democracy," March 7, 2007, www.worldpublicopinion.org/pipa/articles/ brlatinamericara/328.php?nid=&id=&pnt=328&lb=brla.

24 Steve Crabtree and Jesús Ríos, "Opinion Briefing: Latin America's Leftists." January 21, 2009, www.gallup.com/poll/113902/opinion-briefing-latin-america-leftists.aspx.

Chapter 1

1 See, for example, Rodríguez Exposito, *Hatuey, El primer libertador de Cuba.*

2 See Yaremko, www.kacike.org/Yaremko.html.

3 Pérez, *Cuba: Between Reform and Revolution*, pp. 38, 46.

4 Bergad *et al.*, *The Cuban Slave Market, 1790–1880*, p. 38.

5 Ortiz, *Cuban Counterpoint*, p. 103.

6 The first quote is from "Mi Raza," published in *Patria* (New York), April 16, 1893. The essay is reproduced in Vitier and García Marruz, *José Martí*; quote is on p. 161. The second comes from a speech delivered at the Liceo Cubano in Tampa, November 26, 1891. See Poyo, *"With All and For the Good of All."*

7 Bolívar, *Selected Writings of Bolívar*, p. 732.

8   José Martí, "Nuestra América," *El Partido Liberal*, Mexico City, January 30, 1891; translated in Shnookal and Muñiz (eds), *José Martí Reader*, pp. 111–20.

9   Opatrný, *U.S. Expansionism and Cuban Annexationism in the 1850s.*

10   Pérez, *Cuba and the United States*, p. 47.

11   Poyo, "Evolution of Cuban Separatist Thought"; Poyo, "*With All and For the Good of All*."

12   Historian Louis A. Pérez, Jr., used the phrase as the title of his book on U.S.–Cuban relations, *Cuba and the United States: Ties of Singular Intimacy.*

13   Helg, *Our Rightful Share.*

14   On the importance of the vote and access to the country's political system for Cuba's black population, see de la Fuente, *A Nation for All.*

15   For the debate surrounding West Indian immigrants in Cuba, see Chomsky, "'Barbados or Canada?'"

16   Pérez, *Cuba: Between Reform and Revolution*, p. 192.

17   Pérez, *Cuba: Between Reform and Revolution*, pp. 197–8.

18   Jenks, *Our Cuban Colony*; Nearing and Freeman, *Dollar Diplomacy.*

19   Bemis, *The Latin American Policy of the United States.*

20   Foner, *The Spanish-Cuban-American War*; Pérez, *Cuba: Between Reform and Revolution*, p. 178.

21   Roig de Leuchsenring, *La Enmienda Platt* and *Análisis y consecuencias de la intervención norteamericana en los asuntos interiores de Cuba*; Healy, "One War from Two Sides." See also Corbitt, "Cuban Revisionist Interpretations of Cuba's Struggle for Independence," Quinn, "Cuban Historiography in the 1960s," and Pérez de la Riva, *La república neocolonial.*

22   Pérez, *Cuba: Between Reform and Revolution*, p. 226.

23   Pérez, *Cuba: Between Reform and Revolution*, p. 201.

24   Díaz-Briquets and Pérez-López, *Corruption in Cuba*, p. 71.

25   Pérez, *Cuba: Between Reform and Revolution*, p. 234.

26   Moore, *Nationalizing Blackness*, p. 105.

27   Pérez, *Cuba: Between Reform and Revolution*, p. 270.

28   Pérez, *Cuba: Between Reform and Revolution*, p. 268.

29   Pérez, *Cuba: Between Reform and Revolution*, p. 269.

30   Pérez, *Cuba: Between Reform and Revolution*, p. 275.

31   See Liss, *Roots of Revolution*, p. 109.

32   Pérez, *Cuba: Between Reform and Revolution*, p. 284.

33   de la Fuente, *A Nation for All*, p. 253.

34   Benjamin, Collins, and Scott, *No Free Lunch*, pp. 2, 3, 5; Pérez, *Cuba: Between Reform and Revolution*, pp. 295, 297.

35   www.time.com/time/time100/heroes/profile/guevara01.html.

36   Cuban artist Sandra Ramos offers a visual image of this salute, in Figure 1.2 and also viewable at www.thefrasergallery.com/artwork/Sandra-Ramos/Webpages/Seremos. html.

37   Carlos Puebla, "Para nosotros siempre es 26."

38   Liss, *Roots of Revolution*, p. 112.

39   The text is available in many versions, including online in the Castro Internet Archive at www.marxists.org/history/cuba/archive/castro/1953/10/16.htm.

40   Sweig, *Inside the Cuban Revolution*, p. 9.

41   Available online at www.granma.cubaweb.cu.

42   Carlos Puebla, "Para nosotros siempre es 26."

43   See Pérez, *Lords of the Mountain*.

44   Feinsilver, *Healing the Masses*, p. 31.

45   Ferrer, *Insurgent Cuba*, p. 43.

46   Quoted, among other places, in "The Cuban Revolution: An Eternal Triumph," in *Sierra Maestra Online, the Official Newspaper of Santiago de Cuba*, July 19th, 2008. See also Castro's January 3, 1959, speech in Santiago, http://lanic.utexas.edu/project/castro/db/1959/19590103.html. Raúl Castro reiterated the sentiment on January 1, 2009, commemorating the 50th anniversary of the triumph. "The Ejército Rebelde [the Rebel Army] took up again the weapons of the *mambises*," he proclaimed. "This time, with Fidel, the *mambises* entered Santiago de Cuba." Raúl Castro speech, January 1, 2009, Santiago de Cuba, www.cuba.cu/gobierno/rauldiscursos/2009/ing/r010109i.html.

47   Sweig, *Inside the Cuban Revolution*.

48   *New York Times*, February 24, 1957; DePalma, *The Man Who Invented Fidel*.

49   See Benjamin, *The United States and the Origins of the Cuban Revolution*; Morley, *Imperial State and Revolution*; Paterson, *Contesting Castro*.

50   Castañeda, "Gone but Not Forgotten."

51   Silverman, *Man and Socialism in Cuba*, p. 5.

52   Juan Antonio Blanco with Medea Benjamin, *Cuba: Talking About Revolution*, p. 18.

53   Gosse, *Where the Boys Are*. The "old left" in the United States and western Europe in the first half of the twentieth century was shaped by the Russian Revolution and the parties that formed from it. The New Left that developed in the 1960s, including the student and anti-war movements, rejected the top-down, authoritarian politics of the USSR and much of the Old Left.

54   "Education in Venezuela: Fatherland, Socialism, or Death: Venezuela's Schools Receive Orders to Create the 'New Man,'" *The Economist*, October 11, 2007.

55   Memorandum of a Conversation, Department of State, Washington, September 18, 1959. Subject: Our Future Relations with Cuba. Participants: R. R. Rubottom Jr., Assistant Secretary; Ambassador Bonsal; CMA [Office of Caribbean and Mexican Affairs, Bureau of Inter-American Affairs, Department of State] – William A. Wieland; ARA [Bureau of Inter-American Affairs, Department of State] – J. C. Hill; CMA – R. A. Stevenson, R. B. Owen.

Chapter 2

1   *Pachanga* refers, literally, to a lively Cuban music/dance form from the 1950s; the phrase recalls anarchist Emma Goldman's protest against the puritanical and

authoritarian nature of revolutionary organizations and her call for a revolution that encompassed freedom, beauty, joy, and dance.

2   For example, see Rostow's classic, *The Stages of Economic Growth*. A third edition was published in 1990.

3   See Prebisch, *The Economic Development of Latin America and its Principal Problems*.

4   See Brunendius, *Revolutionary Cuba*, pp. 10–12; Hamilton, "The Cuban Economy."

5   Brunendius, *Revolutionary Cuba*, p. 13.

6   Brunendius, *Revolutionary Cuba*, p. 14.

7   Quoted in Pérez, *On Becoming Cuban*, p. 368.

8   Roger de Lauria, quoted in Pérez, *On Becoming Cuban*, p. 355.

9   José Martí, "Our America," *El Partido Liberal* (Mexico City), March 5, 1892.

10 Pérez, *Between Reform and Revolution*, pp. 320–1.

11 Benjamin, Collins, and Scott, *No Free Lunch*, p. 17.

12 Feinsilver, *Healing the Masses*, p. 157.

13 Fagen, *The Transformation of Political Culture in Cuba*, p. 35.

14 Leiner, "The 1961 Cuban National Literacy Campaign," pp. 174–5.

15 See Quiroz, "Martí in Cuban Schools," in Font and Quiroz, *The Cuban Republic and José Martí*, p. 81.

16 Feinsilver, *Healing the Masses*, p. 32.

17 Fidel Castro speech, September 28, 1960, cited in Fagen, *Transformation of Political Culture*, p. 69.

18 Fagen, *Transformation of Political Culture*, pp. 70–1.

19 Fagen, *Transformation of Political Culture*, p. 73.

20 March 1968 speech, quoted in Benjamin, Collins, and Scott, *No Free Lunch*, p. 110.

21 Alfredo Prieto, "Otra vez los soviéticos," July 3, 2009, http://7dias.com.do/app/article.aspx?id=54772.

22 Eckstein, *Back from the Future*, pp. 47, 58.

23 Domínguez, *Cuba: Order and Revolution*, p. 202.

24 Benjamin, Collins and Scott, *No Free Lunch*, chapter 5.

25 Feinsilver, *Healing the Masses*, p. 37.

26 Feinsilver, "Cuban Medical Diplomacy."

27 Kozol, *Children of the Revolution*, pp. 105–6.

28 Dilla Alfonso, "Cuba: The Changing Scenarios of Governability," p. 60.

29 Roca, "The *Comandante* in His Economic Labyrinth," p. 91. He describes rectification as "centralist, personalist, anti-market, anti-incentive, with heavy emphasis on ideological and political values."

30 See LeoGrande and Thomas, "Cuba's Quest for Economic Independence"; Eckstein, *Back from the Future*, chapter 3. Eckstein concludes that "a major reason for launching the 'rectification process' was fiscal" (p. 79).

31 Lockwood, *Castro's Cuba, Cuba's Fidel*, p. 136.

32 Fornet, "El quinquenio gris: revisitando el término."

33 González Echevarría, "Criticism and Literature in Revolutionary Cuba," p. 168. For other summaries of Cuba's cultural policies and cultural production since the revolution, see Craven, "Cuban Art and Culture"; Ripoll, "Writers and Artists in Today's Cuba"; Casal, "Literature and Society."

Chapter 3

1   Silvio Rodríguez, "Canción urgente para Nicaragua."

2   Bonsal, *Cuba, Castro, and the United States*, pp. 42–3.

3   Braddock to Department of State, January 6, 1959. *Foreign Relations of the United States (FRUS) 1958–60*, VI, p. 346. These same businessmen had previously urged that the United States support a military coup to prevent a revolutionary victory; in that case, the Ambassador decided not to follow their advice, although he agreed that the United States "should not be [a] silent spectator." Instead of a coup, he urged the State Department to convince Batista to relinquish the presidency to a civilian backed by the military – perhaps a difference more semantic than real. This incident is described in Paterson, *Contesting Castro*, p. 201.

4   Bonsal, *Cuba, Castro, and the United States*, p. 28.

5   Memorandum by the Assistant Secretary of State for Inter-American Affairs' Special Assistant (Hill). "Briefing Memorandum-Cuba" February 6, 1959. *FRUS 1958–60*, p. 397.

6   Director of the Office of Mexican and Caribbean Affairs (Weiland) to Assistant Secretary of State for Inter American Affairs (Rubottom), February 19, 1959. *FRUS, 1958–60*, VI, p. 406.

7   Telegram from Embassy in Cuba to the Department of State, May 11, 1959. *FRUS 1958–60*, VI, pp. 507–8.

8   Pérez, *Cuba: Between Reform and Revolution*, p. 320.

9   Bonsal, *Cuba, Castro, and the United States*, p. 72.

10 Telegram from the Department of State to the Embassy in Cuba, May 22, 1959. *FRUS 1958–60*, VI, p. 510.

11 Telegram from the Embassy in Cuba to the Department of State, May 23, 1959. *FRUS 1958–60*, VI, pp. 511–12.

12 Memorandum of Conversation, June 1, 1959, *FRUS 1958–60*, VI, p. 518.

13 Telegram from the Embassy in Cuba to the Department of State, June 12, 1959, *FRUS 1958–60*, VI, pp. 529–30.

14 Note from Minister of State Roa to the Ambassador in Cuba (Bonsal), June 15, 1959. *FRUS 1958–60*, pp. 531–34.

15 Telegram from the Department of State to the Embassy in Cuba, June 25, 1959. *FRUS 1958–60*, VI, p. 543. The meeting with Robert Kleberg, proprietor of the

King Ranch in Texas, and Jack Malone, the manager of his Cuban properties, is described in Memorandum of Conversation, Department of State, Washington, June 24, 1959. *FRUS 1958–60*, VI, pp. 539–41. In his telegram to the Embassy, Herter specifically noted that "of serious concern Department is report of seizure Kleberg and other U.S. cattle properties" (p. 543).

16   Memorandum by the Director of the Office of Inter-American Regional Ecnomic Affairs, July 1, 1959. *FRUS 1958–60*, pp. 546–51; the quote is from p. 548.

17   Telegram from the Embassy in Cuba to the Department of State, July 7, 1959. *FRUS 1958–60*, pp. 553–54.

18   Telegram from the Embassy in Cuba to the Department of State, September 4, 1959. *FRUS 1958–60*, VI, p. 596.

19   Memorandum of a Conversation between the Ambassador in Cuba (Bonsal) and Minister of State Roa, July 23, 1959. *FRUS 1958–60*, p. 572.

20   Airgram from the Embassy in Cuba to the Department of State, August 2, 1959. *FRUS 1958–60*, VI, pp. 581–2.

21   Assistant Secretary of State for Inter-American Affairs' Special Assistant John C. Hill, September 18, 1959. *FRUS 1958–60*, VI, p. 605.

22   December 28, 1959. *FRUS 1958–60*, VI, pp. 716–20.

23   Paterson, "Fixation with Cuba," p. 126. He is citing Robert Anderson, Memorandum, January 19, 1961.

24   Rubottom, January 14, 1960. *FRUS 1958–60*, VI, p. 743.

25   November 4, 1959. *FRUS 1958–60*, VI, p. 652.

26   This document was quoted in U.S. Congress, Senate, *Alleged Assassination Plots*, p. 92.

27   For example, Fidel Castro gave Senator George McGovern a list of 24 assassination attempts against him. The CIA admitted "operational relationships" with nine of the would-be assassins, but claimed that it had not explicitly arranged these assassination attempts. Thus the Committee did not include these nine in its investigation (U.S. Congress, Senate, *Alleged Assassination Plots*, p. 71). Information has slowly emerged concerning CIA sponsorship of other assassination attempts, including one by Felix Rodriguez during CIA training for the Bay of Pigs invasion. See Rodriguez and Weisman, *Shadow Warrior*, pp. 65–6. According to Fabián Escalante of Cuba's Department of State Security, Cuban intelligence uncovered 634 plots with CIA involvement between 1958 and 2000. See "La lucha político-ideológica fue en todas partes," entrevista al General (r) Fabián Escalante", *Temas* 56 (Sept–Dec, 2008).

28   U.S. Congress, Senate, *Alleged Assassination Plots*, p. 85.

29   U.S. Congress, Senate, *Alleged Assassination Plots*, p. 74.

30   For example, one CIA contact who had agreed to place the poison in Castro's meal was fired from his position in Castro's office before he could carry out the murder. See Escalante, *CIA Targets Fidel*, p. 41.

31   November 26, 1959. *FRUS 1958–60*, VI, pp. 680–1.

32   December 4, 1959. *FRUS 1958–60*, VI, pp. 689–91.

33 Department of State–Joint Chiefs of Staff meeting, January 8, 1960. *FRUS 1958–60*, VI, pp. 731–4.

34 Press conference, January 26, 1960. *FRUS 1958–60*, VI, p. 767.

35 See Escalante, *The Cuba Project* and Escalante's introduction to, and the heavily censored, *CIA Targets Fidel*.

36 U.S. Congress, Senate, *Alleged Assassination Plots*, pp. 92–3.

37 Paper prepared by the 5412 Committee, March 16, 1960. *FRUS 1958–60*, VI, pp. 850–1.

38 Turkel, July 1, 1959. *FRUS 1958–60*, VI, pp. 546–8.

39 *New York Times*, February 20, 1960; February 19, 1960. Also cited in Blum, *Killing Hope*.

40 *New York Times*, March 5, 1960; March 6, 1960.

41 For a useful chronology of events, with access to many declassified documents, see the National Security Archives website at George Washington University, www.gwu.edu/~nsarchiv/bayofpigs/chron.html. See also Kornbluh, *Bay of Pigs Declassified*.

42 Hunt, *Give Us This Day*, p. 40.

43 Hunt, *Give Us This Day*, p. 45.

44 He describes this month-long infiltration in Rodriguez and Weisman, *Shadow Warrior*, pp. 71–82. CIA agent Rolando Martínez, who I have quoted elsewhere, was the one who picked him up and brought him back to the United States (p. 82).

45 Rodriguez and Weisman, *Shadow Warrior*, p. 84.

46 Hunt, *Give Us This Day*, p. 38.

47 Paterson, "Fixation with Cuba," p. 133. He cites an interview with Richard Bissell by Lucien Vandenbroucke, May 18, 1984, in U.S. Congress, Senate, *Alleged Assassination Plots*, and Thomas Powers, "Inside the Department of Dirty Tricks," *Atlantic Monthly* CCXLIV (August 1979), p. 40.

48 Nitze Report, quoted in Schoultz, *That Infernal Little Cuban Republic*, p. 172.

49 Branch and Crile, "The Kennedy Vendetta," p. 50.

50 McNamara testimony, July 11, 1975, in U.S. Congress, Senate, *Alleged Assassination Plots*, p. 158.

51 Corn, *Blond Ghost*, is a comprehensive biography of Shackley. Chapter 4 details the period during which he directed the Miami station.

52 Branch and Crile, "The Kennedy Vendetta," pp. 51–2. Rodriguez confirms the immense, and unique, nature of the Miami operation: "Miami station was the only full-service CIA operation ever based in the continental United States … In the mid-sixties, it had hundreds of employees … Scores of safe houses and literally hundreds of Cuban exiles like me who worked as agents for our American case officers" (Rodriguez and Weisman, *Shadow Warrior*, pp. 100–1).

53 Rodriguez and Weisman, *Shadow Warrior*, p. 52.

54 Branch and Crile, "The Kennedy Vendetta," p. 56.

55 Branch and Crile, "The Kennedy Vendetta," p. 58.

56 U.S. Congress, Senate, *Alleged Assassination Plots*, p. 140.

57 SGA Minutes, August 10, 1962, in U.S. Congress, Senate, *Alleged Assassination Plots*, p. 163.

58 Corn, *Blond Ghost*, p. 87. He cites declassified CIA memoranda by John McCone and McGeorge Bundy.

59 Garthoff, *Reflections on the Cuban Missile Crisis*, pp. 16–18. He cites U.S. Congress, Senate, *Alleged Assassination Plots*, pp. 139–43; Prados, *Presidents' Secret Wars*, pp. 210–13; and Schlesinger, *Robert Kennedy and His Times*, pp. 477–80 for general information on MONGOOSE; and the Central Intelligence Agency, "Memorandum of MONGOOSE Meeting Held on Thursday, October 4, 1962" (now declassified), cited in Prados, *Presidents' Secret Wars*, p. 213 and U.S. Congress, Senate, *Alleged Assassination Plots*, p. 147, for the October 4th meeting.

60 Corn, *Blond Ghost*, p. 62. The two were captured and confessed essentially the same story that Martínez corroborated to Crile and Branch 10 years later. See Corn, p. 90n.

61 Garthoff, *Reflections on the Cuban Missile Crisis*, pp. 78–9. He cites the translation of the letter cabled to Washington by the United Nations (telegram no. 1802, USUN to State, November 15, 1962, p. 3, Secret; now declassified).

62 Memo by Helms, 10/16/62, in U.S. Congress, Senate, *Alleged Assassination Plots*, p. 146; Gilpatric testimony, July 8, 1975, in U.S. Congress, Senate, *Alleged Assassination Plots*, p. 159.

63 See Chang and Kornbluh, *The Cuban Missile Crisis, 1962*.

64 Some of the publications that resulted from this movement include Blight and Welch, *On the Brink*; Blight, *The Shattered Crystal Ball*; Allyn, Blight, and Welch, *Back to the Brink* and *Cuba On the Brink*.

65 Several online collections of documents are available, at the JFK Library, www.jfklibrary.org/Historical+Resources/JFK+in+History/Cuban+Missile+Crisis.htm; the National Security Archive (including declassified Cuban, Soviet, and Eastern bloc documents), www.gwu.edu/~nsarchiv/nsa/cuba_mis_cri/index.htm; and at the Library of Congress, www.loc.gov/exhibits/archives/colc.html.

66 Schoultz, *That Infernal Little Cuban Republic*, pp. 186–7.

67 McNamara, "Forty Years after Thirteen Days" and "A Conversation in Havana"; Schoultz, *That Infernal Little Cuban Republic*, p. 187.

68 Alfredo Prieto, personal communication, January 2010.

69 Landsdale Memo, October 30, 1962; Bundy testimony, July 11, 1975, in U.S. Congress, Senate, *Alleged Assassination Plots*, pp. 148, 170. See Corn, *Blond Ghost*, p. 94, for the role of the Missile Crisis in MONGOOSE's demise. Bundy testimony, July 11, 1975, in U.S. Congress, Senate, *Alleged Assassination Plots*, p. 170.

70 Memorandum for the Special Group, June 19, 1963, in U.S. Congress, Senate, *Alleged Assassination Plots*, p. 173. CIA Review Staff to Select Committee, July

11, 1975, in U.S. Congress, Senate, *Alleged Assassination Plots*, p. 173; Ayers, *The War that Never Was*, pp. 100, 147–8, 166; Corn, *Blond Ghost*, pp. 103, 109–29.

71 This episode is described in U.S. Congress, Senate, *Alleged Assassination Plots*, pp. 86–90, and Escalante, *CIA Targets Fidel*, pp. 78–103.

72 Escalante, *CIA Targets Fidel*, p. 90.

73 Escalante, *CIA Targets Fidel*, pp. 97–102.

74 McClintock, *Instruments of Statecraft*, p. 205, citing Marchetti and Marks, *The CIA and the Cult of Intelligence*, p. 290n; and Powers, *The Man who Kept the Secrets*, p. 199.

75 Memorandum of the Special Group, April 7, 1964, in U.S. Congress, Senate, *Alleged Assassination Plots*, p. 177.

76 Corn, *Blond Ghost*, pp. 111–12, citing declassified CIA documents. Ayers was told that his commando group would be "given a security debriefing and be terminated with one month's pay in advance" (Ayers, *The War that Never Was*, p. 197). He himself was given the option of continuing to work with infiltration teams, but only for intelligence gathering, as commando operations were being phased out (p. 206).

77 Corn describes some of the later crimes committed by Cuban former CIA assets (*Blond Ghost*, pp. 117–18).

78 Marks, *The Search for the "Manchurian Candidate,"* pp. 197–8.

79 Garthoff, *Détente and Confrontation*, p. 88.

80 Ronald Reagan, "Address to the Nation on the Situation in Nicaragua," March 16, 1986. Ronald Reagan Presidential Library, www.reagan.utexas.edu/archives/speeches/1986/31686a.htm.

81 *New York Times*, December 12, 1964.

82 Stein, "Inside Omega 7." This "murderous legacy" is also described in Hinckle and Turner, *Deadly Secrets*, chapter 10.

83 Dinges and Landau, *Assassination on Embassy Row*, p. 251.

84 Dinges and Landau, *Assassination on Embassy Row*, p. 251n.

85 Stein, "Inside Omega 7."

86 For example, Garfield and Santana, "The impact of the economic crisis and the U.S. embargo on health in Cuba"; Kirkpatrick, "Role of the USA in Shortage of Food and Medicine in Cuba"; Kuntz, "The Politics of Suffering"; American Association of World Health, *Denial of Food and Medicine.*

Chapter 4

1 Portes and Stepick, *City on the Edge*, p. 100.

2 Domínguez, "Cuba since 1959," p. 100.

3 Pérez, *Between Reform and Revolution*, p. 266.

4 Pew Hispanic Center, Fact Sheet, "Cubans in the United States," August 25, 2006.

5 García, "Exiles, Immigrants, and Transnationals," p. 149.

6 García, *Havana USA*, p. 14.

7 Chomsky, *They Take Our Jobs!*, p. 68.

8 García, *Havana USA*, p. 23. On Operation Peter Pan, see also Torres, *The Lost Apple* and Conde, *Operation Pedro Pan*. Both of these authors were "Peter Pan children" themselves, who went on to study and write about the events that had shaped their own lives.

9 Portes and Stepick, *City on the Edge*, p. 17.

10 Masud-Piloto, *From Welcomed Exiles to Illegal Immigrants*, pp. 80–3.

11 García, *Havana USA*, pp. 93–4.

12 Sawyer, *Racial Politics in Post-Revolutionary Cuba*, p. 160.

13 Portes and Stepick, *City on the Edge*, p. 33.

14 Portes and Stepick, *City on the Edge*, p. 139.

15 Portes and Stepick, *City on the Edge*, p. 33.

16 Quoted in Gleijeses, "Cuba's First Venture in Africa," p. 161.

17 Fanon, *Black Skin, White Masks* and *The Wretched of the Earth*; James, *The Black Jacobins*; Williams, *Capitalism and Slavery*; Rodney, *How Europe Underdeveloped Africa*.

18 Parascandola, *Look for Me All Around You*, p. 2.

19 "Introduction," in Brock and Castañeda Fuertes, *Between Race and Empire*, pp. 1–2.

20 Gosse, *Where the Boys Are*, pp. 121, 123, 151.

21 Marable, "Race and Revolution in Cuba," p. 91.

22 Marable, "Race and Revolution in Cuba," p. 90.

23 Gleijeses, "Moscow's Proxy," p. 98.

24 See Risquet, "La epopeya de Cuba en Africa Negra," p. 104.

25 Dominguez, "Cuba's Foreign Policy."

26 Gleijeses, "Moscow's Proxy," pp. 103, 144.

27 See Moore, *Castro, the Blacks, and Africa*.

28 Gleijeses, *Conflicting Missions*, p. 392; "Moscow's Proxy," p. 98. See also Falk, "Cuba in Africa."

29 Zimmermann, *Sandinista*, p. 9.

30 Domínguez, *To Make a World Safe for Revolution*, p. 4.

31 Gleijeses, *Conflicting Missions*, pp. 31, 32.

32 Gleijeses *Conflicting Missions*, p. 392.

33 Feinsilver, *Healing the Masses*, p. 157 and Feinsilver, "Cuban Medical Diplomacy."

34 Ospina, "Cuba Exports Health"; Chávez, "Cuban Doctors Help Treat Injured."

35 Feinsilver, "Cuban Medical Diplomacy."

36 Feinsilver, "Cuban Medical Diplomacy."

Chapter 5

1 Bunck, *Quest for a Revolutionary Culture in Cuba*, p. xi.
2 Fernandes, *Cuba Represent!*, p. 2.
3 Bunck, *Quest for a Revolutionary Culture*, p. 42; Fagen, *Transformation of Political Culture*, p. 17.
4 Bunck, *Quest for a Revolutionary Culture*, p. 17.
5 Fagen, *Transformation of Political Culture*, p. 67.
6 Craven, *Art and Revolution in Latin America*, p. 85.
7 Domínguez, *Cuba: Order and Revolution*, p. 198.
8 Fernandes, *Cuba Represent!*, p. 3.
9 González Echevarría, "Criticism and Literature," pp. 154–5.
10 Carpentier, "On the Marvelous Real in America," p. 85.
11 Carpentier, "On the Marvelous Real in America," p. 83.
12 González Echevarría, "Criticism and Literature," p. 169.
13 Smorkaloff, *Readers and Writers in Cuba*, pp. 73, 102, 155.
14 Reina María Hernández, "One Hundred Years of Solitude: The Most Popular Book at the Havana Book Fair," cubanow.net, www.cubanow.cult.cu/pages/loader.php?sec=7&t=2&item=4327.
15 Luis, "Lunes de Revolución y la Revolución de Lunes."
16 Luis, "Lunes de Revolución y la Revolución de Lunes."
17 "In Hard Times," in Padilla, *Fuera del juego*, p. 130.
18 Padura, *Havana Black: A Lieutenant Mario Conde Mystery*, p. 12.
19 Burgos, "The Story of a Testimonio," p. 53.
20 González Echevarría, "Criticism and Literature," p. 161.
21 Craven, *Art and Revolution in Latin America*, p. 81.
22 Berthier, "Memorias del subdesarrollo/Memories of Underdevelopment," pp. 99, 100.
23 López and Humy, "Sergio Giral on Filmmaking in Cuba," in Martin, *Cinemas of the Black Diaspora*, p. 277. Originally published in *Black Film Review* 3:1 (1986–1987), 4–6.
24 "La pasión del cine: conversando de esto y aquello con Sergio Giral," n.d., Ediciones La Gota de Agua, www.edicioneslagotadeagua.com/Archivo/entrevistaconser.html.
25 Fernandes, *Cuba Represent!*, pp. 118–19.
26 Roberto Zurbano, cited in Fernandes, *Cuba Represent!*, p. 120.
27 Fernandes, *Cuba Represent!*, p. 122.
28 Wunderlich, "Hip Hop Pushes the Limits," pp. 70–71.
29 Pettavino and Pye, *Sport in Cuba*.
30 Interview with the International Association of Athletics Federations, www2.iaaf.org/insideiaaf/Structure/Council/JuantorenaBis.html.

31 Anderson, "Sports of the Times: El Duque's Man Stashes Two More."
32 PBS, "Stealing Home: The Case of Contemporary Cuban Baseball," www.pbs.org/stealinghome/debate/defections.html#mot.
33 Campoy, "Dancers Who Stretch the Limits," p. 96.
34 www.folkcuba.cult.cu/history.htm.
35 Daniel, *Dancing Wisdom*, p. 47.
36 Campoy, "Dancers Who Stretch the Limits," p. 98–9.
37 Campoy, "Dancers Who Stretch the Limits," pp. 99, 102–3.
38 Hernández and Dilla, "Political Culture and Popular Participation," p. 38.
39 Blanco, *Talking About Revolution*, p. 65.
40 Azcuy, "Democracia y derechos humanos," p. 47.
41 Valdés, "Democracia y sistema político," p. 54.
42 Valdés, "Democracia y sistema político," p. 56.
43 Dilla Alfonso, "¿Cuál es la democracia deseable?," p. 186.
44 Valdés, "Democracia y sistema político," pp. 48–9.
45 Prieto, "Made in América," p. 11.
46 Blanco, *Talking About Revolution*, pp. 54–6.
47 Blanco, *Talking About Revolution*, p. 65.
48 Suárez Salazar, "El sistema electoral cubano: apuntes para una crítica," pp. 215, 216, 213.
49 Dilla Alfonso, "¿Cuál es la democracia deseable?," p. 186.
50 Azcuy Henríquez, "Estado y sociedad civil en Cuba," p. 108.
51 Azcuy Henríquez, "Estado y sociedad civil en Cuba," p. 107.
52 Benjamin, Collins, and Scott, *No Free Lunch*, pp. 7–8.
53 Alfredo Prieto, personal communication, January 2010.
54 Perez, *Caring for Them from Birth to Death*, p. 125.
55 Benjamin, Collins, and Scott, *No Free Lunch*, p. 114.

Chapter 6

1   de la Fuente, *A Nation for All*, pp. 262, 263.
2   Serviat, "Solutions to the Black Problem," p. 89.
3   Moore, "Black Music in a Raceless Society," p. 8.
4   Gosse, "The African American Press Greets the Cuban Revolution," pp. 277–8.
5   Clytus, *Black Man in Red Cuba*, pp. 157–8.
6   Brent, *Long Time Gone*, p. 145.
7   Brent, *Long Time Gone*, pp. 150, 151.
8   Brent, *Long Time Gone*, p. 203.
9   Brent, *Long Time Gone*, p. 174.
10 Sawyer, *Racial Politics in Post-Revolutionary Cuba*, p. 100.
11 Kainz and Vernon-Feagans, "The ecology of early reading development for children in poverty." See also Kozol, *The Shame of the Nation*; Frankenberg, Lee,

and Orfield, *A Multiracial Society with Segregated Schools*; Orfield and Lee, *Why Segregation Matters*; Orfield and Yun, *Resegregation in American Schools*.

12   de la Fuente, "Race and Discrimination in Cuba's Special Period," p. 319.

13   de la Fuente, "Race and Discrimination in Cuba's Special Period," p. 319.

14   de la Fuente, "Race and Discrimination in Cuba's Special Period," p. 319.

15   Moore, *Castro, the Blacks, and Africa*, p. 16.

16   Sawyer, *Racial Politics in Post-Revolutionary Cuba*, p. xx.

17   Moore, *Castro, the Blacks and Africa*, p. 28.

18   Sawyer, *Racial Politics in Post-Revolutionary Cuba*, p. 6.

19   Smith and Padula, *Sex and Revolution*, p. 45.

20   Randall, *To Change the World*, pp. 103–4.

21   Family Code, Article 27.

22   Smith and Padula, *Sex and Revolution*, chapters 8–9.

23   Safa, *The Myth of the Male Breadwinner*, p. 154.

24   Smith and Padula, *Sex and Revolution*, p. 133.

25   Benjamin, Collins and Scott, *No Free Lunch*, p. 28.

26   The American Psychological Association defined homosexuality as a psychiatric disorder until 1973. Despite the prominence of a gay rights movement in the United States, the United States did not completely decriminalize homosexuality until 2003, and continues to defend discriminatory practices in marriage, the military, etc. As late as December, 2008, the United States had refused to sign a UN declaration calling for the decriminalization of homosexuality, though President Obama reversed this decision in July 2009.

27   Lumsden, *Machos, Maricones and Gays*, p. 29.

28   Lancaster, *Life Is Hard*, p. 238.

29   Lekus, "Queer Harvests," p. 255.

30   Lockwood, *Castro's Cuba, Cuba's Fidel*, p. 107.

31   Smith and Padula, *Sex and Revolution*, p. 39.

32   Bunck, *Fidel Castro and the Quest for a Revolutionary Culture in Cuba*, p. 135.

33   Valdés, *Dear First Love*. See also Espin, "Leaving the Nation and Joining the Tribe."

34   See especially his oral history, José Barreiro, *Panchito: cacique de montaña*.

35   See Barnet, *Afro-Cuban Religions*.

36   See Yaremko, *U.S. Protestant Missions in Cuba*.

37   Pérez states that by the 1950s, 400,000 Cubans were Protestants, and there were more Protestant churches and ministers than Catholic churches and priests on the island. Margaret Crahan, however, cites studies from 1957 and 1960 showing that between 50 and 75 percent of Cubans identified themselves as Catholics, and less than 10 percent as Protestants. Pérez, *Cuba and the United States: Ties of Singular Intimacy*; Crahan, "Cuba: Religion and Revolutionary Institutionalization," p. 321.

38   Article 54 of the Constitution.

39   See, for example, Gonzalez, *Afro-Cuban Theology*.

40 Pixley, "Baptists and Liberation Theology".
41 For further details on Suárez and the Centro, see Institute for Human Rights and Responsibilities, "Centro Memorial Martin Luther King, Jr., in Havana, Cuba," www.kingiannonviolence.info/cmmlk.html, and the Center's own website, www.cmlk.com, especially the section on the history of the Ebenezer Baptist Church.

Chapter 7

1   The dollar stores operated on the principle of a 140 percent markup on all items sold. See Eckstein, "Dollarization and its Discontents," p. 320.
2   Eckstein, "Dollarization and its Discontents, p. 313.
3   Dilla Alfonso, "Cuba: The Changing Scenarios of Governability," p. 65.
4   Enríquez, "Economic Reform and Repeasantization," p. 204.
5   Corrales, "The Gatekeeper State," p. 50. Uriarte says 73 percent were employed in the state sector in 2000 (Uriarte, "Social Policy Responses").
6   Díaz-Briquets and Pérez-López, *Corruption in Cuba*, p. 97.
7   Eckstein, "Dollarization and its Discontents," p. 321.
8   Mesa-Lago, *Economic and Social Disparities*, pp. 3, 4.
9   Uriarte, "Social Policy Responses," p. 110.
10 Eckstein, "Dollarization and its Discontents," p. 325.
11 Uriarte, "Social Policy Responses," p. 109.
12 Eckstein, "Dollarization and its Discontents," p. 325; Uriarte, "Social Impact of the Economic Measures," p. 289; Uriarte, "Social Policy Responses," p. 112.
13 Uriarte, "Social Policy Responses," p. 106.
14 Monreal, "Development as an Unfinished Affair," p. 75.
15 Feinsilver, "Cuban Medical Diplomacy."
16 Uriarte, "Social Policy Responses," pp. 116, 117.
17 Uriarte, "Social Policy Responses," pp. 115–16.
18 Corrales, "The Gatekeeper State," pp. 44, 45.
19 Corrales, "The Gatekeeper State," p. 45.
20 Uriarte, "Social Policy Responses," p. 109.
21 Ritter and Rowe, "Cuba: From 'Dollarization' to 'Euroization' or 'Peso Reconsolidation?'"
22 Mesa-Lago, *Economic and Social Disparities*, p. 4.
23 Mesa-Lago, *Economic and Social Disparities*, p. 6.
24 Corrales, "The Gatekeeper State," pp. 57, 59.
25 Enríquez, "Economic Reform and Repeasantization," p. 206.
26 Rossett and Benjamin, *The Greening of the Revolution*.
27 Enríquez, 'Economic Reform and Repeasantization," p. 216.
28 Díaz-Briquets and Pérez-López, *Conquering Nature*.
29 Whittle and Rey Santos, "Protecting Cuba's Environment," p. 77.
30 Whittle and Rey Santos, "Protecting Cuba's Environment," p. 84.

31 Houck, "Thinking about Tomorrow".
32 Eckstein, "Dollarization and its Discontents," p. 323. In the 2000 census, 84 percent of the over one million Cubans in the United States identified as white. See Blue, "The Erosion of Racial Equality in the Context of Cuba's Dual Economy," p. 57.
33 See McGarrity and Cárdenas, "Cuba"; de la Fuente and Glasco, "Are Blacks 'Getting Out of Control'?"; Pérez Sarduy, "¿Qué tienen los negros en Cuba?"
34 Blue, "The Erosion of Racial Equality," pp. 46–7.
35 Htun, "Gender Equality in Transition Policies," p. 137.
36 Shayne, *The Revolution Question*, p. 143.
37 Fusco, "Hustling for Dollars," p. 157.
38 Fusco, "Hustling for Dollars," p. 165.
39 Human Rights Watch, "Cuba: Repression," p. 7.
40 Daniel Williams, "Suddenly, the Welcome Mat Says 'You're Illegal,'" *Washington Post*, August 20, 1994.
41 "12,000 Remain at Guantánamo," *Washington Post*, August 19, 1995.
42 José Pertierra, "The Cuban Five: A Cold War Case in a Post-Cold War World, *Counterpunch* (July 10–12, 2009), www.counterpunch.org/pertierra07102009.html.
43 Tom Miller commentary on Latino USA, KUT Radio, Austin, Texas, May 5, 2006. Podcast available at www.utexas.edu/coc/kut/latinousa/stationservices/podcast/2006/05/0505_06_lusa_podcast.mp3. Transcript by Walter Lippman available at www.walterlippmann.com/docs608.html.
44 Stephenson, "International Educational Flows between the United States and Cuba (1959–2005)," p. 139.
45 Although this is still a relatively rare phenomenon, see Smith and Morales Domínguez, *Subject to Solution*; Coatsworth and Hernández, *Culturas encontradas*; Dominguez and Hernández, *U.S.-Cuba Relations in the 1990s*; Dominguez, Pérez Villanueva and Barberia, *The Cuban Economy at the Start of the Twenty-First Century* (Harvard University Press, 2004); Tulchin *et al.*, *Changes in Cuban Society since the 1990s*.
46 Dilla, "Changing Scenarios of Governability," p. 61.
47 Díaz-Briquets and Pérez-López, *Corruption in Cuba*, pp. 111–13.
48 "Report of the Cuban Communist Party (PCC) Politburo approved at the fifth PCC Central Committee plenum on 24 March; read by Army General Raul Castro." FBIS Translated Text, March 28, 1996.
49 Randall, *To Change the World*, p. 111.
50 Randall, *To Change the World*, p. 112.
51 *Reforma*, May 14, 1996.
52 Mimi Whitefield and Juan O. Tamayo, Knight-Ridder News Service, "Raúl Castro's attack on intellectuals stirs backlash," May 6, 1996.
53 Whitefield and Tamayo, "Raúl Castro's attack on intellectuals stirs backlash."
54 See IPS, "Inusual debate sobre la prostitución abre órgano de prensa," April 22, 1996.

Chapter 8

1   "Violenta crítica de Raúl Castro contra académicos y periodistas," *La Jornada* [Mexico], March 28, 1996. www.jornada.unam.mx/1996/03/28/cuba.html.

2   Javier Corrales called 1993–95 "the peak of economic reform." See Corrales, "The Gatekeeper State."

3   Mesa-Lago, *The Cuban Economy Today*, p. 25.

4   Pérez-López, "Rectification Redux? Cuban Economic Policy at the End of 2005," p. 1.

5   Pérez-López, "The Cuban Economy in 2005–2006," p. 13.

6   Mesa-Lago, *The Cuban Economy Today*, p. 25.

7   González Corzo, "Cuba's De-Dollarization Program," p. 59.

8   Mesa-Lago, *The Cuban Economy Today*, p. 27.

9   Díaz-Briquets and Pérez-López, *Corruption in Cuba*, p. 18.

10   Corrales, "The Gatekeeper State," p. 48.

11   Mesa-Lago, *The Cuban Economy Today*, p. 29.

12   See Pérez-López, "The Cuban Economy in 2005–2006," p. 10.

13   Corrales, "The Gatekeeper State," pp. 36, 46.

14   Ritter, "Cuba's Strategic Economic Re-orientation," p. 140.

15   See, for example, the essays by Pedro Monreal and Julio Carranza in Monreal (ed.), *Development Prospects in Cuba.*

16   Ritter, "Cuba's Strategic Economic Re-orientation," pp. 147–9.

17   Ritter, "Cuba's Strategic Economic Re-orientation," p. 148.

18   González, "A New 'Cold War'?" p. 65.

19   Ritter, "Cuba's Strategic Economic Re-orientation," p. 151.

20   Díaz-Briquets and Pérez-López, *Corruption in Cuba*, p. 129.

21   Benjamin, Collins and Scott, *No Free Lunch*, p. 46.

22   Mesa-Lago, *The Cuban Economy Today*, pp. 30–1.

23   Mesa-Lago, *The Cuban Economy Today*, pp. 13–14.

24   Mesa-Lago, *The Cuban Economy Today*, p. 14.

25   Díaz-Briquets and Pérez-López, *Corruption in Cuba*, pp. 114–15.

26   Lumsden, *Machos, Maricones, and Gays*, p. 102.

27   Wintz, "The Church in Cuba."

28   Catholic Relief Services, "Cuba," http://crs.org/cuba/.

29   Hagedorn, *Divine Utterances*, chap. 9; Catherine Bremer, "Santería Lures Tourist Cash to Cuba," www.reuters.com/article/idUSN2936782720070507.

30   Martínez Furé, "Modas y modos: pseudofolklorismo y folklor," p. 24.

31   Fernandes, *Cuba Represent!*, p. 46.

32   Stock, *On Location in Cuba*, p. 15, 16.

33   www.oswaldopaya.org/es/up/VARELA%20PROJECT.pdf.

34   "Press Conference by Foreign Minister," www.granma.cu/documento/ingles03/012.html.

35 Dilla, "The Changing Scenarios of Governability," p. 66.
36 International Republican Institute, "Cuban Public Opinion Survey, March 14–April 12, 2008," www.iri.org/lac/cuba/pdfs/2008%20June%205%20Survey%20of%20Cuban%20Public%20Opinion,%20March%2014-April%2012,%202008.pdf.
37 Mesa-Lago, *The Cuban Economy Today*, p. 20.
38 Glionna, "Bush's Cuban American Support May Be Slipping."
39 Bustillo and Williams, "Cuban Americans' Attitudes Shift."
40 Eckstein, *Back from the Future*, pp. 95–6.
41 Feinsilver, "Cuban Medical Diplomacy."
42 Mesa-Lago, "The Cuban Economy in 2006–2007," p. 10.
43 Roig-Franzia, "Raul Castro Urges Students to Debate 'Fearlessly,'" *Washington Post*, December 22, 2006.
44 The Lexington Institute's Philip Peters, quoted in Tim Padgett, "Hints of More Reform in Cuba," *Time* (April 30, 2008), www.time.com/time/world/article/0,8599,1736186,00.html. As of early 2010, though, the Congress had still not been held or scheduled.
45 Ballvé, "On the 50th Anniversary of the Cuban Revolution, Obama should signal an end to the embargo," *The Progressive*, December 29, 2008, www.progressive.org/mp/balve122908.html.
46 CNN, "Poll: Three-quarters favor relations with Cuba," April 10, 2009, www.cnn.com/2009/POLITICS/04/10/poll.cuba/.
47 Freedom House, "Another 'Special Period' in Cuba? How Cuban Citizens View their Country's Future," March 25, 2009, www.freedomhouse.org/template.cfm?page=383&report=78.
48 Alfredo Jam, Director of Macroeconomic Analysis at the Ministry of the Economy and Planning, quoted in Nick Miroff, "Cubans Face Dire Formula," *Global Post*, June 25, 2009, www.globalpost.com/dispatch/the-americas/090624/cuba-economy?page=0,1.
49 Lacey, "In Cuba, Hopeful Tenor Toward Obama is Ebbing."

Conclusion

1 Amnesty International, "The U.S. Embargo Against Cuba," www.amnesty.org/en/library/asset/AMR25/007/2009/en/7859386a-e9b2-431c-acf7-e0610b7aba9f/amr250072009en.pdf.

Bibliography

Adorno, Rolena. "Havana and Macondo: The Humanities in U.S. Latin American Studies, 1940–2000." In *The Humanities and the Dynamics of Inclusion Since World War II*, edited by David A. Hollinger. Baltimore: Johns Hopkins University Press, 2006.

Allyn, Bruce J., James G. Blight, and David A. Welch. *Back to the Brink: The Moscow Conference on the Cuban Missile Crisis*. Lanham, MD: University Press of America, 1991.

Allyn, Bruce J., James G. Blight, and David A. Welch. *Cuba on the Brink: Fidel Castro, the Missile Crisis and the Collapse of Communism*. New York: Pantheon, 1993.

American Association of World Health. *Denial of Food and Medicine. The Impact of the U.S. Embargo on Health and Nutrition in Cuba*. Washington, DC: American Association of World Health, 1997.

Amnesty International. "The U.S. Embargo Against Cuba: Its Impact on Economic and Social Rights." Amnesty International Publications, 2009.

Anderson, Dave. "Sports of the Times: El Duque's Man Stashes Two More." *New York Times*, February 11, 1999.

Ayers, Bradley Earl. *The War that Never Was: An Insider's Account of CIA Covert Operations against Cuba*. Indianapolis: Bobbs Merrill, 1976.

Azcuy, Hugo. "Democracia y derechos humanos." In *Cuba en las Américas: una perspectiva sobre Cuba y los problemas hemisféricos*, edited by Centro de Estudios sobre América. Havana: Centro de Estudios sobre América, 1995.

Azcuy Henríquez, Hugo. "Estado y sociedad civil en Cuba." *Temas* 4 (1995).

Barnet, Miguel. *Afro-Cuban Religions*. Princeton: Markus Wiener, 2001.

Barreiro, José. *Panchito: cacique de montaña*. Santiago de Cuba: Ediciones Catedral, 2001.

Bemis, Samuel Flagg. *The Latin American Policy of the United States: An Historical Interpretation*. New York: Harcourt, Brace, 1943.

Benjamin, Jules R. *The United States and the Origins of the Cuban Revolution: An Empire of Liberty in an Age of National Liberation*. Princeton: Princeton University Press, 1990.

Benjamin, Medea, Joseph Collins, and Michael Scott. *No Free Lunch: Food and Revolution in Cuba Today*. San Francisco: Institute for Food and Development Policy, 1984.

Bergad, Laird W., Fe Iglesias García, and María del Carmen Barcia. *The Cuban Slave Market, 1790–1880*. Cambridge: Cambridge University Press, 1995.

Berthier, Nancy. "Memorias del subdesarrollo/Memories of Underdevelopment." In *The Cinema of Latin America*, edited by Alberto Elena and María Díaz López. London: Wallflower Press, 2003, pp. 99–108.

Black, Jan Knippers. "Introduction: Understanding the Persistence of Inequity." In *Latin America, its Problems and its Promise: A Multidisciplinary Introduction*, 4th ed. Edited by Jan Knippers Black. Boulder: Westview Press, 2005.

Blanco, Juan Antonio, with Medea Benjamin. *Cuba: Talking About Revolution*. Melbourne, Australia: Ocean Press, 1994.

Blight, James G. *The Shattered Crystal Ball: Fear and Learning in the Cuban Missile Crisis*. Savage, MD: Rowman and Littlefield, 1990.

Blight, James G., and David A. Welch. *On the Brink: Americans and Soviets Reexamine the Cuban Missile Crisis*. New York: Hill and Wang, 1989.

Blue, Sarah A. "The Erosion of Racial Equality in the Context of Cuba's Dual Economy." *Latin American Politics & Society* 49:3 (Fall 2007), 35–68.

Blum, William. *Killing Hope: U.S. Military and CIA Interventions Since World War II*. Updated ed., Monroe, ME: Common Courage Press, 2008.

Bolívar, Simón. *Selected Writings of Bolívar*, vol. II, compiled by Vicente Lecuna and edited by Harold A. Bierck, Jr. London: Colonial Press, 1951.

Bonsal, Philip Wilson. *Cuba, Castro, and the United States*. Pittsburgh: University of Pittsburgh Press, 1971.

Bourne, Peter G. *Fidel: A Biography of Fidel Castro*. New York: Dodd, Mead and Company, 1986.

Branch, Taylor, and George Crile III. "The Kennedy Vendetta: How the CIA Waged a Silent War against Cuba." *Harpers Magazine* CCLI (August 1975).

Brent, William Lee. *Long Time Gone: A Black Panther's True-Life Story of His Hijacking and Twenty-Five Years in Cuba*. New York: Random House/Times Books, 1996.

Brock, Lisa, and Digna Castañeda Fuertes, eds. *Between Race and Empire: African-Americans and Cubans before the Cuban Revolution*. Philadelphia: Temple University Press, 1998.

Brunendius, Claes. *Revolutionary Cuba: The Challenge of Economic Growth with Equity*. Boulder: Westview Press, 1984.

Bunck, Julie. *Fidel Castro and the Quest for a Revolutionary Culture in Cuba*. University Park: Penn State University Press, 1994.

Burgos, Elisabeth. "The Story of a Testimonio." *Latin American Perspectives* 26:6 (November 1999), 53–63.

Bustillo, Miguel and Williams, Carol J. "Cuban Americans' Attitudes Shift." *Los Angeles Times*, February 26, 2008.

Campoy, Ana. "Dancers Who Stretch the Limits." In *Capitalism, God, and a Good Cigar*, edited by Lydia Chávez. Durham: Duke University Press, 2005.

Carpentier, Alejo. "On the Marvelous Real in America." In *Magical Realism: Theory, History, Community*, edited by Wendy B. Faris and Lois Parkinson Zamora. Durham: Duke University Press, 2003.

Casal, Lourdes. "Literature and Society." In *Revolutionary Change in Cuba*, edited by Carmelo Mesa-Lago. Pittsburgh: University of Pittsburgh Press, 1971.

Castañeda, Jorge J. "Gone but Not Forgotten: Che's Ideology Outlived Him, to Devastating Effect." *Newsweek* (web edition), October 13, 2007.

Chang, Laurence, and Peter Kornbluh, eds. *The Cuban Missile Crisis, 1962: A National Security Archive Documents Reader*. 2nd ed. New York: The New Press, 1998.

Chávez, Juan Carlos. "Cuban Doctors Help Treat Injured." *Miami Herald*, January 23, 2010, www.miamiherald.com/news/americas/haiti/story/1441144.html.

Chomsky, Aviva. "'Barbados or Canada?' Race, Immigration, and Nation in Early Twentieth Century Cuba." *Hispanic American Historical Review* 80:3 (August 2000), 415–62.

Chomsky, Aviva. *They Take Our Jobs! And 20 Other Myths about Immigration*. Boston: Beacon Press, 2007.

Clytus, John. *Black Man in Red Cuba*. Coral Gables, FL: University of Miami Press, 1970.

Coatsworth, John H., and Rafael Hernández, eds. *Culturas encontradas: Cuba y los Estados Unidos*. Havana: Centro Juan Marinello and Cambridge: Harvard University Press, 2001.

Coltman, Leycester. *The Real Fidel Castro*. New Haven: Yale University Press, 2005.

Conde, Yvonne M. *Operation Pedro Pan: The Untold Exodus of 14,048 Cuban Children*. New York: Routledge, 1999.

Corbitt, Duvon C. "Cuban Revisionist Interpretations of Cuba's Struggle for Independence." *Hispanic American Historical Review* 43 (August 1963), 395–404.

Corn, David. *Blond Ghost*. New York: Simon and Schuster, 1994.

Corrales, Javier. "The Gatekeeper State: Limited Economic Reforms and Regime Survival in Cuba." *Latin American Research Review* 39:2 (2004), 35–65.

Crahan, Margaret E. "Cuba: Religion and Revolutionary Institutionalization." *Journal of Latin American Studies*, 17:2 (1985), 319–40.

Craven, David. "Cuban Art and Culture." In *Cuba: A Different America*, edited by Wilber A. Chaffee and Gary Prevost. Rev. ed. Lanham, MD: Rowman and Littlefield, 1992.

Craven, David. *Art and Revolution in Latin America, 1910–1990*. New Haven: Yale University Press, 2006.

Daniel, Yvonne. *Dancing Wisdom: Embodied Knowledge in Haitian Vodou, Cuban Yoruba, and Bahian Candomblé*. Champaign: University of Illinois Press, 2005.

Davis, Shelton H. *Victims of the Miracle: Development and the Indians of Brazil*. Cambridge: Cambridge University Press, 1977.

de la Fuente, Alejandro. *A Nation for All: Race, Inequality and Politics in Twentieth-Century Cuba.* Chapel Hill: University of North Carolina Press, 2001.

de la Fuente, Alejandro. "Recreating Racism: Race and Discrimination in Cuba's Special Period." In *A Contemporary Cuba Reader*, edited by Philip Brenner, Marguerite Rose Jiménez, John M. Kirk, and William M. LeoGrande. Lanham, MD: Rowman and Littlefield, 2007.

de la Fuente, Alejandro, and Laurence Glasco. "Are Blacks 'Getting Out of Control'? Racial Attitudes, Revolution, and Political Transition in Cuba." In *Toward a New Cuba? Legacies of a Revolution*, edited by Miguel A. Centeno and Mauricio Font. Boulder: Lynne Rienner, 1997.

DePalma, Anthony. *The Man Who Invented Fidel: Castro, Cuba, and Herbert L. Matthews of the New York Times.* New York: Public Affairs/Perseus, 2006.

Díaz-Briquets, Sergio, and Jorge Pérez-López. *Conquering Nature: The Environmental Legacy of Socialism in Cuba.* Pittsburgh: University of Pittsburgh Press, 2000.

Díaz-Briquets, Sergio, and Jorge Pérez-López. *Corruption in Cuba: Castro and Beyond.* Austin: University of Texas Press, 2006.

Dilla Alfonso, Haroldo. "¿Cuál es la democracia deseable?" In *La democracia en Cuba y el diferendo con los Estados Unidos*, edited by Haroldo Dilla Alfonso and William I. Robinson. Havana: Centro de Estudios sobre América, 1995.

Dilla Alfonso, Haroldo. "Cuba: The Changing Scenarios of Governability." *boundary 2* 29:3 (2002), 55–75.

Dinges, John, and Saul Landau. *Assassination on Embassy Row.* New York: Pantheon, 1980.

Domínguez, Jorge I. *Cuba: Order and Revolution.* Cambridge, MA: Harvard University Press, 1978.

Dominguez, Jorge I. "Cuba's Foreign Policy." *Foreign Affairs* (Fall 1978).

Domínguez, Jorge I. *To Make a World Safe for Revolution: Cuba's Foreign Policy.* Cambridge, MA: Harvard University Press, 1989.

Domínguez, Jorge I. "Cuba since 1959." In *Cuba: A Short History*, edited by Leslie Bethell. Cambridge: Cambridge University Press, 1993.

Dominguez, Jorge I., and Rafael Hernández, eds. *U.S.–Cuba Relations in the 1990s.* Boulder: Westview Press, 1989.

Dominguez, Jorge I., Omar Everleny Pérez Villanueva, and Lorena Barberia, eds. *The Cuban Economy at the Start of the Twenty-First Century.* Cambridge, MA: Harvard University Press, 2004.

Eckstein, Susan. *Back from the Future: Cuba under Castro.* New York: Routledge, 2003.

Eckstein, Susan. "Dollarization and its Discontents: Remittances and the Remaking of Cuba in the Post-Soviet Era." *Comparative Politics* 36:3 (April 2004), 313–30.

Enríquez, Laura. "Economic Reform and Repeasantization in Post-1990 Cuba." *Latin American Research Review* 38:1 (2003), 202–18.

Escalante, Fabián. *CIA Targets Fidel: The Secret Assassination Report.* Melbourne: Ocean Press, 2002.

Escalante, Fabián. *The Cuba Project: CIA Covert Operations 1959–1962*. Melbourne: Ocean Press, 2004.

Espin, Olivia M. "Leaving the Nation and Joining the Tribe: Lesbian Immigrants Crossing Geographical and Identity Borders." In *Sexualities*, edited by Marny Hall. Binghamton, NY: The Hayworth Press, 1996, pp. 99–107.

Everleny, Omar. "Ciudad de La Habana: desempeño económico y situación social." In *La economía cubana en el 2000: desempeño macro-económico y transformación empresarial*. Havana: CEEC, 2001.

Fagen, Richard R. *The Transformation of Political Culture in Cuba*. Stanford, CA: Stanford University Press, 1969.

Fagen, Richard R. "Studying Latin American Politics: Some Implications of a *Dependencia* Approach." *Latin American Research Review* 12:2 (1977), 3–26.

Fagen, Richard R. "Latin America and the Cold War: Oh For the Good Old Days?" *LASA Forum* 26 (1995), 5–11.

Falk, Pamela S. "Cuba in Africa." *Foreign Affairs* 65:5 (summer 1987), 1077–96.

Fanon, Frantz. *The Wretched of the Earth*. Translated by Richard Philcox, New York: Grove Press, 2004.

Fanon, Frantz. *Black Skin, White Masks*. Translated by Richard Philcox, New York: Grove Press, 2008.

Feinsilver, Julie. *Healing the Masses: Cuban Health Politics at Home and Abroad*. Berkeley: University of California Press, 1993.

Feinsilver, Julie. "Cuban Medical Diplomacy: Where the Left Got It Right." Council on Hemispheric Affairs, 2006, www.coha.org/2006/10/cuban-medical-diplomacy-when-the-left-has-got-it-right/.

Fernandes, Sujatha. *Cuba Represent! Cuban Arts, State Power, and the Making of New Revolutionary Cultures*. Durham: Duke University Press, 2006.

Ferrer, Ada. *Insurgent Cuba: Race, Nation, and Revolution, 1868–1898*. Chapel Hill: University of North Carolina Press, 1999.

Foner, Philip S. *The Spanish–Cuban–American War and the Birth of American Imperialism, 1895–1902* (Vols. 1, 2). New York: Monthly Review Press, 1972.

Fornet, Ambrosio. "El quinquenio gris: revisitando el término." *Criterios* (2006), 5, www.criterios.es/pdf/fornetquinqueniogris.pdf.

Frankenberg, E., C. Lee, and G. Orfield. *A Multiracial Society with Segregated Schools: Are We Losing the Dream?* Cambridge. MA: The Civil Rights Project at Harvard University, 2003.

Fusco, Coco. "Hustling for Dollars: *Jineterismo* in Cuba." In *Global Sex Workers: Rights, Resistance, and Redefinition*, edited by Kamala Kempadoo and Jo Doezema. New York: Routledge, 1998.

García, María Cristina. *Havana USA: Cuban Exiles and Cuban Americans in South Florida, 1959–1994*. Berkeley: University of California Press, 1996.

García, María Cristina. "Exiles, Immigrants, and Transnationals: The Cuban Communities of the United States." In *The Columbia History of Latinos in the*

United States since 1960, edited by David G. Gutiérrez. New York: Columbia University Press, 2006.

Garfield, Richard, and S. Santana. "The Impact of the Economic Crisis and the U.S. Embargo on Health in Cuba." *American Journal of Public Health* 87 (1997), 15–20.

Garthoff, Raymond L. *Reflections on the Cuban Missile Crisis*. Washington, DC: The Brookings Institution, 1987.

Garthoff, Raymond L. *Détente and Confrontation: American–Soviet Relations from Nixon to Reagan*. Rev. ed. Washington, DC: The Brookings Institution, 1994.

Gerassi, John. *Fidel Castro: A Biography*. Garden City, NY: Doubleday, 1973.

Geyer, Georgie Ann. *Guerrilla Prince: The Untold Story of Fidel Castro*. 3rd ed. Kansas City, MO: Andrews McMeel, 2001.

Gleijeses, Piero. "Cuba's First Venture in Africa: Algeria, 1961–1964." *Journal of Latin American Studies* 28:1 (1996), 159–95.

Gleijeses, Piero. *Conflicting Missions: Havana, Washington, and Africa, 1959–1976*. Chapel Hill: University of North Carolina Press, 2002.

Gleijeses, Piero. "Moscow's Proxy? Cuba and Africa, 1975–1988." *Journal of Cold War Studies* 8:4 (2006), 98–146.

Glionna, John M. "Bush's Cuban American Support May Be Slipping." *Los Angeles Times*, September 21, 2004.

Gonzalez, Michelle A. *Afro-Cuban Theology: Religion, Race, Culture and Identity*. Gainesville: University Press of Florida, 2006.

González, Mónica. "A New 'Cold War'?" *Berkeley Review of Latin American Studies* (Spring 2008), 65–7.

González Corzo, Mario A. "Cuba's De-Dollarization Program: Principal Characteristics and Possible Motivations." In Association for the Study of the Cuban Economy, *Cuba in Transition* 16. Proceedings of the Sixteenth Annual Meeting of the ASCE, August 2006.

González Echevarría, Roberto. "Criticism and Literature in Revolutionary Cuba." In *Cuba: Twenty-Five Years of Revolution, 1959–1984*, edited by Sandor Halebsky and John M. Kirk. New York: Praeger, 1985.

Gosse, Van. *Where the Boys Are: Cuba, Cold War America and the Making of a New Left*. London: Verso, 1993.

Gosse, Van. "The African American Press Greets the Cuban Revolution." In *Between Race and Empire: African-Americans and Cubans before the Cuban Revolution*, edited by Lisa Brock and Digna Castañeda Fuertes. Philadelphia: Temple University Press, 1998.

Hagedorn, Katherine J. *Divine Utterances: The Performance of Afro-Cuban Santería*. Washington, DC: Smithsonian Institution Press, 2001.

Hamilton, Nora. "The Cuban Economy: Dilemmas of Socialist Construction." In *Cuba: A Different America*, edited by Wilber A. Chaffee, Jr. and Gary Prevost. Lanham, MD: Rowman and Littlefield, 1989.

Healy, David. "One War from Two Sides: The Cuban Assessment of U.S.–Cuban Relations." *Cercles* 5 (2002), 31–8.

Helg, Aline. *Our Rightful Share: The Afro-Cuban Struggle for Equality, 1886–1912.* Chapel Hill: University of North Carolina Press, 1995.

Hernández, Rafael, and Haroldo Dilla. "Political Culture and Popular Participation." In *The Cuban Revolution into the 1990s: Cuban Perspectives*, edited by Centro de Estudios Sobre América. Boulder: Westview Press, 1992.

Hersh, Seymour M. *The Price of Power: Kissinger in the Nixon White House.* New York: Summit Books, 1984.

Hinckle, Warren and William W. Turner. *Deadly Secrets: The CIA–Mafia War against Castro and the Assassination of J.F.K.* New York: Thunder's Mouth Press, 1993.

Houck, Oliver A. "Thinking about Tomorrow: Cuba's 'Alternative Model' for Sustainable Development." *Tulane Environmental Law Journal* 16. Special Issue: *Environmental Law and Sustainable Development in 21st Century Cuba* (summer 2003), 521–32.

Htun, Mala. "Gender Equality in Transition Policies: Comparative Perspectives on Cuba." In *Looking Forward: Comparative Perspectives on Cuba's Transition*, edited by Marifeli Pérez-Stable. Notre Dame: University of Notre Dame Press, 2007.

Human Rights Watch. *Cuba: Repression, the Exodus of August 1994, and the U.S. Response.* New York: Human Rights Watch, 1994.

Hunt, E. Howard. *Give Us This Day.* New York: Arlington House, 1973.

James, C. L. R. *The Black Jacobins: Toussaint L'Ouverture and the San Domingo Revolution.* London: Secker and Warburg, 1938.

Janos, Leo. "The Last Days of the President." *Atlantic* (July 1973).

Jenks, Leland H. *Our Cuban Colony: A Study in Sugar.* New York: Vanguard Press, 1928.

Kainz, K., and Vernon-Feagans, L. "The Ecology of Early Reading Development for Children in Poverty." *The Elementary School Journal*, 107:5 (2007), 407–27.

Kirk, John, and Peter McKenna. "Trying to Address the Cuban Paradox." *Latin America Research Review* 34:2 (1999), 214–26.

Kirkpatrick, A. F. "Role of the USA in Shortage of Food and Medicine in Cuba." *The Lancet* 348 (1996), 1489–91.

Kohan, Nestor, and Nahuel Scherma. *Fidel: A Graphic Novel Life of Fidel Castro.* New York: Seven Stories Press, 2008.

Kornbluh, Peter, ed. *Bay of Pigs Declassified: The Secret CIA Report on the Invasion of Cuba.* New York: The New Press, 1998.

Kozol, Jonathan. *Children of the Revolution: A Yankee Teacher in the Cuban Schools.* New York: Dell, 1978.

Kozol, Jonathan. *The Shame of the Nation: The Restoration of Apartheid Schooling in America.* New York: Random House, 2005.

Kuntz, D. "The Politics of Suffering: The Impact of the U.S. Embargo on the Health of the Cuban People. Report of a Fact-Finding Trip to Cuba, June 6–11, 1993. *International Journal of Health Services* 24 (1994), 161–79.

Lacey, Marc. "In Cuba, Hopeful Tenor Toward Obama is Ebbing." *New York Times*, December 30, 2009.

Lancaster, Roger N. *Life Is Hard: Machismo, Danger, and the Intimacy of Power in Nicaragua*. Berkeley: University of California Press, 1993.

Leiner, Marvin. "The 1961 Cuban National Literacy Campaign." In *National Literacy Campaigns: Comparative and Historical Perspectives*, edited by Robert F. Arnove and Harvey J. Graff. New York: Plenum Press, 1987.

Lekus, Ian. "Queer Harvests: Homosexuality, the U.S. New Left, and the Venceremos Brigades to Cuba." In *Imagining Our Americas: Toward a Transnational Frame*, edited by Sandhya Rajendra Shukla and Heidi Tinsman. Durham: Duke University Press, 2007.

LeoGrande, Leo M., and Julie M. Thomas. "Cuba's Quest for Economic Independence." *Journal of Latin American Studies* 34:2 (May 2002), 325–63.

Leonard, Thomas M. *Fidel Castro: A Biography*. Westport, CT: Greenwood Press, 2004.

Liss, Sheldon B. *Roots of Revolution: Radical Thought in Cuba*. Lincoln: University of Nebraska Press, 1987.

Lockwood, Lee. *Castro's Cuba, Cuba's Fidel: An American Journalist's Inside Look at Today's Cuba in Text and Picture*. New York: Vintage Edition, 1967.

López, Ana M., and Nicholas Peter Humy. "Sergio Giral on Filmmaking in Cuba." In *Cinemas of the Black Diaspora: Diversity, Dependence, and Oppositionality*, edited by Michael T. Martin. Detroit: Wayne State University Press, 1995, pp. 274–80. Originally published in *Black Film Review* 3:1 (1986–87), 4–6.

Luis, William. "Lunes de Revolución y la Revolución de Lunes." *Otro Lunes: Revista Hispanoamericana de Cultura* 1, May 2007, www.otrolunes.com/hemeroteca-ol/numero-01/html/sumario/este-lunes/este-lunes-n01-a07-p01-200705.html.

Lumsden, Ian. *Machos, Maricones, and Gays: Cuba and Homosexuality*. Philadelphia: Temple University Press, 1996.

Lutjens, Sheryl L. "Restructuring Childhood in Cuba: The State as Family." In *Children in the Streets of the Americas*, edited by Roslyn Arlin Mickelson. New York: Routledge, 2000.

Marable, Manning. "Race and Revolution in Cuba: African American Perspectives." In *Dispatches from the Ebony Tower: Intellectuals Confront the African American Experience*, edited by Manning Marable. New York: Columbia University Press, 2000.

Marchetti, Victor, and John D. Marks. *The CIA and the Cult of Intelligence*. New York: Dell, 1974.

Marks, John. *The Search for the "Manchurian Candidate": The CIA and Mind Control, the Story of the Agency's Secret Efforts to Control Human Behavior*. New York: Times Books, 1979.

Martí, José. "Nuestra América." *El Partido Liberal (Mexico City)*, March 5, 1892.

Martínez Furé, Rogelio. "Modas y modos: pseudofolklorismo y folklor." Interview by Evangelina Chio, *Revolución y Cultura* 33:5 (September–October 1994), 32–5.

Masud-Piloto, Felix Roberto. *From Welcomed Exiles to Illegal Immigrants: Cuban Migration to the U.S., 1959–1995.* Lanham, MD: Rowman and Littlefield, 1996.

McClintock, Michael. *Instruments of Statecraft.* New York: Pantheon, 1992.

McGarrity, Gayle, and Osvaldo Cárdenas. "Cuba." In *No Longer Invisible: Afro-Latin Americans Today,* edited by Minority Rights Group. London: Minority Rights Publications, 1995, pp. 77–107.

McNamara, Robert S. "A Conversation in Havana." *Arms Control Today,* November 2002, www.armscontrol.org/act/2002_11/cubanmissile.

McNamara, Robert S. "Forty Years after Thirteen Days." *Arms Control Today,* November 2002, www.armscontrol.org/act/2002_11/cubanmissile.

Mesa-Lago, Carmelo. *Growing Economic and Social Disparities in Cuba: Impact and Recommendations for Change.* Miami: University of Miami Institute for Cuban and Cuban-American Studies/Cuba Transition Project, 2002.

Mesa-Lago, Carmelo. *The Cuban Economy Today: Salvation or Damnation?* Miami: University of Miami Institute for Cuban and Cuban-American Studies/Cuba Transition Project, 2005.

Monreal, Pedro. "Development as an Unfinished Affair: Cuba after the 'Great Adjustment' of the 1990s." *Latin American Perspectives* 29:3 (May 2002), 75–90.

Monreal, Pedro, ed. *Development Prospects in Cuba: An Agenda in the Making.* London: Institute of Latin American Studies, University of London, 2002.

Moore, Carlos. *Castro, the Blacks, and Africa.* Los Angeles: Center for Afro-American Studies, UCLA, 1988.

Moore, Robin. *Nationalizing Blackness: Afrocubanismo and Artistic Revolution in Havana, 1920–1940.* Pittsburgh: University of Pittsburgh Press, 1997.

Moore, Robin. "Black Music in a Raceless Society: Afro-Cuban Folklore and Socialism." *Cuban Studies* 37 (2006), 1–32.

Morley, Morris H. *Imperial State and Revolution: The United States and Cuba 1952–1986.* Cambridge: Cambridge University Press, 1987.

Nearing, Scott, and Joseph Freeman. *Dollar Diplomacy: A Study in American Imperialism.* New York: B. W. Heubsch and the Viking Press, 1925.

Opatrný, Josef. *U.S. Expansionism and Cuban Annexationism in the 1850s.* Lewiston, NY: E. Mellen Press, 1993.

Orfield, G., and C. Lee. *Why Segregation Matters: Poverty and Educational Inequality.* Cambridge, MA: The Civil Rights Project at Harvard University, 2005.

Orfield, G., and J. T. Yun. *Resegregation in American Schools.* Cambridge, MA: The Civil Rights Project at Harvard University, 1999.

Ortiz, Fernando. *Cuban Counterpoint: Tobacco and Sugar.* Translated by Harriet de Onis. New York: Alfred Knopf, 1947 Reprint ed. Durham, NC: Duke University Press, 1995.

Ospina, Hernando Calvo. "Cuba Exports Health." *Le Monde Diplomatique* International Edition, August 2006, http://mondediplo.com/2006/08/11cuba.

Padilla, Heberto. "Fuera del juego." Translated by Jorge Guitart. *Dissent Magazine* (spring 1973).

Padura, Leonardo. *Havana Black: A Lieutenant Mario Conde Mystery*. London: Bitter Lemon Press, 2006.

Parascandola, Louis J. *Look for Me All Around You: Anglophone Caribbean Immigrants in the Harlem Renaissance*. Detroit: Wayne State University Press, 2005.

Paterson, Thomas G. "Fixation with Cuba: The Bay of Pigs, Missile Crisis, and Covert War against Castro." In *Kennedy's Quest for Victory: American Foreign Policy, 1961–1963*, edited by Thomas G. Paterson. New York: Oxford University Press, 1989.

Paterson, Thomas G. *Contesting Castro: The United States and the Triumph of the Cuban Revolution*. New York: Oxford University Press, 1994.

Perez, Christina. *Caring for Them from Birth to Death: The Practice of Community-Based Cuban Medicine*. Plymouth, UK: Lexington Books, 2008.

Pérez, Louis A., Jr. *Lords of the Mountain: Social Banditry and Peasant Protest in Cuba, 1878–1918*. Pittsburgh: University of Pittsburgh Press, 1989.

Pérez, Louis A., Jr. "History, Historiography, and Cuban Studies: Thirty Years Later." In *Cuban Studies since the Revolution*, edited by Damián Fernández. Gainesville: University Press of Florida, 1992.

Pérez, Louis A., Jr. *Cuba: Between Reform and Revolution*. 2nd ed. New York: Oxford University Press, 1995.

Pérez, Louis A., Jr. *On Becoming Cuban: Identity, Nationality and Culture*. Chapel Hill: University of North Carolina Press, 1999.

Pérez, Louis A., Jr. *Cuba and the United States: Ties of Singular Intimacy*. 3rd ed. Athens: University of Georgia Press, 2003.

Pérez de la Riva, Juan. *La república neocolonial* (Anuario de Estudios Cubanos vols. 1 and 2). Havana: Instituto Cubano del Libro/Editorial de Ciencias Sociales, 1973, 1979.

Pérez Sarduy, Pedro. "¿Qué tienen los negros en Cuba?" *América Negra* 15 (1998), 217–28.

Pérez-López, Jorge F. "Rectification Redux? Cuban Economic Policy at the End of 2005." *Cuban Affairs* 1:1 (January 2006).

Pérez-López, Jorge F. "The Cuban Economy in 2005–2006: The End of the Special Period?" Association for the Study of the Cuban Economy. *Cuba in Transition* 16. Proceedings of the Sixteenth Annual Meeting of the ASCE, August 2006, 1–13.

Pérez-Stable, Marifeli. "Review: The Field of Cuban Studies." *Latin American Research Review* 26:1 (1991), 239–50.

Pettavino Paula, and Geralyn Pye. *Sport in Cuba: The Diamond in the Rough*. Pittsburgh: University of Pittsburgh Press, 1994.

Pixley, Jorge. "Baptists and Liberation Theology: Mexico, Central America, and the Caribbean." *Baptist History and Heritage* (Winter 2000).

Portes, Alejandro, and Alex Stepick. *City on the Edge: The Transformation of Miami*. Berkeley: University of California Press, 1993.

Powers, Thomas. "Inside the Department of Dirty Tricks." *Atlantic Monthly* CCXLIV (August 1979).

Powers, Thomas. *The Man who Kept the Secrets: Richard Helms and the CIA*. New York: Pocket Books, 1979.

Poyo, Gerald E. "Evolution of Cuban Separatist Thought in the Emigré Communities of the United States, 1848–1895." *Hispanic American Historical Review* 66:3 (August 1986), 485–507.

Poyo, Gerald E. *"With All, and for the Good of All": The Emergence of Popular Nationalism in the Cuban Communities of the United States*. Durham: Duke University Press, 1989.

Prados, John. *Presidents' Secret Wars: CIA and Pentagon Secret Operations since World War II*. New York: William Morrow, 1986.

Prebisch, Raúl. *The Economic Development of Latin America and its Principal Problems*. New York: United Nations, 1950.

Prieto, Alfredo. "Made in América: la imagen de Cuba en el exterior." In *Cuba en las Américas: una perspectiva sobre Cuba y los problemas hemisféricos*, edited by Centro de Estudios sobre América. Havana: Centro de Estudios sobre América, 1995.

Quinn, Kate. "Cuban Historiography in the 1960s: Revisionists, Revolutionaries, and the Nationalist Past." *Bulletin of Latin American Research* 26:3 (2007), 378–98.

Quirk, Robert E. *Fidel Castro*. New York: W. W. Norton, 1995.

Quiroz, Alfonso W. "Martí in Cuban Schools." In *The Cuban Republic and José Martí: Reception and Use of a National Symbol*, edited by Mauricio Augusto Font and Alfonso W. Quiroz. Lanham, MD: Lexington Books, 2006.

Ramonet, Ignacio. *Fidel Castro: My Life: A Spoken Autobiography*. New York: Scribner, 2008.

Randall, Margaret. *To Change the World: My Years in Cuba*. New Brunswick, NJ: Rutgers University Press, 2009.

Ripoll, Carlos. "Writers and Artists in Today's Cuba." In *Cuban Communism*, edited by Irving Louis Horowitz. 7th ed. New Brunswick, NJ: Transaction Publishers, 1989.

Risquet, Jorge. "La epopeya de Cuba en África negra." In *Cuba y Africa: historia común de lucha y sangre*, edited by Piero Gleijeses, Jorge Risquet, and Fernando Remírez. Havana: Editorial de Ciencias Sociales, 2007.

Ritter, Archibald R. M. "Cuba's Strategic Economic Re-orientation." Association for the Study of the Cuban Economy, *Cuba in Transition* 16. Proceedings of the Sixteenth Annual Meeting of the ASCE, August 2006, 140–54.

Ritter, Archibald R. M., and Nicholas Rowe. "Cuba: From 'Dollarization' to 'Euroization' or 'Peso Reconsolidation?'" *Latin American Politics and Society* (summer 2002), 99–123.

Roca, Sergio G. "The *Comandante* in His Economic Labyrinth." In *Conflict and Change in Cuba*, edited by Enrique A. Baloyra and James A. Morris. Albuquerque: University of New Mexico Press, 1993.

Rodney, Walter. *How Europe Underdeveloped Africa*. London: Bogle-L'Ouverture Publications, 1972.

Rodriguez, Felix I., and John Weisman. *Shadow Warrior: The CIA Hero of a Hundred Unknown Battles*. New York: Simon and Schuster, 1989.

Rodríguez Exposito, Cesar. *Hatuey, El primer libertador de Cuba*. Havana: Cubanacán, 1944.

Roig de Leuchsenring, Emilio. *La Enmienda Platt: su interpretación primitiva y sus aplicaciones posteriores hasta 1921*. Havana: Siglo XX, 1922.

Roig de Leuchsenring, Emilio. *Análisis y consecuencias de la intervención norteamericana en los asuntos interiores de Cuba*. Havana: Siglo XX, 1923.

Rossett, Peter, and Medea Benjamin. *The Greening of the Revolution: Cuba's Experiment with Organic Agriculture*. Melbourne: Ocean Press, 1995.

Rostow, Walt W. *The Stages of Economic Growth: A Non-Communist Manifesto*. Cambridge: Cambridge University Press, 1960.

Safa, Helen. *The Myth of the Male Breadwinner: Women and Industrialization in the Caribbean*. Boulder: Westview Press, 1995.

Sawyer, Mark Q. *Racial Politics in Post-Revolutionary Cuba*. New York: Cambridge University Press, 2006.

Schlesinger, Arthur M., Jr. *Robert Kennedy and His Times*. Boston: Houghton Mifflin, 1978.

Schoultz, Lars. *That Infernal Little Cuban Republic: The United States and the Cuban Revolution*. Chapel Hill: University of North Carolina Press, 2009.

Serviat, Pedro. "Solutions to the Black Problem." In *AfroCuba: An Anthology of Cuban Writing on Race, Politics and Culture*, edited by Pedro Pérez Sarduy and Jean Stubbs. Melbourne: Ocean Press, 1993.

Shayne, Julie D. *The Revolution Question: Feminisms in El Salvador, Chile, and Cuba*. New Brunswick, NJ: Rutgers University Press, 2004.

Shnookal, Deboarah, and Mirta Muñiz, eds. *José Martí Reader: Writings on the Americas*. Melbourne: Ocean Press, 1999.

Silverman, B., ed. *Man and Socialism in Cuba: The Great Debate*. New York: Atheneum, 1971.

Skierka, Volker. *Fidel Castro: A Biography*. Cambridge: Polity, 2004.

Smith, Lois M., and Alfred Padula. *Sex and Revolution: Women in Socialist Cuba*. New York: Oxford University Press, 1996.

Smith, Peter H. "Memoirs from LASA's 14th President." *LASA Forum* XXXVII (spring 2006), 20.

Smith, Wayne S., and Esteban Morales Domínguez, eds. *Subject to Solution: Problems in Cuban-U.S. Relations*. Boulder: Lynne Rienner, 1988.

Smorkaloff, Pamela Maria. *Readers and Writers in Cuba: A Social History of Print Culture, 1830s–1990s*. New York: Garland Reference Library of the Humanities, 1997.

Stein, Jeff. "Inside Omega 7." *Village Voice*, March 10, 1980.

Stephenson, Skye. "International Educational Flows between the United States and Cuba (1959–2005): Policy Winds and Exchange Flows." *Cuban Studies* 37 (2006), 122–55.

Stock, Ann Marie. *On Location in Cuba: Street Filmmaking during Times of Transition.* Chapel Hill: University of North Carolina Press, 2009.

Suárez Salazar, Luis. "El sistema electoral cubano: apuntes para una crítica." In *La democracia en Cuba y el diferendo con los Estados Unidos*, edited by Haroldo Dilla Alfonso and William I. Robinson. Havana: Centro de Estudios sobre América, 1995.

Sweig, Julia E. *Inside the Cuban Revolution: Fidel Castro and the Urban Underground.* Cambridge, MA: Harvard University Press, 2002.

Szulc, Tad. *The Illusion of Peace: Foreign Policy in the Nixon Years.* New York: Viking Press, 1978.

Szluc, Tad. *Fidel: A Critical Portrait.* New York: Morrow, 1986.

Torres, María de los Ángeles. *The Lost Apple: Operation Pedro Pan, Cuban Children in the US and the Promise of a Better Future.* Boston, MA: Beacon Press, 2003.

Tulchin, Joseph S., Lilian Bobea, Mayra P. Espina Prieto, and Rafael Hernández, eds. *Changes in Cuban Society since the 1990s.* Woodrow Wilson International Center for Scholars, 2005.

Uriarte, Miren. "Social Policy Responses to Cuba's Economic Crisis of the 1990s." *Cuban Studies* 35 (2004), 105–36.

Uriarte, Miren. "Social Impact of the Economic Measures." In *A Contemporary Cuba Reader: Reinventing the Revolution*, edited by Philip Brenner, Marguerite Rose Jiménez, John M. Kirk, and William LeoGrande. Lanham, MD: Rowman and Littlefield, 2007, pp. 285–91.

Valdés, Juan. "Democracia y sistema político." In *Cuba en las Américas: una perspectiva sobre Cuba y los problemas hemisféricos*, edited by Centro de Estudios sobre América. Havana: Centro de Estudios sobre América, 1995.

Valdés, Zoé. *Dear First Love: A Novel.* Translated by Andrew Hurley. New York: Harper Collins, 2002.

Vilas, Carlos M. "Is Socialism Still an Alternative for the Third World?" *Monthly Review* (July–August 1990).

Whittle, Daniel, and Orlando Rey Santos. "Protecting Cuba's Environment: Efforts to Design and Implement Effective Environmental Laws and Policies in Cuba." *Cuban Studies* 37 (2006), 73–103.

Williams, Eric. *Capitalism and Slavery.* Chapel Hill: University of North Carolina Press, 1944.

Winn, Peter, ed. *Victims of the Chilean Miracle: Workers and Neoliberalism in the Pinochet Era, 1973–2002.* Durham: Duke University Press, 2004.

Wintz, Jack. "The Church in Cuba: Is a New Day Dawning?" *St. Anthony's Messenger Magazine*, May 1996 (online edition), www.americancatholic.org/Messenger/May1996/feature1.asp.

Wunderlich, Annelise. "Hip Hop Pushes the Limits." In *Capitalism, God, and a Good Cigar: Cuba Enters the Twenty-First Century*, edited by Lydia Chávez. Durham: Duke University Press, 2005.

Yaremko, Jason M. *U.S. Protestant Missions in Cuba: From Independence to Castro*. Gainesville: University Press of Florida, 2000.

Zimmermann, Matilde. *Sandinista: Carlos Fonseca and the Nicaraguan Revolution*. Durham: Duke University Press, 2001.

Several online collections of documents are available, at the JFK Library (www.jfklibrary. org/Historical+Resources/JFK+in+History/Cuban+Missile+Crisis.htm), the National Security Archive, including declassified Cuban, Soviet, and eastern bloc documents (www.gwu.edu/~nsarchiv/nsa/cuba_mis_cri/index.htm), and at the Library of Congress (www.loc.gov/exhibits/archives/colc.html).

Index